PLANNING AND RURAL RECREATION IN BRITAIN

Planning and Rural Recreation in Britain

David Groome

Avebury

Aldershot • Brookfield USA • Hong Kong • Singapore • Sydney

© David Groome 1993

Published by
Avebury
Ashgate Publishing Limited
Gower House
Croft Road
Aldershot
Hants GU11 3HR

Ashgate Publishing Company
Old Post Road
Brookfield
Vermont 05036
USA

British Library Cataloguing in Publication Data

Groome, David
    Planning and Rural Recreation in Britain
    I. Title
    711

ISBN 1 85628 454 9

Printed and Bound in Great Britain by
Hartnolls Limited, Bodmin, Cornwall.

Contents

List of tables

List of figures

List of plates

Preface and acknowledgements

In the last 30 years there have been several surges of interest in country-side recreation from perspectives which have ranged from behavioural studies to interpretation and marketing. Yet little investigation has been made of the way in which the British planning system has responded to the increased pressures for using the countryside for rural recreation. At first glance, plans and policies for rural areas suggest that the statutory planning system has shown little concern with recreation provision in the countryside. A central aim of this book has been to explore how far this is in fact the case and to test the notion that recreation is the 'Cinderella' of rural planning. The method adopted to do this has been to examine the various mechanisms and tools used by planners and to consider how far recreation features in them.

An important avenue of investigation has been that of bringing together various ideas developed by the author in recent years on access to the countryside, dealing in particular with the impact of the car on the countryside. The problems of living with the motor car are mostly focused on urban and inter-urban travel. Yet the insidious effect of increases in traffic volumes and greater dependence on the private motor car promise quite alarming prospects for national parks and other rural areas subject to heavy visitor pressure. Of all the issues raised by increased leisure use of the countryside, the problem of handling the car is likely to be a preoccupation of importance in future years.

Planning and providing for rural recreation is in a period of rapid change. Many assumptions made, for example, about the roles of local authorities in providing rural recreation facilities are now subject to challenge. A review at this stage can provide a benchmark to compare public providers' performances in service delivery with providers from the private and voluntary sectors.

Lastly, sea changes in agricultural policy-making have swept across the countryside of Britain in recent years and have brought in their train pressures to promote recreation on a hitherto unheard-of scale. In considering the future of rural recreation, thought also has to be given to those pressures and the extent to which the countryside is the right setting for them. As a factor for change, recreation itself will have an important effect on the future form of the countryside. It could influence the extent to which countryside takes on a 'tamed' appearance into which recreation is gently assimilated or whether it becomes a rural playground – a sort of rustic theme park.

In writing this book I would like to express my thanks to my colleagues at Manchester University's Department of Planning and Landscape for allowing me a period of sabbatical leave to undertake a substantial part of the research for this book and, particularly, to Professor Chris Wood for his encouragement to pursue my investigations. I am indebted also to undergraduate and postgraduate students at Manchester University who attended courses on countryside and recreational planning and who provided much lively stimulus. Can I express my thanks, too, to the many officers working in local authority planning offices, the Countryside Commissions and the voluntary sector who went to considerable trouble to assist me in my investigations.

My lasting thanks are due to Moira for showing great tolerance towards me whilst writing this book.

Chapter 1

The study framework

This book examines the role played by the planning system in influencing the way in which the British countryside is used for outdoor recreation. In undertaking the investigation the following assumptions have been made about the nature of planning.

1. Planning exists as a form of decision-making which involves intervention by the state in the development process.
2. Statutory planning demonstrates a number of different 'styles', reflecting the ways in which planning has adapted to changing political and institutional settings.
3. Particular techniques are available to planners as aids to decision-making, including identification of aims and prescription of future states.
4. An important characteristic of planning is that a constantly changing balance sheet exists between central control and local claims of interests.
5. An increasing concern of planning is with wider environmental and energy issues and with the promotion of policies which foster sustainable development.

PLANNING AS A FORM OF DECISION-MAKING

The central theme of this book is the way in which planning concepts and ideology have featured in rural recreation provision. The term 'planning' can be taken to have a number of meanings. It can be said to involve making plans, either in the form of drawings or statements of intent; as a type of decision-making, it is a process of preparing decisions for action in the future and achieving goals by optimal means; it can involve organizing change or implementing plans, offering societal guidance and incorporating sets of laws, institutions and procedures in particular countries (Cross, 1983, p. 288).

A feature of planning which makes it different from other forms of intervention is that it seeks to influence where development takes place, determining patterns of development in forms other than those that developers intended; and at times other than those when it would otherwise have taken place (Reade, 1987, p. xii).

The form taken by planning has evolved considerably since its modern origins in the early 20th century. Its role as a mechanism for achieving minimal standards of layout of industrial cities evolved into a preoccupation in the inter-war period with coping with suburban expansion and regional imbalances. This concern was reflected in legislation in the form of the Town and Country Planning Act 1932, which for the first time extended the scope of planning schemes to rural areas. However, the main provisions of that Act were permissive only and it is to the Town and Country Planning Act 1947 that the basic framework of the present-day system in Britain can be traced. The National Parks and Access to the Countryside Act 1949 complemented the Planning 1947 Act with provision for the creation of national parks and other statutory protection of the countryside. The 20 years following the 1947 Act were marked by a number of refinements to the system, reflected in the search for new methods, administrative procedures and institutions.

In the later 1960s and 1970s there was growing awareness of the problems of social change, economic growth and development with the focusing of policy initiatives on the inner city. In the 1980s planning had the task of adjusting to the major political changes of that era, including the emergence of 'new right' policies under the Thatcher administrations with planning seen as restrictive, distorting the economy and slowing down job creation (Ehrman, 1988, p. 1).

Rural recreation therefore needs to be seen as part of these wider movements in pursuit of a 'desired state': the orderly physical layout of town and countryside and the achievement of defined social and economic objectives. In addition, planning has necessarily been perceived as a statutory mechanism and form of public administration comprising a body of instruments and procedures (Solesbury, 1974, pp. 4–7).

STYLES OF PLANNING

Researchers have observed that public policy-making and the planning system in particular have not been static but have evolved constantly. For example, McKay and Cox have recorded that land-use planning history in Britain can be divided into a number of phases ranging from strongly interventionist planning models on the one hand to 'non-planning' on the other. Thus, an 'indicative' style of planning would indicate the objectives towards which public and private resources should be harnessed. 'Regulative' styles suggest control or regulation of initiatives by the private sector. 'Non-planning' would enable the private sector to influence change at will. 'Indicative' planning would indicate the objectives towards which public and private resources should be harnessed (McKay and Cox, 1979, pp. 25–26).

Others, too, have been able to identify a number of 'styles' of planning which include:

- public-led statutory development plans and control by local authorities supported by public investment planning;
- 'popular' planning, emphasizing the role of the private sector and limited local authority input;
- 'leverage' planning and 'private management' planning (Cherry, 1988, p. 189).

The notion of there being several styles of planning has probably been most fully developed by Brindley, *et al.* (1989), on which Table 1.1 is based. Such styles of planning may be applicable only in certain types of geographical area and will reflect a response to local problems. In addition, they are likely to be closely related to the political complexion of the party in power at a particular time.

However, such a typology can be of value in helping to explain the nature of the constraints under which the planning system operates. In terms of the focus of this particular study, other typologies may also emerge, sharing some of the characteristics of the styles of planning identified here.

Table 1.1   Styles of planning

Form of Planning	Characteristics
Regulative planning	Reacting to private development interests, based on hierarchy of statutory plans and use of development control powers
Trend planning	Applies minimal planning powers to facilitate in line with market processes; exemplified in simplified planning zones
Positive planning	Used to bring problem areas up to standards of surrounding areas; the role of planning is to stimulate change needed
Popular planning	Public sector dominant but acting through the community
Leverage planning	Major role played by public sector but private sector is important agent of change, 'highly interventionist', can 'stimulate a weak market'
Public investment planning	Public sector arena, significant levels of investment, e.g. new towns; use of compulsory purchase powers
Private management planning	Private sector agencies take control of tasks that were part of the public sector

Source: based on Brindley, *et al.* (1989)

PLANNING TECHNIQUES

A feature of the planning system which has evolved in Britain since the Second World War has been the use of planning techniques to assist in the preparation of plans and policies. Such techniques generally reflect an attempt to produce a more rational basis for decision-making and have been examined at length elsewhere (Roberts, 1974). There has been continued interest in the use of analytical and predictive methods in urban planning (Field and McGregor, 1987). Texts dealing specifically with rural resource planning have stressed the need for planning techniques which successfully coordinate different rural activities (Thomas and Coppock, 1981; Bunce and Barr, 1988). In terms of actual planning practice, attention to methodology has varied considerably. The introduction of the structure plan as a statutory instrument in the late 1960s coincided with much discussion on the role of urban systems planning and the use of quantitative methods to assist in forecasting urban change. Techniques developed in the late 1960s and the early 1970s were often designed to describe complex social economic and spatial relationships (Briscoe, 1983, p. 112). For many involved in the planning process numerical description was a convenient shorthand for excessive complexity and its policy consequences.

Many of these techniques were abandoned in subsequent years. Reasons for this included, firstly, the difficulties of anticipating rapid and unpredictable changes in population, economic growth, and social customs. Secondly, there was a growing consciousness and increasing emphasis on the importance of political choice and public participation in planning decisions (Briscoe, 1983, p. 112).

Recent years have seen the adoption of less ambitious and more 'opportunistic' or pragmatic approaches to plan-making. A change of image of planning has been accompanied by less reliance on extensive quantitative bases for plans. The focus has moved to a concern with devising ways in which plans, having been made, might be implemented.

This concern with the implementation of plans paralleled a growing awareness of the limitations of planning. As one commentator has noted.

- State power seemed inefficient in regulating development and in providing guidance for the future and was compared unfavourably with more adaptive private market intelligence.
- Disillusionment revolved around the inability of planning to implement what was promised, resulting in pressure for retreat from government and accompanied by erosion of local authority responsibilities (Cherry, 1988, p. 140).

CENTRE–LOCAL RELATIONS

Central government generally sets the broad framework within which locally inspired planning policies and initiatives can operate. Yet the centre has been often reluctant to release power to lower-tier organizations or to transfer responsibilities that are seen to belong to one ministry to another (Cherry, 1975, pp. 83–85). In addition, government has been unwilling to allow local authorities to venture outside a narrowly defined arena of physical planning when drawing up statutory structure and local plans (Cross and Bristow, 1983, p. 312). In addition, there has been a number of examples of government ministries coming into conflict with each other. This reflects the increasing complexity of relations between state agencies, markedly in the case of the Ministry of Agriculture and the Department of the Environment, resulting in local authorities receiving confused messages from central government (Cloke, 1987, p. 25).

Centre–local relations changed in a number of respects in the 1980s in Britain. A trend was for government to attempt to break the control of local authorities in environmental planning by such measures as the creation of urban development corporations and groundwork trusts. The squeeze on local government was accompanied by measures to enhance the power of consumers through increasing access to local authority documents, seen, for example, in provisions of the Local Government (Access to Information) Act 1985. In addition, government sought to strengthen the power of organized groups against local authorities with a result that the latter found themselves squeezed between central government intervention and increased demands and powers from local communities (Parkinson, 1987, p. 7). Attempts to increase accountability have been sought through the short-lived Community Charge introduced in England and Wales in 1990. In addition, a vigilant Audit Commission scrutinizes the value for money of local-authority-provided services through use of performance indicators which enable comparisons to be made between councils from one year to another (Audit Commission, 1991).

All these changes mean that an examination of planning in Britain now takes place within a different context to that of 10 or 15 years ago. Planners find that the rules within which they operate are subject to sudden change. Increasingly, the control of central government and its agencies has been extended in order to reduce overall public spending. In the case of rural recreational planning, national policies may not exist in Britain, but the centre is increasingly able to ensure that local policies

conform to centrally accepted views, with local government fiscal regimes encouraging local policy-making to conform to centrally approved
forms.

Although leisure and recreation provision has been regarded in the
past as politically neutral, this has been challenged on a number of
occasions. After the upheavals in planning in the 1970s and 1980s,
Eisenschitz questions whether planning is attempting to recapture some
of its lost innocence in what seems the unambiguously beneficial sphere
of leisure and tourism (Eisenshitz, 1988, p. 14). This critique draws
attention to the way in which pressure for provision of commercial
leisure intensifies tensions and heightens conflicts in leisure theory and
practice.

A further critical review of recreation and tourism planning records
that although there are ample statistics as to how far people stray from
their cars, 'the nature of how recreation "demand" by itself is determined or influenced by the state's organization of it, physically, politically
and ideologically is rarely considered' (Bouquet and Winter, 1987, p. 6).
Planning, it is argued, has tended to accommodate market mechanisms
rather than encourage reallocation or redistribution of resources.

PLANNING AND ENVIRONMENTAL CHANGE

A fifth theme to help in constructing a context for rural recreational
planning concerns the future of towns, cities and countryside in the long
term. In periods of rapid social and economic change there has been
justifiable caution in attempting to plan ahead more than 5 or 10 years.
However, the growth of environmentalism has encouraged planners to
take a longer-term view of change and this standpoint has been increasingly asserted (Lock, 1991, p. 9). Attention is being paid to devising
planning policies which promote 'sustainability', taking account of the
true environmental costs of development and of safeguarding resources.
Yet, in one survey it was shown that only just over a third of strategic
planning authorities and 18 per cent of planning authorities with development control functions paid specific attention to energy-efficiency
issues in policy-making (Owens, 1991, p. 48). In 1992, government introduced a requirement for statutory plans to incorporate sustainable development policies (Department of the Environment, 1992b). While this
overdue measure may raise 'green' issues higher on to the local policy-

making agenda, pursuit of sustainability itself is not without apparent contradictions. In referring to the concept of the 'compact city' the task is that of 'closing the environmental circle' of desirable lifestyles, the economies, future form and function of cities (Breheny, 1991, p. 1).

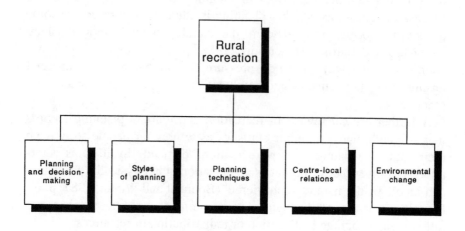

Figure 1.1   The study framework

THE STRUCTURE OF THE BOOK

The themes noted above suggest a number of questions which might be posed about the role and form of recreational planning. How effective are various statutory and informal planning mechanisms in achieving specific goals for rural recreation? Can distinctive 'styles' of recreational planning be identified? Or, to what extent does there exist, and to what extent is use made of, a distinct body of techniques in rural recreation planning? What is the nature of the relationships between the different 'actors' in rural recreational planning and those in other areas of central and local decision-making? As a consumer of significant quantities of resources, how do rural recreation policies relate to current concepts of sustainable development?

Seeking answers to such questions as these has helped to provide a study framework for considering in more detail the precise nature of rural recreation planning.

Chapter 2 examines the information needs of planners concerned with rural recreation. The chapter provides information on the characteristics of rural recreational activities, identifies trends in demand, and summarizes the planning issues associated with various pursuits.

Chapter 3 considers how such data might be used in the process of preparing rural recreation plans and records possible methodologies and techniques which might be adopted by planners.

Chapter 4 examines the different statutory and informal mechanisms by which rural recreation planning is undertaken. Formal plan-making *for* rural recreation is taken to include prescriptions for rural recreation achieved via statutory mechanisms such as structure and local plans. However, informal plan-making for rural recreation can be important and may vary greatly in form, ranging perhaps from a local authority *ad hoc* policy on access to the countryside to wide-ranging countryside strategies.

Formal and informal plans often provide only a limited indication of policies towards rural recreation. Much also depends on the response of the development-control system to proposals for rural recreation. Examined in Chapter 5 is the role of development control in policy-making, local authority responses to planning applications and the results of appeal decisions. Reviewed, too, is the role of environmental assessment procedures in Britain.

Much informal planning of rural recreation has taken place under the broader heading of 'countryside management'. Several land and property disciplines, including professional planners, are likely to be involved in undertaking countryside management. Planners, in particular, are likely to be concerned with identifying the relationship between overall planning policies and the role of area-wide and site-management plans. Chapter 6 reviews principles of layout, design and management that are commonly employed in the preparation of management plans and which planners need to be aware of in drawing up design briefs or plans.

Chapter 7 records the existence of different notions of access: as rights assigned to the ownership of property or wider rights allowing the individual to walk on land which belongs to someone else. It considers the recent shift of recreation policies away from site-based planning in the form of country parks to provision based on networks of trails, paths and access to the wider countryside. The problems of effectively channelling recreational pressures away from sensitive areas, whether users are on foot or in a car, are addressed and attention is paid to ways in which policies might reduce the environmental impact of the car on the countryside.

The call for planners to explain 'who gets what?' as a result of intervention policies has led to a reappraisal of the distributional effects of planning. In the case of rural recreation, social objectives have sought to ensure that opportunities are made available to as wide a section of the community as possible. What form might such objectives take? How are they most likely to be effective? Chapter 8 poses these questions and considers a number of approaches to widening opportunities for enjoying the countryside.

The last ten years have seen a surge of interest in promoting rural tourism, linked to agricultural diversification. Local planning authorities have faced conflicting and sometimes confusing guidance from other agencies on how to respond to the new and often highly promotional stances of rural tourism. Chapter 9 considers the implications of these developments for the planning system and, against a background of concern about the environmental and social impacts of tourism and commercial recreation, the role that might be played by 'green' tourism.

The delivery of rural recreation services has normally been seen as a responsibility of local authorities or as a by-product activity of public agencies such as the Forestry Commission or, in England and Wales, the former regional water authorities. Operating under new administrative and financial regimes introduced during the Thatcher years from 1979 onwards, such assumptions can no longer be made. The notion of the countryside being a 'free' commodity is being challenged as public agencies gain greater degrees of financial independence. Chapter 10 examines the challenge for planners in establishing relationships with new 'actors' in recreational planning and the ways in which policies need to take account of newly evolving centre–local relations.

Attitudes towards the role that the voluntary sector can play in developing rural recreation sometimes seem conflicting. Government has encouraged 'non-profit' organizations to take on tasks which were formerly handled by local authorities. At the same time, central and local funding support to many voluntary organizations bears little relationship to the scale of tasks which they are expected to undertake. Chapter 11 examines the diversity of the voluntary sector activities which range from being scrutineers of policy-making to acting as providers of rural recreation facilities. The voluntary-sector contribution to policy-making can be considerable but a number of limitations of that involvement are also identified in this chapter.

RURAL RECREATION: A 'THREAT' OR AN 'OPPORTUNITY'?

An underlying theme in rural recreation planning has been that outdoor recreation is a threat to the environment. Indeed, a major justification for the planning of rural recreation has been the need to limit the impacts of large numbers of people visiting the countryside. The theme was central in the debates associated with the *Countryside in 1970* conferences held in 1963, 1965 and 1970 (Royal Society of Arts, 1970). The problems caused by the effects of recreation on the countryside in Britain have also been highlighted by the activities of bodies such as the Recreation Ecology Research Group. Knightsbridge expresses the views of many by reminding that although people and wildlife can coexist, pressures from visitors also have a detrimental effect on the nature conservation value of sites (Knightsbridge, 1986, pp. 31–32).

It is of interest that in the 1980s rural recreation began to be seen as rather less of a threat. Increased concern with the need to improve social and economic opportunities in the countryside led to recognition of the value of recreation and tourism (English Tourist Board, 1988b). In addition, reviews of the impact of recreation on wildlife suggested that there was more room for compromise than was advocated by some interest groups (Sidaway, 1988, p. iv). Rather than recreation being seen as an activity for residual areas of land only, there was growing interest in adopting a more positive stance in policy-making in order to cater for the increasing demands of certain types of sporting and recreational activity in the countryside (Sports Council, 1990). In addition, it is now recognized that rural recreation resources themselves need to be protected from development, as guidelines on undertaking environmental assessment remind (Countryside Commission, 1991a).

This change in perception of rural recreation planning provides a further context for the present study.

THE LITERATURE OF RURAL RECREATIONAL PLANNING

Rural recreation has been dealt with at length by a number of researchers since the early 1970s (Patmore, 1970, 1983; Lavery, 1974; Coppock and Duffield, 1975; Smith, 1983; Pigram, 1983; Glyptis, 1991). These studies provide thorough coverage of the subject, in particular in offering an understanding of patterns of activity and consequent demands on land

and water resources. Owens provides a particularly valuable overview of academic research undertaken in the field of rural recreation (Owens, 1984).

Recent studies relating specifically to the preparation of rural recreation plans are few although planning studies are considered to a limited extent in two texts which are primarily concerned with countryside management (Miles and Seabrooke, 1977; Bromley, 1990).

Of a number of evaluative studies of rural recreational planning and policy making, that of Curry deserves mention for the critical analysis it offers of sites policy (Curry, 1985). Rural recreation has, of course, featured quite prominently in major policy reviews of planning and the countryside (Countryside Review Committee, 1977). The topic has been dealt with at length in inquiries into national parks (National Parks Policy Review Committee, 1974; National Parks Review Panel, 1991). In addition, the history of rural recreational policy has featured significantly in two studies (Cherry, 1975; Sheail, 1981).

The body of literature on rural recreation is considerable, particularly if inclusion is made of evaluative and prescriptive studies undertaken by the Countryside Commissions, local authorities, the Sports Councils, tourist boards and other bodies. Nevertheless, many such studies deal with only quite specialist areas of study. They include site and visitor surveys but few deal with the ways in which recreation is planned either within the statutory planning system or through the preparation of informal plans and policies.

At first glance, readers might conclude that statutory planning has had little to do with the problems and opportunities created by increased rural recreation. Planning for countryside recreation has been regarded as a 'Cinderella' area of policy-making. To an extent this can be explained by the very limited extent of planning controls over most activities in the countryside. In addition, the slight reference to rural recreation could be said to reflect planning's preoccupation with change and development in urban areas.

The extent to which these views are generally true is now examined.

Chapter 2

Enjoying the countryside

In planning for rural recreation, account needs to be taken of wider patterns of participation in leisure in society as a whole. The aim of this chapter is to discuss the factors which can influence the present scale and future development of rural recreation. Readers should note that discussion of these aspects of countryside recreation, and of behaviour patterns in particular, has been explored elsewhere (Coppock and Duffield, 1975; Patmore, 1983; Glyptis, 1991). In this present review discussion on this topic is limited and readers are recommended to these texts for fuller treatment of this theme.

Although the terms 'leisure' and 'recreation' are often used in an interchangeable manner, the terminology used in this book recognizes leisure as 'the time available to an individual when the disciplines of work, sleep and other basic needs have been met'; recreation is taken to consist of 'any pursuit engaged upon during leisure time, other than those to which people are normally highly committed' (Kenyon, 1970, p. 1). Pursuits to which people might be 'highly committed' are taken to include such activities as optional shopping, overtime, house repairs, car maintenance and others. Recreation is thus only one of a number of examples of leisure activity and countryside recreation itself is but one component of the overall pattern of recreation.

DATA ON LEISURE AND RECREATION

Information on how we use our leisure time has only become available on a large scale over the last 30 years. In reviewing the development of our knowledge of rural recreation, Sidaway notes that in the 1960s research in the field hardly existed and was limited to basic fact-finding

(Sidaway, 1982, p. 4). A major stimulus and boost to interest was generated by the investigations into leisure use by the American Outdoor Recreation Resources Review Commission (Patmore, 1983, p. 55).

Two major surveys undertaken in the 1960s were to prove important benchmarks. They were the National Pilot Recreation Survey, the first report of which was published in 1967, and Leisure in Britain in 1969. Both surveys providing comprehensive overviews of people's leisure activities at that time (Rodgers, 1967; Sillitoe, 1969).

At this time attempts were also made to provide a more detailed picture of leisure in the regions of England and Wales with surveys undertaken in the north, north west, and south east of England (North Regional Planning Committee, 1969; Patmore and Rodgers, 1972; Countryside Commission, 1977). In addition, in 1973, 1977, 1980, 1983, 1986 and 1987 the General Household Survey included a series of questions on leisure and recreation (Office of Population Censuses and Surveys, 1989a). The 1987 survey contained major revisions to questions on leisure and although the findings present a more accurate picture of leisure patterns, comparison with earlier years is more difficult (Matheson, 1991, p. 1). A major survey of leisure day visits in Britain was undertaken for the Employment Department and the British Tourist Authority/ English Tourist Board in 1988–1989 (Dodd, 1991, p. ix). Leisure was taken here to include such activities as shopping and pub visits, but the data also refers to different types of countryside visits, too.

Specifically in relation to rural recreation there has been a major series of national surveys undertaken by the Countryside Commission in 1977, 1980, 1984 and 1990. In Scotland, several investigations into national leisure patterns have been undertaken, including the Scottish countryside day trips surveys in 1987, 1988 and 1989 (Countryside Commission for Scotland 1990). An important characteristic of national and regional investigations is that most have been based on home-based questionnaire surveys, although in some regional surveys site interviews have also been undertaken. Surveys have sometimes provided only limited information on the use of the countryside. For example, in the General Household Survey, information is provided on activities such as walking or jogging which might take place in the countryside, but information about trips to the countryside features only in a very general way. A feature of the regional studies has been to identify future trends in demand for recreation. This has involved the use of regression analysis as a way of identifying the planning implications of survey findings

(Patmore and Rodgers, 1972, p. 198). However, only small recordings are made of some activities and analysis or forecasting needs to be treated with considerable care (Owens, 1984, p. 160).

A major problem in comparing surveys is that despite clear guidance being offered from a number of sources on how surveys should be carried out, survey information tends to be difficult to compare between one survey and another (Elson, 1977, p. 6). This is true of all the types of survey described above, both national and regional as well as local site surveys. Even when repeat surveys have been undertaken, modifications to questions and poor matches of samples mean that it is often difficult to achieve effective comparisons over time.

A source of data which planners are likely to use is locally undertaken surveys, most probably site-based but also in some cases involving household questionnaires. Over the last 30 years, hundreds of site surveys have been undertaken throughout Britain. For the most part they have been designed to assist managers and policy-makers in resolving problems arising at particular sites (Owens, 1984, p. 159). Although site surveys may have confirmed, or less frequently, overturned, managers' views, there has been little attempt to ask questions that are comparable at the same sites (over time) or with other sites in other counties or regions. A further criticism of site surveys is that they have only focused on people who are actually able to get to a site and have been concerned with expressed rather than with potential demand. Household surveys which explore the characteristics of those who do *not* visit the countryside have been much rarer although some examples exist (Leicestershire County Council, 1986).

A detailed critique of the approaches used in site surveys undertaken for the Countryside Commission identified many of the shortcomings, particularly inconsistencies, noted above (Elson, 1977). It is doubtful whether many additional advances have been made since then although some efforts have been made to achieve greater order in site survey methodology. For example, a recreation site survey manual usefully provides a number of ground rules for survey directors and designers (Tourism and Recreation Research Unit, 1983b). The manual provides a straightforward account of the main techniques used in site surveys, including model forms for designing and administering questionnaire and observation surveys. It draws attention to the need for proper design of sampling frames for interviews, an aspect of survey design which has been weakly understood in the past in Britain.

15

NATIONAL PATTERNS OF LEISURE

Most commentators on national trends in recreation have drawn attention to the fact that we are moving into a leisure age. It is an age heralded by a general increase in the opportunities to enjoy leisure and is associated with such factors as increased real income, greater longevity, a shorter working week, better education and increased personal mobility (Dower, 1965, p. 5). Evidence presented to the *Countryside in 1970* conferences demonstrated that there had been a significant growth in outdoor recreation during the period of increased prosperity in Britain in the 1950s and particularly during the 1960s (Royal Society of Arts, 1970).

Plate 2.1   The 1960s saw a major growth in car based recreation in Britain: Derwent Reservoir, Northumberland, 1970

This evidence of change was indicated at the time as being due to certain long-term social and economic changes taking place in society, including a better-educated and more mobile population. This view represents an oversimplification of the case and leisure patterns can be seen to reflect a more complex interaction of factors rather than being explained in terms of one or two variables. However, practitioners and researchers are able to draw attention to several indicators that can be described as having an influence on patterns of recreation. Some of the indicators are now outlined.

Taking the case of hours of work as a reason often advanced for increased leisure, then overall there would appear to be some evidence of a general reduction in hours. Normal basic hours of work have reduced from just under 42.8 in 1961 to 38.9 hours in 1988 (Figure 2.1). However, it will be seen that around 1980, there was a noticeable increase in the actual hours worked including overtime.

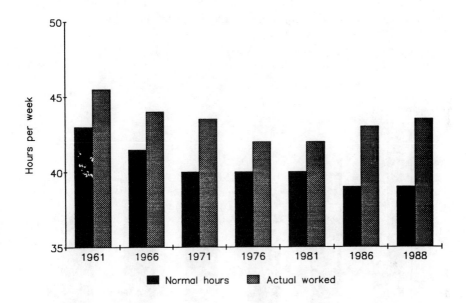

Figure 2.1   United Kingdom: weekly hours of work, 1961–1988
Source: Central Statistical Office (1990), p. 152

Paid holidays have also increased in length. In 1961, 97 per cent of full-time manual workers had an entitlement of only two weeks. Entitlements increased during the 1960s and 1970s. By 1988, 99 per cent of full-time manual workers had four weeks' or more paid holiday. How-

17

ever, here we are reminded that holiday entitlement is not necessarily a choice open to an individual, and worker–employer agreements may require workers to work during holiday periods (Gratton and Taylor, 1985, p. 24).

A factor which has not changed in the way that might have been expected in the 1960s is the pattern of unemployment, which rose gradually in the 1970s and then very sharply in the 1980s. There was a sudden fall in 1986, but a significant rise occurred from 1989 onwards. There is the prospect of a permanent pool of unemployed people who are unable to share in the 'leisure explosion' which was promised at one time.

Where there has been an increase in employment from 1986 onwards, then much of that has been in part-time work, often involving women. An increase in women's employment may result in the amount of leisure

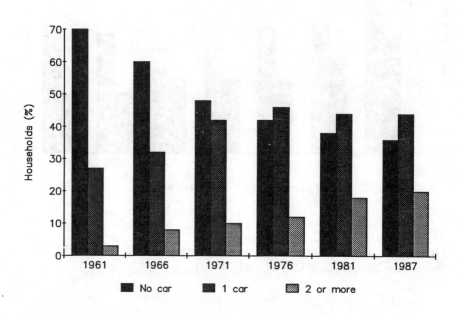

Figure 2.2   Great Britain: households with and without use of a car, 1961–1987
Source: based on Central Statistical Office (1990), p. 141

time available to a family being significantly reduced, particularly since leisure is a shared activity, with an important social function which tends to be jointly undertaken by all or most members of a family.

Another factor considered to have a major influence on an individual's use of leisure time is ownership of the private motor car. Increase in ownership has resulted in over 60 per cent of households in Britain having access to at least one car (Figure 2.2). However, access by women, children and older members of a household is likely to be limited.

There are other influences which help shape people's use of their leisure time. Longitudinal surveys of leisure habits can help identify these factors. Involved here are age, sex, social class, cultural differences and the several stages of an individual's life cycle (Parker, 1976, p. 51). Thus a young person's leisure habits are likely to be modified substantially on transfer from school to work. The move to work would be likely to include early starts, late returns and shorter holidays. For compensation, a wage or salary will be more than pocket money, but overall there is likely to be a decrease in leisure once he or she has left school. At parenthood, responsibilities normally increase with a reduction in the amount of time that can be spent on leisure. With increasing age and the departure of children, then the release from domestic responsibilities is matched by more free time. In the case of the elderly, then it might be assumed that an individual may be entering a new leisured age. However, poor health and impaired mobility, reduced income, loss of family and friends may result in a population with plenty of leisure time but frustrated because of the difficulties in actually using that leisure (Parker, 1976, p. 60).

Although many share in the opportunities created by the growth in leisure time, there exists a number of barriers faced by others which act as a 'filter', influencing whether or not an individual is likely to take up a particular recreational pursuit. An individual's sex, social class and stage reached in the life cycle are of importance but, as was indicated in a study of sporting opportunities in Cleveland, confidence or familiarity with a leisure pursuit, and primary and secondary education are also relevant factors (Boothby et al., 1981, pp. 52–53).

LEISURE AND RURAL RECREATION

The General Household Survey provides limited information on the popularity and characteristics of participants in sports, games and physical activities. The problems in interpreting these data have been referred to on a number of occasions (Veal, 1979, p. 80; Patmore, 1983, p. 57). Despite these difficulties, practitioners and researchers are likely to make regular use of the information contained in questions focused on sport and recreation. The popularity of sport and recreational pursuits can be interpreted by using the various measures of participation used in the General Household Survey:

- participation rates: the percentages of people who took part in an activity in the four weeks prior to interview;
- participation rates based on average percentages over each calendar quarter;
- frequency of participation: the average number of occasions on which participants take part in an activity during the four weeks prior to an interview;
- frequency of participation per adult per year, based on the total number of occasions of participation in an activity per year divided by the whole sample of adults rather than by the sample of participants.

From this categorization it will be seen that particular activities will have a higher ranking under some headings than others. Highly seasonal activities such as outdoor swimming might feature modestly in activity rates per year, but would feature prominently during the most popular quarter. Sometimes, in order to give a rounded picture of participation in an activity, two or more of the measures outlined above may be used. In order to indicate volumes of users, one approach might be to multiply the number of people participating in countryside activities in the 4-week period prior to interview by the numbers of times in which they actually participate (Sports Council, 1990, p. 5). The differences in rank ordering are reflected in the table of popularity of outdoor pursuits listed in Figure 2.3.

Walking, including rambling and hiking over distances of 2 miles, is by far the most popular of all outdoor pursuits. This is true in the case of the percentage participating in the previous 4 weeks (column 1) and

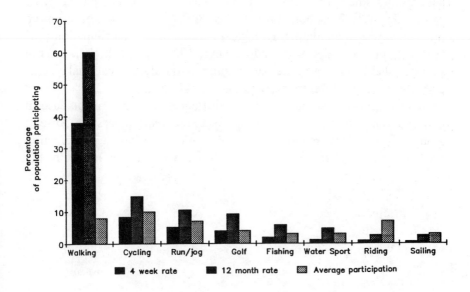

Figure 2.3   Great Britain: popularity of countryside outdoor pursuits (persons of 16 years or over), 1987
Source: Matheson (1991), p. 13

annual participation rates (column 2). Using the measure of the average number of occasions of participation per participant (column 3) then walking is overtaken by cycling, closely followed by running/jogging and riding. In other words, amongst walkers and cyclists, respondents who actually cycled were likely to participate in that activity more frequently than those who cited walking as a recreational activity. However, such distinctions cannot disguise the overall popularity of walking as a recreational pursuit. Even other rural recreational pursuits such as fishing which can claim much popular support fare only modestly on the basis of the General Household Survey, while horse riding and sailing emerge as minority activities.

The General Household Survey also allows comparison over time and it is possible to identify trends in various activities. Here, some caution

21

should be exercised in interpreting the data since relatively few participants were interviewed for some activities and the sample size was
accordingly small. In addition, changes have been made over the years
to the General Household Survey including the introduction of more
precise ways of calculating averages of frequency of participation (Office of Population Censuses and Surveys, 1989a, p. 214). Variations in
weather also influence participation quite markedly and can make comparisons between different activities a difficult task.

However, certain trends can be identified with a general increase in
participation in many countryside sports and recreation pursuits. Absent,
though, is any demonstration of the dramatic increases in participation
predicted by some researchers and policy-makers in the 1960s. In the

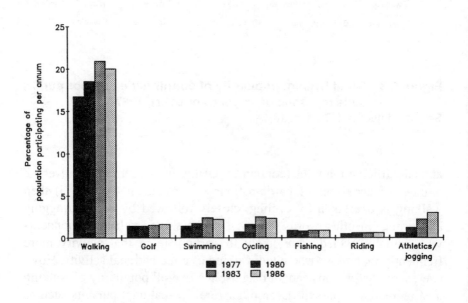

**Figure 2.4 Great Britain: average frequency of participation per
adult per annum in countryside sport and recreation,
1977–1986**
Source: Office of Population Censuses and Surveys (1989), p. 224

case of walking, taking the average number of occasions of participation per adult per year amongst the whole interview population, then this activity has shown a gradual increase in participation. Noticeable increases have taken place in cycling, although there was a slight reduction in participation between 1983 and 1986 (Figure 2.4).

Regional patterns of rural recreation within Britain reflect a number of departures from the overall picture. An early investigation, the National Pilot Recreation Survey, was valuable in pointing out the great differences in regional rates of participation (Rodgers, 1969, p. 31). Golf, for example, demonstrates high levels of participation in Scotland. Sailing, on the other hand, tends to have highest levels of participation in southern coastal locations in England. In part, regional variations can be explained by particular recreational traditions but, to a great extent, the availability of opportunities for participation must be a major factor in influencing levels of participation. Such opportunities might be reflected by the presence or absence of a resource such as water which can be used for fishing; open space to which there might be *de facto* or *de jure* access; or the existence of a good rail transport network enabling people to gain relatively easy access to the countryside. Given the prominent part played by local authorities and other public bodies in providing for rural recreation, then their role must be a significant factor in shaping patterns of participation.

WHO USES THE COUNTRYSIDE?

Several studies, including the Countryside Commission national countryside recreation surveys of 1977, 1980, 1984 and 1990, have demonstrated that not all sections of society make equal use of the countryside for recreational purposes. In examining the factors which could in part influence the extent to which people use the countryside, then the surveys confirm an association between access to a car and visits by individuals to the countryside. Thus, in England and Wales, 82 per cent of trips are made by the 66 per cent of households in which there is that vital piece of countryside 'equipment': a car.

The survey findings remind us, too, that participation in countryside recreation seems related to the social class of respondents. Social class B (professional and higher managerial) appear to be the most frequent trip-makers, although the actual volume of trip-making is dominated by

23

groups C1 and C2 (clerical and skilled manual workers). Other findings indicate higher rates of participation amongst respondents who belong to countryside organizations and those who own recreational 'equipment' such as a horse or tent. Amongst those who have overcome barriers to participation such as lack of ownership of a car, then there are generally less differences in trip-making characteristics between different social classes. Thus, car owners who had made a recent trip to the countryside demonstrated much less difference in relative frequency in trip-making between social class B and unemployed people (Countryside Commission, 1985(d), p. 6).

Reviews of site survey results suggest replication at the local scale of general national patterns of participation (Curry and Comley, 1986b, pp. 11–12). Analysis of occupational groups at a range of site surveys confirms the generally higher proportions of managerial and professional groups who participate in rural recreation.

Even so, local data demonstrate that there can be considerable variations in social class of visitors to recreational sites. In studies of four Glasgow parks and in visitor surveys in east Cheshire, variations in the social class of visitors emphasized the tendency for visitors' characteristics to mirror the social composition of neighbouring areas, particularly where catchments are quite local (Tourism and Recreation Research Unit, 1980, p. 91; Groome, 1988, p. 40). Assertions that pursuit of rural recreation is entirely a middle-class activity should be viewed with some caution in the light of findings from these local studies.

THE CHARACTERISTICS OF THE VISIT TO THE COUNTRYSIDE

The National Countryside Recreation Survey 1984, sought information on the mode of transport used to travel from home to recreational sites. For the majority, some 72 per cent, the trip was made by car, although in the case of those going on long walks, walking itself was the main mode of transport for 35 per cent of respondents. Public transport and cycling were only of very minor importance as modes of transport (Figure 2.5).

Despite the importance of recreation attractions with strong regional appeal and located some distance from major centres of population, the local countryside appears to be of particular importance with over a third

24

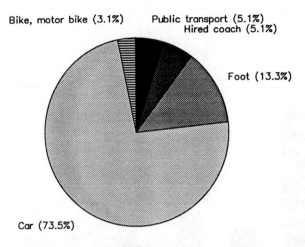

Bike, motor bike (3.1%)   Public transport (5.1%)
                          Hired coach (5.1%)

Foot (13.3%)

Car (73.5%)

**Figure 2.5   England and Wales: mode of transport used to reach
the countryside, 1984**
Source: Countryside Commission (1985a), p. 9

of trips having a round distance of less than 10 miles, and a half of trips
having a round distance of under 20 miles; in other words, the countryside around towns is the major destination for visitors (Figure 2.6).

There are, of course, departures from these national patterns. In the
1978 metropolitan green belt recreation study it was shown that, in some
urban fringe areas, walking can be an important mode of transport used
by visitors in order to reach sites (Harrison, 1983, p. 299). In a major
conurbation-wide survey of urban fringe sites in Greater Manchester
variations in transport mode were noted, with walking, cycling and
public transport reaching much higher proportions than might normally
be expected (Figure 2.7).

Duffield has drawn attention to the relationship between distance
travelled to the countryside and mode of transport which might be used
by visitors to the countryside (Duffield, 1982, p. 124). For walkers, 86
per cent of journeys cover return distances of less than 5 miles. The
more energetic cyclist is able to travel within a wider compass while the
freedom and choice for car owners enable them to travel considerable
distances within limited periods of time when compared with other
modes of transport.

25

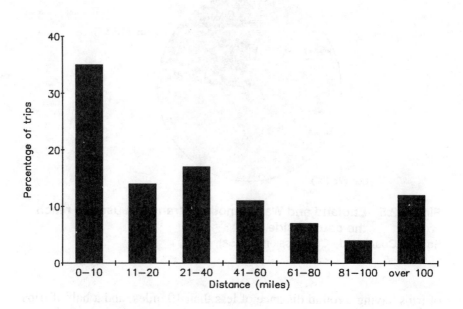

**Figure 2.6   England and Wales: distance travelled on countryside
            trips, 1984**
Source: Countryside Commission (1985a), p. 9

With regard to trip purpose, the National Countryside Recreation Survey recorded these as follows: drives, outings, picnics, long walks or hikes (over 2 miles in length), visiting friends and relatives in the countryside and informal sport. Probably the most significant finding here is the importance of 'unmanaged' countryside compared with managed sites such as country parks, with three times as many visiting the former as visit the latter (Figure 2.8).

The national pattern will tend to be replicated locally, although variations should be expected. In the case of the Peak District National Park, the appeal of the wider open countryside of hills and moors and lakes is very evident (Peak Park Joint Planning Board, 1988, p. 21). Also popular, too, at levels considerably above the national figures, are visits to the

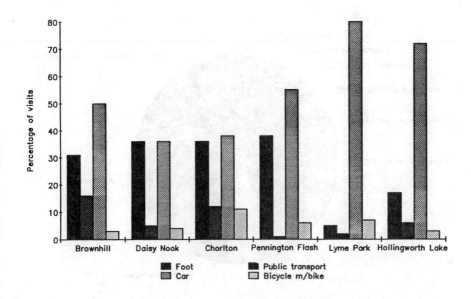

Figure 2.7 Greater Manchester: mode of transport used by visitors to selected urban fringe recreation sites, 1984

Source: based on Pawson and Groome (1987), p. 96

'built-on' countryside, notably to villages (16 per cent as against 6 per cent nationally).

TRENDS IN PARTICIPATION IN RURAL RECREATION ACTIVITIES

In the account which follows, brief portraits are provided of some of the most popular rural sporting and recreation pursuits. Much of the information described is aggregated from national data and local variations in many cases may be quite different. Sources for the section which follows draw on the Sports Council's *Digest of Sports Statistics for the UK*, which provides a comprehensive review of sports and recreation activities

27

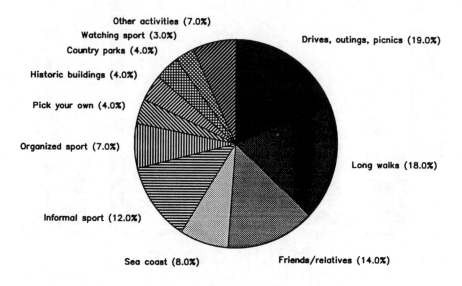

Other activities (7.0%)
Watching sport (3.0%)
Country parks (4.0%)
Historic buildings (4.0%)
Pick your own (4.0%)
Organized sport (7.0%)
Informal sport (12.0%)
Sea coast (8.0%)
Drives, outings, picnics (19.0%)
Long walks (18.0%)
Friends/relatives (14.0%)

**Figure 2.8   England and Wales: visits to the countryside, trip
purpose, 1984**
Source: based on Countryside Commission (1985a), p. 8

(Centre for Leisure Research, 1986(a)). Other sources, where used, have
also been identified.

Walking

Although walking as a mode of transport to reach the countryside features in national surveys in only a minor way, it is the most popular
physical recreation activity, pursued regularly by 22 per cent of the adult
population (Matheson, 1991, p. 8). It has a wide appeal across all age
ranges, even though only a very small proportion of walkers actually
belong to walking organizations (Centre for Leisure Research, 1986a, p.
138). The rapid increase in membership of the main walkers' organization,
the Ramblers' Association, from just over 22 000 in 1970 to over 90 000

28

in 1990 is an indication of growing interest in this activity. Most walking, defined as walks of 2 miles or over, consists of informal wandering in the countryside and 'serious' walkers are in a minority. Visitors seek out 'natural' settings for walking on paths, on fields and farmland and in woodland. However, no less than a third of respondents in a national survey for the Countryside Commission's 1987 *Recreation 2000* review walked on country roads and lanes used by cars, pavements on the side of roads and roads through villages (Countryside Commission, 1987(a), p. 10). This may reflect the absence of off-highway paths in particular localities, but it may also reflect the confidence that people have in using a clearly indicated surface rather than meeting possible difficulties in using a poorly marked right of way on farmland. An attractive feature of walking is that it requires little expenditure in the form of equipment, although costs of private and public transport are likely to act as a deterrent to participation.

Driving for pleasure

For most visitors travelling to the countryside by car, it can be reasonably assumed that the drive itself is a not insignificant part of the trip experience. A 1972 report by consultants on traffic in the Lake District National Park observed:

> Their (tourists') desire is to find pleasant roads with good scenery rather than to find the shortest possible route between two points. To travel on winding roads, up hill and down dale is part of the pleasure of arrival in the Park, in contrast to the need for speed in reaching it from large urban areas. (Wilson and Womersley, 1972, p. 6)

However, evidence from the General Household Survey reminds us that open-air outings, including outings by car/motor cycle or boat, are subject to variations in levels of participation. Visits to the countryside have shown an actual decrease of average trips per adult per year (Office of Population Censuses and Surveys, 1989a, p. 239). A number of reasons can be advanced for this trend: the decrease in domestic holiday-making, the effect of economic recessions and, to an extent, the introduction of more precise methods of calculating averages of rates of participation.

A number of studies of the effect of petrol price increases on recreational motoring indicate that sudden rises may have a short-term effect of decreasing trip distances but this is followed by recovery (Country-side Commission, 1985(a), p. 16). Thus drives and outings appeared to fall by a third between 1977 and 1980, a period when petrol prices increased by 40 per cent in real terms. They had recovered to their 1977 levels by the time of the National Countryside Recreation Survey in 1984 but the data may well have been influenced by the hot summer of that year in Britain.

Cycling

After many years in decline, there is evidence of an increase in the use of the bicycle both as a mode of transport used to reach the countryside and as a recreational pursuit in its own right (Groome, 1986, pp. 14–16).

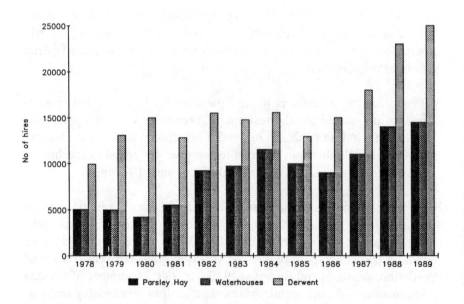

Figure 2.9   Peak District National Park: trends in use of hire cycles, 1978–1989

Source: Peak Park Joint Planning Board, correspondence

The 1986 General Household survey indicated that 2.3 per cent of the population over the age of 16 took part in recreational cycling with some degree of regularity. This figure should be compared with 0.9 per cent in 1977 (Office of Population Censuses and Surveys, 1989(a), p. 224). However, the revised questions on leisure included in the 1987 General Household Survey suggest that those figures had seriously underestimated levels of recreational cycling (Matheson, 1991, p. 13). Further indication of trends in cycling include membership of the Cyclists' Touring Club which increased from 19 000 in 1970 to 40 000 in 1990; and through hires at cycle-hire centres (Figure 2.9). Only a small proportion, some 9 per cent of all regular recreational cyclists, belong to a cycling governing body (Tourism and Recreation Research Unit, 1983a, p. viii). 'Barriers' to recreational cycling in the countryside include the growth in fast, heavy levels of traffic, increased distances between town and the start of the countryside and difficulties of travelling by train with a bicycle. Attempts to provide for recreational cycling include the creation of off-highway paths on disused railway lines. However, the success of such schemes is often dependent on planning authorities' safeguarding potential routes from development. Much will depend, too, on the extent to which cycling is more fully integrated with other modes of transport and how far it is promoted for the health, economic and environmental advantages it confers (Hillman, 1992, pp. 126–127).

Future developments are also likely to be influenced by continued interest in popular rugged 'mountain bikes' which are designed for off-road (often competitive) cycling and on the pace at which new facilities, are provided for cyclists. Mountain bikes accounted for 40 per cent of 2.4 million United Kingdom cycle sales in 1990. There is evidence of increasing conflict between mountain bike riders and other visitors to the countryside (Friends of the Earth, 1984; Cyclists' Touring Club, 1990).

Angling

There are over a million regular participants and over three million people participate at some time during the course of a year in Britain. An important feature of angling is the division of the activity into several specialist areas including sea, coarse and game angling with strong leisure and competitive dimensions. The *Digest of Sport Statistics* records the relatively high proportion of participants who belong to clubs and associations, although this varies between different branches of the sport.

31

There is a seasonal pattern to angling, with a major influence being 'close' seasons but with a clear summer peak in the July to September quarter (Matheson, 1991, p. 14).

The General Household Survey records some fluctuation in the numbers taking part in angling but with none of the significant increases noticed in activities such as walking and cycling. The activity is characterized by a relatively high turnover in participants who move on to other activities.

Plate 2.2   The future for angling is closely related to river and canal water quality and the stocking and pricing policies of providers: Macclesfield Canal, Poynton, 1988

Angling is a very male-dominated activity with minimal participation by women. A towing-path survey of anglers on the Leeds and Liverpool Canal revealed that 97 per cent of participants were male (British Waterways Board, 1989, p. 30). However, the *Digest* suggests that, nationally, there has been a gradual increase in women participating in angling.

The need for quiet undisturbed conditions and clean, accessible water makes angling particularly vulnerable to interference from other users. A national survey of inland waterways in 1984 revealed considerable concern by anglers about the impact of most other types of activity, particularly pleasure boaters and cyclists (British Waterways Board, 1986, p. 25). Highly resource-dependent, the future of angling is closely related to improvements being made to river and canal water quality, the stocking and pricing policies of providers, the creation of new fishing areas such as abandoned wet mineral workings reservoirs, and resolution of conflict between different users of water space.

Field sports

These activities include wild-fowling, grouse and pheasant shooting, and rough shooting. The *Digest* records a substantial and continual growth in membership of field sport organizations. Although not strictly speaking a field sport, clay pigeon shooting saw an increase in clubs and membership of the Clay Pigeon Shooting Association from 157 clubs and 550 members in 1965 to 860 and 13 000 respectively in 1985.

Plate 2.3   Recreational landscapes of the 1990s: clay pigeon shooting site near Rowlands Castle, Hampshire, 1991

The value of letting sporting rights on land can be considerable and an important influence on the growth of field sports will be the availability of appropriate land. A chartered surveyor's annual review of 1989/90 recorded 'astonishingly high prices' being paid for Scottish sporting estates with red deer stalking maintaining a strong appeal to the European market (Smiths Gore, 1990, p. 8).

Competition for the use of land for field sports can give rise to conflicts. The requirements of field sports such as deer stalking can be used as a reason for excluding walkers (Shoard, 1987, p. 290). In addition, aside from any debate about the rights or wrongs of blood sports, environmental conflicts have arisen over the construction of access roads to deer lands in Scotland. Disturbance over the use of land for clay pigeon shooting, including the erection of shooting towers, can also give rise to conflict (Planning Appeal Decisions, 1985, pp. 65–66).

It seems likely that interest in field sports will continue to increase. An influence on future trends will be the expansion of corporate entertainment in the countryside and the extent to which it extends to both angling and shooting. Seen as a way of cementing business relationships in relaxed surroundings, future development of these sporting activities will have implications for rural recreation planning and management.

Riding

Horse riding can be divided into several different classes of activity, although in terms of rural recreation the planning and management issues will tend to focus on hacking/informal riding and trekking.

The General Household Survey indicates that riding is undertaken by about 0.9 per cent of the England and Wales population aged 16 years or over (Matheson, 1991, p. 13). There does not appear to be a clear seasonal variation in riding although there is a suggestion that it takes place on a more frequent basis in winter than during the rest of the year.

The *Digest* noted that as evidenced by increases in numbers belonging to riding clubs, there has been a slight increase in participation. It records that the activity retains an image of being a pursuit for the white-collar, higher-income groups, with a particular popularity in the south of England. Needed for the enjoyment of riding is land for the keeping, hire, exercising and housing of horses used for recreation. The land needs for such activities can be quite extensive, particularly if developed commercially and can result in the fragmentation of farm holdings and suburbanization of the countryside (Council for the Protection of Rural England, 1989, para. 35; Department of the Environment, 1991c, p. 23).

Plate 2.4   Growth in riding in the future will be influenced by the availability of bridleways. A national trail which is used by riders, cyclists and walkers is the South Downs Way, shown here at Kingston, near Lewes, East Sussex, 1991

Future enjoyment of riding opportunities will also depend on the improvement, protection and extension of the bridleway network (Graham, 1988, p. 1). Stress is placed on the need for carefully designed paths and tracks that are free of fast or heavy road traffic. More so perhaps than in the case of cycling is the incompatibility between riding and other recreation pursuits and the need for riders to be clearly segregated from other users (Grimshaw, 1988, p. 49). Complaints may arise that large investments which have been made for a small number of off-highway

35

routes may tend to be used largely by commercial riding schools, with very little use by the casual rider (Centre for Leisure Research, 1986c, p. 113).

Visiting stately homes, gardens and ancient monuments

There has been a major growth in buildings and gardens open to the public in recent years. Participation rates to historic buildings, sites and towns increased from 2.9 visits a year in 1977 to 3.8 in 1980, fell back in 1983 to 3.0 and then increased to 3.7 visits in 1986 (Office of Population Censuses and Surveys, 1989a, p. 239). These variations can probably be explained by long-term changes in patterns of holiday-making and the incidence of adverse or fine weather. Outside holiday areas there is a

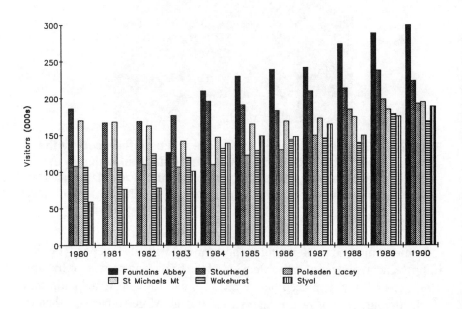

**Figure 2.10   England and Wales: visits to National Trust proper-
ties, 1980–1990**
Source: based on National Trust annual reports, 1980–1990

general upward trend in visitors to historic sites and buildings. Visits to National Trust properties have shown local variations, but there is a general upward trend in numbers (Figure 2.10; National Trust, 1990).

Camping and caravanning

Camping, particularly when carried out in conjunction with walking and cycling, has placed affordable recreation within easy reach of many people. The *Digest* records the importance of caravanning and camping as family activities, with interest being maintained over long periods of people's lives.

The old image of caravan holidays has changed considerably in the case of both touring and static caravans. Caravan holiday homes intended for seasonal use represent upgraded versions of the traditional holiday caravan site. From the perspective of the rural recreational planner and manager, there are significant problems in accommodating sites within rural areas. However, there have been noticeable improvements in quality of site management with an increasing emphasis being placed on attractiveness, design of layout, cleanliness and associated recreational and sporting facilities. Some caravan holiday home parks have been replaced by cabins in a landscaped setting.

The main participants' organization is the Camping and Caravan Club, which has approximately 170 000 members, including both caravanners (who form the bulk of members), motor caravanners, tented campers and trailer tents. The Club can own or lease sites and site rules are imposed in respect of matters such as vehicle speeds, rubbish disposal and general site management. Sites which are certified by the Club have exemption from planning controls under the Caravan Sites and Control of Development Act 1960. Under the General Development Order 1988, landowners do not need to obtain planning permission for using land for camping and caravanning for up to 28 days in a calendar year (Department of the Environment, 1989e).

Golf

The *Digest* records that golf is a popular sport with a widespread appeal to different age groups. However, it appears to have only limited appeal to women and to the less well-off. The 1987 General Household Survey indicates that 3.9 per cent of the population of Great Britain had played golf in the 4 weeks prior to interview (Matheson, 1991, p. 13).

Some 80% of present facilities in Britain are private members' clubs. However, there has been a trend to open these up to golfing societies whose business can be lucrative (Royal and Ancient Golf Club of St Andrews, 1989, p. 3). Buoyant demand for golf and long waiting lists are matched by much interest from the private sector into the development of courses. A recent trend has been the growth of syndicated golf clubs in which club members are shareholders and controllers of club policy. Such schemes can incorporate ancillary activities (restaurants, meeting rooms) and can occupy extensive areas of land with the largest extending to 100 ha or more.

Planning authorities are likely to recognize that golf courses can revert to agricultural use and that they can offer some diversity in terms of wildlife value (Green and Marshall, 1987; Nature Conservancy Council, 1989). However, the level of built development and the suburban character suggests that golf courses are really urban land uses located in the countryside. They are prone to attract growth, with ailing clubs seeing advantages in developing leisure facilities as a way of supporting the course (Chatters, 1991, p. 22).

The question of viability has to be addressed by planning authorities who are likely to require a market assessment so as to assess the financial and operational issues. Although much will depend on the particular circumstances of individual applications, planning authorities now offer guidelines in order to minimize the impact of golf schemes on the countryside (Leicestershire County Council, 1991, pp. 8–9).

Based on a notional standard of one course per 25 000 people, it has been suggested that 691 facilities will need to be built in the United Kingdom by the year 2000 (Royal and Ancient Golf Club of St Andrews, 1990, p. 3). Assuming an area of around 50 ha for an 18-hole course, the land-take for the required 91 courses in the West Midlands could be some 4 550 ha. In London and the South East, the land requirement could be 15 000 ha for an estimated shortfall of 300 courses.

Motor sports

The General Household Survey records this as an activity in which just under half a per cent of the adult population of England and Wales participate in the 4 weeks before interview (Matheson, 1991, p. 13). The activity includes both two- and four-wheeled motor sports which are carried out under off-highway conditions, and which are generally based on competition, although recreational off-highway motoring and motorcycling are also important. Many of the issues affecting the development of motor sports are discussed in a major review of these pursuits (Elson *et al.*, 1986).

The *Digest* notes a continued growth in popularity of motor sports in terms of both participation and in watching, but a major constraint is the lack of suitable facilities. However, assertions that the number of sites has actually reduced in recent years is not borne out by some evidence. Clubs, it seems, are using more sites but less frequently in order to avoid conflict and disturbance with others (Northern Motorsports Project, 1989, p. 10). Concern is expressed about the damage which can occur to paths and bridleways as well as the introduction or motor vehicles and their accompanying noise into quiet areas. The presence of highly articulate populations in the countryside can produce formidable opposition to motor sports (Hampshire County Council, 1989, p. 10). Motorsports user groups are sensitive to the attitudes of others, feeling that the legitimacy of their activity is being questioned. They are faced with 'opposition from the well-financed, well-staffed and well-marshalled body of opinion which is actively seeking to obliterate or severely restrict our leisure pursuits' (Northern Motorsports Project, 1989, p. 11).

War games/paint-ball games

Prospects of farm diversification have led landowners to consider many ways of obtaining alternative incomes from varied enterprises, including war games. The activity involves competition between teams dressed in camouflage clothing and armed with paint-pellet guns, who seek to attack defensive positions. War games take place in woods of 16–40 ha in extent with a mix of open space and cover and with exclusive access to which the general public is excluded. Other recreational activities can be undertaken since the activities tend to be confined to weekends (Smiths Gore, 1989, p. 16). Under the General Development Order 1988, planning permission is not required if activities take place on no more than 28 days in a calendar year. However, war games can constitute development: for example, if new accesses are required or buildings are erected. Applications for planning permission to use sites for war games can be the subject of local controversy and conservationists are particularly concerned about the effects of war games. Considerable, and in some cases permanent, damage occurs in woodlands after quite small amounts of activity (Hatton, 1991, p. 27).

Yachting

Under this heading is included a wide range of activities from powered and sail vessels used in coastal areas to narrowboats used on canals and inland waterways. The *Digest* records a number of characteristics of yachting, including its popularity amongst a wide range of ages and its appeal, in particular, to white-collar workers. Yachting has expanded markedly as a leisure pursuit since the Second World War, although participation appears to have levelled off. The requirements for yachting activities are primarily for accessible coastal or inland waters. The *Digest* records little increase in opportunities for sailing on water supply reservoirs, but in practice there is still considerable scope for yachting in some regions (Water Authorities Association, 1988, p. 52).

A number of planning issues arise in providing for yachting. In the case of coastal yachting, there exists considerable pressure for the use of estuaries for mooring and boat storage. On the extensive 3 500 km network of inland waterways in Britain, there are problems of congestion and conflict between boat users and anglers and, in certain instances such as the Basingstoke Canal in Hampshire and Surrey, conservationists (Sidaway, 1988, p. 87). In the case of water supply reservoirs conflict can arise between sailing and protection of wildlife habitats; management plans for reservoirs may designate areas for particular types of activity (Eachus Huckson Partnership, 1988, pp. 17–19)

A feature of yachting is that it can take relatively inexpensive forms, although anxiety has been expressed about big increases in mooring charges as owners try to realize the development potential of sites for marinas and other projects. Numbers of marinas in south and south-east England increased significantly between 1981 and 1990, with a virtual doubling of capacity, 8 000 berths being provided in that period (Sidaway, 1991, p. 5)

ATTITUDES TO RURAL RECREATION

There seems little doubt that countryside, however defined, is important in people's minds. Nearly two thirds of visitors who go to the countryside do so because it is countryside rather than because it is a convenient place to pursue a particular activity (Countryside Commission, 1985 (a), p. 13). Trips from home appear to be split equally between places specifically singled out for a visit and others selected on a casual basis with the motivation of simply getting out into the country.

An important point to emerge from recreation behaviour studies is that researchers and practitioners have often tried to demonstrate that a causal relationship exists between the various factors that may influence rural recreation. However, the conclusions which are drawn have often been simplistic and the underlying relationships have not been fully understood (Owens, 1984, p. 160). The interrelationships between the different factors are really quite complex and the attempts to refine our knowledge of rural recreation suggest that rather than catering for 'Mr and Mrs Average', there exists a wide range of differences between the characteristics of various types of visitor.

Consideration also needs to be given to the significant proportion of the population for whom the countryside does not play a particularly significant role in their recreational pursuits. Surveys undertaken for the Countryside Commission for its *Recreation 2000* initiative in 1987 demonstrated that in relation to people's local countryside then over a third of the population regarded it as being a place in which there is 'not very much' or 'nothing at all' to do.

To what extent is the perception of what the countryside has to offer a reflection of constraints or barriers or of personal preferences? An analysis of the 1984 National Countryside Recreation Survey sought to identify which of these was of greatest influence (Curry and Comley, 1986b, p. 15). The investigation involved analysis of the questions in the Survey which asked respondents to indicate the following:

- those activities they would be *interested in undertaking* in the countryside;
- *how easy* it would be for them actually to do those pursuits.

For going on drives or outings, the ratio between the two responses produced a relatively close match of 55 and 67 per cent. In other words, a significant proportion of respondents felt that it would be relatively easy to take up a stated activity. Similarly, in the case of visiting country parks and going on long walks, around two thirds of respondents considered that it would be easy for them to pursue those activities. However, in the case of specialist activities such as visiting nature reserves, riding and angling, pursuits for which there was a clear interest amongst respondents, significant proportions saw difficulty in participating in the activities concerned. Analysis of responses amongst different social groups reveals that in social groups A, B and C1, the ease of participating in countryside recreation overall was higher than the respondent's interest in activities (Curry and Comley, 1986b, p. 15). In social groups C2, D and E, there was a noticeably smaller general interest in countryside recreation generally, but there was a noticeable increase in the degree of difficulty that respondents felt they would experience in pursuing rural recreation activities. The investigation reminds us of the importance of individual preferences or antipathy towards particular activities as well, of course, as the influence of other constraints such as lack of personal mobility.

A criticism of large-scale national countryside recreation surveys is that for the most part they have dealt with broad statistical aggregates and not with individual groups of countryside visitors. For example, it has been argued that the 1977 National Survey of Countryside Recreation could be of only limited help in extending our understanding of the meaning of recreation to the individual (Sidaway, 1982, p. 14). Like most of the surveys discussed, it provided only a limited indication of how rural recreation fitted in to the wider pattern of activities in a person's life.

This theme has been explored further by Glyptis in a study of Holderness which attempted to relate individual life-styles to enjoyment of the countryside (Glyptis, 1981). The investigation recorded that participation patterns had to be seen in relation to a diverse pattern of underlying values, motivations and preferences. Much would seem to revolve around 'life-style', defined as the aggregate pattern of day-to-day activities which make up an individual's way of life. Time-budget diaries issued to respondents were used to help identify common elements to life-styles amongst countryside visitors. By use of 'association analysis' the research demonstrated a high degree of life-style 'specialization'. In the case of countryside visitors, then trip-making, sport, walking and classes appeared to hold an unusual importance in peoples' lives. In the case of home-based activities, then there appeared to be an affiliation with reading, hobbies, home and car maintenance and games. The research concludes that 'life-style similarities for countryside visitors transcend social-class differences and car ownership' (Glyptis, 1981, p. 324).

The perception of countryside and green space in people's minds has been explored by other researchers, too. A study of attitudes to the countryside amongst residents in the London Borough of Greenwich suggested that there was a wide range of interest in countryside amongst people from different social backgrounds (Harrison, Limb and Burgess, 1986, p. 20). However, people seek a variety of countryside experiences. For some, the countryside offers a place for solitary enjoyment. For others, enjoyment of the countryside is something which is invariably shared with others.

It would appear that demand and need for countryside recreation is a complex issue. There is a strong irrational element in demand which is not possible to explain by quantified factors (Coopers and Lybrand, 1979, p. 18). The information and advice available to the practitioner on an individual's attitudes to the use of the countryside may appear contradictory and difficult to relate to practice. It is likely, however, that an ability to enjoy the countryside is something which is acquired gradually and it is learned.

FUTURE TRENDS IN PEOPLE'S ENJOYMENT OF THE COUNTRYSIDE

The opportunities, constraints and preferences noted here will continue to influence the future use of the countryside for recreation. Their significance was explored in scenarios developed as part of the Countryside Commission's *Recreation 2000* investigation. A number of possibilities were suggested.

- Demographic changes are likely to result in increased demand for recreation from an expanding 30–44 age group, offset by a decline from groups aged 16–29. Increases in one-person and one-parent households could foster a decline in countryside use because of the essentially social nature of the recreational visit and because trips are rarely undertaken alone.
- Depopulation of inner city areas could see a further 3–5 million people housed in peripheral areas by the end of the century, resulting in a greater ability and inclination to visit the countryside.
- Mobility will increase with a continued but slower rise in car ownership accompanied by a decline in public transport; increase

43

in incomes for those in work could be accompanied by an increase of leisure time for the whole population by an estimated 5 per cent.

- A key factor will be the attraction of the countryside relative to other leisure destinations: for example, social and community leisure, eating out and attending local events. Despite the attraction of home-centred leisure in a safe environment, natural experiences will be gained in the countryside *per se* rather than in 'para' countryside.
- Increasing public awareness of environmental issues suggest that the countryside will grow in importance as something of increasing interest to be enjoyed and conserved (Countryside Commission, 1987(a), pp. 24–25).

Such scenarios as these can help to highlight possible directions for change in the use of the countryside. However, certain of the ideas explored need to be refined further. In the case of mobility, traffic forecasts now suggest major increases of between 83 and 142 per cent in vehicular traffic volumes from 1988 to 2025 (Department of Transport, 1989, p. 1). In addition, questions remain over future changes in population and residential choice and these could have a marked influence on the form of future demand for rural recreation. City 'cramming' policies now result in up to 60 per cent of new housing being infilling in built-up areas. However, in the future a large proportion of new housing will need to be built outside existing urban areas, as suburban extensions or as new settlements (Breheny, 1991, p. 11). The extent to which different concepts of urban form are incorporated into planning policy will clearly be of importance in influencing future ease of access to and enjoyment of the countryside.

Thus, of interest are proposals for strategic policies for the countryside promoted by the Town and Country Planning Association (Green and Holliday, 1991). Amongst the ingredients of a new order of countryside planning would be the following:

- incorporating the concept of sustainable development, emphasizing the continuity of cycles of development, decline and regeneration, supported by a full audit of countryside resources;
- continuing dispersal of people from city to countryside met by the

creation of sustainable and efficient new settlements ('social cities') linked to public transport;

- continued support for farming and forestry but with the introduction of new controls over them, integration into other economic activities and wider frameworks of community development;
- new countryside strategies taking policies beyond what is currently included in structure and local plans, including, for example, energy, recreation, new hamlets, villages and small towns, all associated with community participation and local initiatives;
- new countryside centres to undertake audits of countryside resources, advise and assess developments, aid local planning authorities in preparing countryside strategies (Green and Holliday, 1991, pp. 19–20).

The concepts outlined in the 'New Countryside' proposals contribute to the debate about the future form of the countryside and the setting within which rural recreation policies will evolve. In particular, its questioning of the continuation of green belt and agriculture policies in their present forms warrants careful consideration. The notion of sustainability is not new but the widespread support that it could attract reminds us that it too might feature prominently in the development of countryside recreation policies.

COMMENT

This review suggests that there is a constantly changing demand for rural recreation. Of note is the apparent levelling-off of demand for passive pursuits and increases for sport and recreation in the countryside which involve physical activity and the use of equipment. Some of these newer activities have all the signs of being 'lifestyle' sports and are often expensive to undertake. Generally, there is every sign of rural recreation having gone 'up market'.

Competition for the use of land or water emerges as a constant theme amongst the problems being faced by countryside recreation users. To an extent the competition is a reflection of the ability of certain groups to pay for their enjoyment of the countryside and to exclude others in bargaining for the use of land or water. Thus, low-cost activities on which a value has not been placed in the past now seem particularly vulnerable to pressures from many sources for the use of land or water to which they have generally had unrestricted access. However, other problems concern managerial issues, finding satisfactory solutions to accommodating different users: for example, in minimizing damage caused to wildlife by paint-ball games on the one hand or separating riders from walkers on the other.

The nature of these conflicts and the increasingly extensive areas of land now required for some activities underline the case for continuing regulation of land uses in the countryside. For the planning practitioner a number of questions will require consideration. To what extent can all the activities discussed in this chaper be described as being 'rural', and appropriate in the countryside? In some cases, the setting would appear to be immaterial and, if sites were available, an urban location for some sports would seem to be quite acceptable. In addition, although some of the activities described are exempt from planning control, is that always going to be advisable if demands for some activities exceed what is considered acceptable in a locality? Lastly, in looking to the future, how might future demands relate to evolving concepts of urban development: in particular, the notion of new rural settlements and continued peripheral growth on the edges of cities?

Chapter 3

Tools for plan-making

It has been shown that a wide range of data about rural recreational pursuits are available to planners. The use of this and other information in actually devising plans is normally considered under two headings: methodology, the sequence in which particular stages in a plan-making process might take place; and techniques, 'tools' of various kinds that might be available to planners in preparing rural recreation plans. In respect of both methodology and techniques, rural recreation has been strongly influenced by movements in the mainstream of planning, with stress being placed in particular on its cyclical nature, as expressed in Figure 3.1.

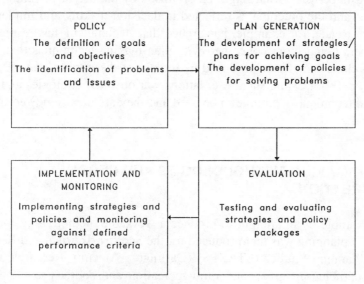

Figure 3.1   The cyclical planning process
Source: Field and MacGregor (1987), p.11

In its various forms, the cyclical process of plan-making features certain repeated elements (Field and MacGregor, 1987, p. 10):

- the definition of objectives in relation to more general goals;
- the generation of strategies to achieve goals and objectives and the formulation of policies to actually achieve them;
- the testing and evaluation of strategies and policy packages;
- implementation and monitoring.

A feature of plan-making, particularly from the early 1960s onwards, was a search for greater rationality with the use of replicable, quantified methods of analysis at each stage of the planning process. This approach has been contrasted with the more informal and intuitive rules of thumb which characterized much British planning in the immediate post-war period and 1950s. Representative of this search for rationality in rural resource planning in the late 1960s and early 1970s, and reflected in a strong emphasis on methodology and systematic use of planning techniques, were the 1968 East Hampshire AONB study and the 1974 Sherwood Forest study (Hampshire County Council *et al.*, 1968; Sherwood Forest Study Group, 1974). Needless to say, there have been marked contrasts between what might be promised by the use of planning techniques and the outcome as reflected in decision-making and implementation. Reade, for example, has argued that 'technicism' has resulted in planners being more concerned with plan-making techniques than with researching the effects produced by the use of these techniques (Reade, 1987, p. 99). Despite such reservations, various methodologies and analytical techniques continue to be used and they are now reviewed in this chapter.

PLAN-MAKING METHODOLOGIES AND RURAL RECREATION

An example of an attempt to produce a workable methodology for recreation planning was that produced for the Scottish Tourism and Recreation Planning Studies (STARPS) (Dartington Amenity Research Trust, 1977). Including urban and rural recreation and sports provision, the methodology can be seen as representative of the different stages that might be followed in preparing rural recreation plans.

The sequence of stages identified was as follows.

1. Clarification of strategic issues for sport, outdoor recreation and tourism. Under this heading are discussed social and economic changes, the aims of national agencies and the relevance of these for individual regions.
2. Analysis of supply and future demands for recreation, including the use of modelling techniques for five categories of demand. Assessment of supply was based on inventories to which capacity formulae were applied.
3. Assessment of the impact of recreation and tourism upon the economy, community and environment.
4. Formulation of aims and objectives relevant to recreation and tourism, cross-referenced to national goals.
5. Development of policies and drawing together an initial strategy.

It will be seen that the process is designed to be cyclical. It allows for feed back-loops, reviews of policy and subsequent policy modification (Figure 3.2). Although the STARPS model was devised for specific conditions in Scotland and was not applied to any great extent, the approach nevertheless offers a useful sequence for analysing the different factors which contribute to policy-making.

A second example of methodology where the cyclical nature of recreational plan-making has also been explored is in guidelines produced for the planning and management of parks and open spaces (Morgan, 1991, p. 11). Although applicable primarily to urban fringe sites and urban parks the principles expressed in this investigation might also be applied to rural recreation strategies. The guidelines outline a process as follows (Figure 3.3).

- Fact-finding surveys, including estimates of the nature of existing use, characteristics of catchment areas, users and non-users; examination of the take-up of facilities by visitors and use of market research techniques to adopt a consumer-oriented approach to open-space provision.
- Supply studies, indicating the location of sites and facilities which are available and highlighting relevant standards where they may be applicable.
- Analysis, including identification of the major issues affecting the

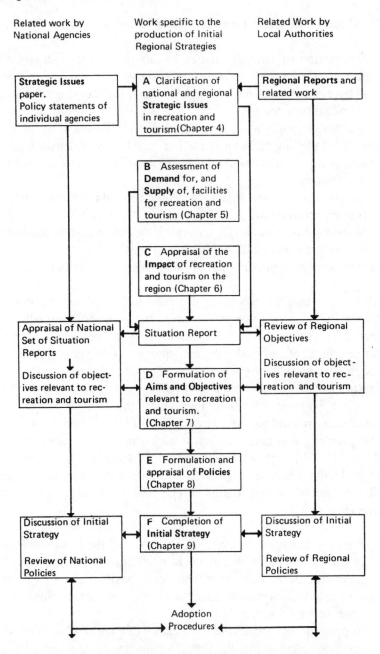

Figure 3.2   The STARPS approach to recreation policy-making
Source: Dartington Amenity Research Trust (1977), p.12

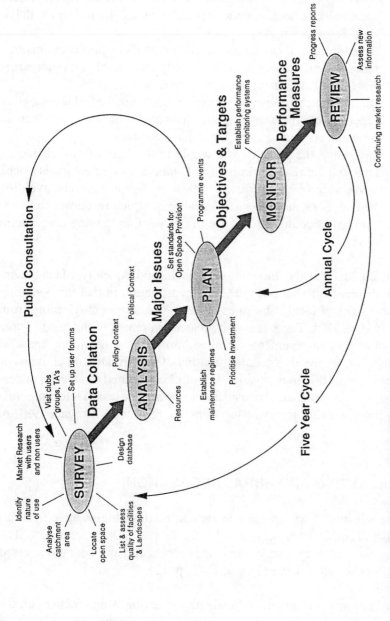

Figure 3.3 The strategic planning process
Source: Morgan (1991), p.12

51

provision of open spaces, reviewing present performance, identifying opportunities for increased provision and recording the national, regional and local policy context for the strategy. Stressed is the need to devise solutions which realistically reflect availability of resources in future years.

- Devising objectives, including such matters as provision, maintenance and programming with a clearly identifiable set of targets at short-, medium- and long-term intervals.
- Monitoring the strategy, reporting back on the achievement of targets, with the use of performance criteria against which to judge the achievement of particular objectives.
- Reviewing the strategy as a whole in the light of new demands, demographic changes, fashion and other factors. Emphasis is placed on the value of major reviews at 3- or 5-year intervals, avoiding the danger of more frequent reviews in which responses to short-term issues could result in the overlook of underlying longer-term trends.

The context for the Institute of Leisure and Amenity Management model differs from that of the DART investigation in that the operating circumstances of local authorities in the 1990s differ considerably from those in the 1970s. There is now a greater awareness of the need to take account of user requirements; local authorities have declining financial bases and are exposed to detailed scrutiny of performance on all items of expenditure. In this light, availability of clearly stated strategies, underpinned by relevant data, is considered to be a significant factor in political decision-making about the use of public resources (Morgan, 1991, p. 18).

FORECASTING AND RURAL RECREATION

Commonly found within rural recreation methodologies have been attempts to forecast likely demands for future uses of the countryside. The central part played by forecasting in the process of plan-making is stressed as follows (Field and MacGregor, 1987, p. 12).

- Planning is a process of analysis and action which focuses on the future. An important feature of planning is the manipulation of procedures and activities to achieve goals. Forecasting is seen to be central to such a process.

- The use of technical methods of analysis, including mathematical models, can help improve understanding of spatial systems and enable predictions to be made of future changes in spatial systems and the effects of policy on these.
- It is important that the forecasts generated by various methods of analysis carry a measure of confidence, reflected in the degree of accuracy and the validity of any models.

What techniques of recreation forecasting might be available to planners? Three of the more familiar techniques are as follows.

- Participation rates: with known participation rates and a population forecast the number of participants can be forecast. For example, if it is shown that 10 per cent of the population take part in a leisure activity on a regular basis, then planning at a local or regional level would attempt to provide support for that level of participation. This approach could be refined to take account of variations in age, so that greater provision is made if the population includes a high proportion of young people. A major problem associated with this approach is that current levels of participation will tend to reflect current provision and suppressed demand is not taken into account. In addition, local social traditions and attitudes are likely to vary greatly and render more difficult forecasting on the basis of participation rates.
- Multiple-regression techniques can be used to forecast participation in particular activities, using estimates of expected changes in a wide range of factors such as age, sex, household structure, car ownership, marital status and hours of work. The approach has been used in a number of studies, including the 1972 investigation into leisure in the north west of England (Patmore and Rogers, 1972). The technique has a number of limitations, notably the assumption that the relationship between the different factors will remain the same during the forecast period.
- The Clawson method places a cost on the visit to a recreational site and explains levels of use in terms of that cost (Clawson, 1981). It involves examining the origins of and distances travelled by visitors to a site and calculating an assumed cost for that trip.

53

The catchment indicated by this will bear a relationship to the costs borne by visitors. Variations in cost, entry fee for example, can be used to forecast levels of use at a site. The approach has mainly been used to forecast likely use of new projects and uses but has a number of serious problems associated with it. Estimating travel costs can be difficult, particularly if the journey is not perceived as 'cost' but is an enjoyable part of the recreation experience; in addition, perceived entrance costs can appear to be more important to the visitor than travel costs (Field and MacGregor, 1987, pp. 179–180).

Recreation forecasting has evolved in several phases. Burton records that it was in the 1950s that trends in increased participation in outdoor recreation became apparent. The response of researchers at the time was a feeling that the causal factors were so numerous and difficult to measure that little could be done: 'even if we could forecast the effects of measurable influences, the results would be subject to such a degree of error to make them of little or no practical value' (Burton, 1971, p. 291). A second phase identified by Burton involved the use of estimates, the 'informed judgement of administrators, planners and other "experts"'. However, 'the problem with this was that estimates soon came to embody perspectives.' In other words, the forecasts became prescriptions for policy. A third phase involved the use of extrapolations based on current trends, which was more scientific in that it was 'based upon an objective mathematical system which excluded value judgement' (Burton, 1971, p. 292).

An important theme which arises in measuring future demands for rural recreation is that publicly provided recreational facilities are essentially collective goods. Consumers are either not asked to pay for them as they use them, or they pay a nominal fee which does not cover the cost of supply (Burton, 1983, p. 229). The problem faced by researchers therefore is that of determining the demand for public goods in a situation where the normal supply-and-demand relationship does not apply.

The record of forecasting in rural recreation can therefore be a hazardous activity, presenting great difficulties in incorporating such matters as taste and fashion (Patmore, 1983, p. 83). Against that background, it is not surprising to learn that recreation 'is an area of activity which has been relatively neglected by land use planners, and is the one (topic)

54

which is furthest from having a standard forecasting methodology' (Field and MacGregor, 1987, p. 159).

For the local authority or consultant planner today confronted with the task of forecasting the demand for rural recreational facility or service, then a pragmatic approach is likely to be adopted. A commonly held view has been that 'whatever facility is provided, it will be used, wherever it is located'. For that reason, little attention has been paid to forecasting demand precisely. Practitioners may rely simply on abstraction of limited data from the regional patterns of participation identified from national surveys such as the National Countryside Recreation Survey 1984. However, such data will be only of limited value and will need verifying at a local level.

There are few current examples of the use of forecasting techniques for rural recreation planning in Britain. At present, the widest comprehensive use of forecasting techniques appears to be in the USA. For example, the 1989 New York State Comprehensive Outdoor Recreation Plan uses analysis zones to identify the relationship between resource location and demands and needs (New York State Office of Parks, Recreation and Historic Preservation, 1989, pp. 2.30–2.36). Like other demand studies it assesses the probability and frequency of present users of recreation facilities, explores their expressed preferences, pressures on the use of existing facilities and ownership of sports and recreation equipment. The demand model projects shifts in population and incorporates variables such as age, travel time and the geographical location of facilities and users. Finally, a 'needs analysis' is used to project demands in relation to existing conditions of supply. For each activity study, capacity information is computed on a county basis and 'pressure indexes' are used to identify areas where there is a need for more provision.

For examples of current British practice, regional sports council studies have probably demonstrated the keenest interest in the use of forecasting techniques. However, studies tend to relate to urban sports and recreation where quantified data are relatively easily obtained. In Wales, a 10-year strategy for sport includes consideration of the demand for golf courses, a major user of rural land (Sports Council for Wales, 1986, p. 79). It uses a mathematical model developed by Planning and Management Development Services (PDMS) with three main ingredients: demand, supply and catchment area. The model uses several variables:

- the desirable levels of participation from the population as a whole according to age and sex;
- the frequency and duration of activities and the extent of the peak period;
- the percentage of outings that take place in peak periods, the radius of catchment areas and the 'at one time' capacity for each facility type.

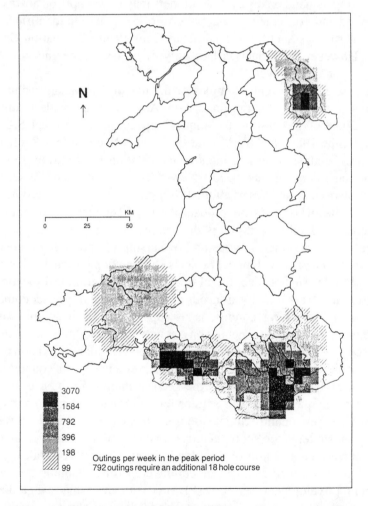

Figure 3.4   Wales: aggregate demand for golf courses, all facilities

Source: Sports Council for Wales (1986), p. 79

The model uses 5 km squares as the basis for the analysis and forecasts. The model can be applied to individual activities for the whole of Wales and for individual local authorities. It identifies present capacity and unsatisfied demand and provides an indication of how many additional users would be attracted to a new facility. The application of the model for golf is illustrated in Figure 3.4.

Although local planning authorities themselves have undertaken few forecasting studies in recent years, consultants' studies for public and private clients have as a matter of course often carried out extensive demand studies. For the most part these have been for single activities or facilities such as theme parks and not for the comprehensive treatment of rural recreation. In an investigation into the benefits of constructing the Trans-Pennine Trail from Liverpool to York, consultants forecast numbers of 'user-days' based on evidence of levels of use of similar facilities elsewhere in Britain (L and R plc *et al.*, 1990, p. 5.14). In situations such as these, the need for demand studies can be quite apparent to client and consultant because of the scale of investment involved and because of competing demands for limited public finance. However, here as in all forecasting, figures need to be handled with caution. It is important, for example, that account is taken of the propensity of new facilities to abstract visitors from other competing sites. A demand study into boating facility provision usefully reminds us of the problems of extrapolating data for forecasting (Sidaway, 1991, p. 34). Some refinement of broad trends can be achieved by market segmentation, identifying the specific requirements of particular types of vessel, such as small sailing cruisers or racing sailboats. But even with such refinements, all assumptions about future growth in demand have to be treated with a healthy scepticism.

It will be clear from this discussion that forecasting of rural recreation demand is beset with difficulties. Practitioners may well abdicate from more than a minimal consideration of the theme but the case for a more systematic approach to demand forecasting still remains. As Gratton and Taylor argue, forecasting is a requirement if responses to recreation demands are to be made efficiently and equitably. 'Forecasting and planning techniques may have their weaknesses, but without them there is an information gap that has serious repercussions for efficient management and policy. Any systematic planning initiatives, therefore, are to be applauded' (Gratton and Taylor, 1985, p. 118).

RECORDING DATA ON RECREATION RESOURCES

The need for a good information base for policy-makers is as relevant to recreation as it is in the use of other rural resources. Relevant information might relate to land used for recreation, together with data on other land uses which might influence or be influenced by rural recreation: agricultural land, forests, wildlife conservation areas, vegetation, geology and other data. Some of such data could form part of an existing wider rural land-use information system, as for example that developed by Highland Regional Council and the Institute of Terrestrial Ecology (Claridge, 1988, p. 21). Otherwise, such information is likely to be assembled on a more *ad hoc* basis and subject to analysis with or without computing facilities.

Compared with drawing up an inventory of different types of agricultural land, rural recreation resources may encompass a very wide range of variables. Included in an inventory might be land dedicated solely to recreation such as a picnic area. But a schedule could also include farmland on which a footpath or bridleway might be a marginal secondary activity; or an area of scenic countryside might be considered as a recreational resource even if there is no public access. Recreation resource inventories may be quite complex and careful consideration will need to be given to the actual way in which site attributes are classified. Thus, besides describing physical characteristics such as soil, slope and vegetation, information will also be required on matters such as ownership, tenancies, statutory designations, access and form of management.

In the STARPS studies, information was assembled on the existing and potential supply of recreation resources (outlets) as shown in Table 3.1.

In assembling data on recreation, an important question which must be addressed is: why is the information needed? Certainly in recent years there has been a reaction against assembling large amounts of data which might be used in the preparation of recreation plans. However, certain minimal information is still needed to develop policies and to build up an understanding of rural and recreational resources. The case for a systematic approach to preparing resource inventories has been stated in the 1990 community forest plan manual (Anderson, 1990, pp. 13–15). Besides land-uses, natural resources, landscape and access, the inventory should extend to include land ownership, land and property values, community organization and the general and specific planning context.

Table 3.1
Resource (supply) categories in rural recreation planning

Type of activity	Outlet (supply)
Active outdoor recreation	Angling waters, water sports areas, pony trekking and organized riding centres
	Hill-walking routes
	Artificial ski slopes
Visits to places of interest	Museums, historic houses, interpretation centres etc
	Tourist information centres
	Gardens, wildlife parks, zoos
	Nature reserves, trails
	Outdoor spectating facilities
Informal countryside recreation	Beach: parking spaces and accessible beach space
	Other coastline, lochside/riverside, woodland, hill and mountain land: (parking spaces, designated picnic areas, accessible areas)
Use of tourist accommodation	Hotels, paying guest, rented accommodation, friends and relatives, second home, youth hostel, camp site, touring caravan, static caravan, other accommodation

Source: based on Dartington Amenity Research Trust (1977), pp. 22–24

LAND CAPABILITY

Besides providing an inventory of what exists, recreation resource data can be considered in terms of the capability of those resources to meet particular user requirements. By recreational capability is understood 'the relationship between land properties and recreational user requirements with the overall aim of maximizing user satisfaction' (Johnstone and Tivy, 1981, p. 90).

In undertaking capability studies, consideration needs to be given to the different requirements of recreationists in terms of both simple quantitative requirements and more subjective requirements such as a visitor's tolerance of specified numbers of other visitors. In drawing an analogy with agriculture it has been observed that the crop yield from farming activity is relatively easy to measure whereas the recreational goal of user satisfaction is very difficult to assess because of factors such as perception, skill, taste and mood (Johnstone and Tivy, 1981, p. 91).

Despite these problems, attempts have been made to identify the capability of land and water resources for particular recreational pursuits (Hampshire County Council, 1968; Sherwood Forest Study Group, 1974). The Mourne Area of Outstanding Natural Beauty recreation strategy makes extensive use of capability analysis techniques (Greer and Murray, 1988, p. 20). The strategy extends over some 570 km^2 of countryside located in the southeast corner of Northern Ireland, including a considerable length of coast, mountains, valleys and lowlands. The methodology involves several stages of investigation, as follows.

- The Mourne Mountains Area of Outstanding Natural Beauty is divided into 63 elements based on landscape, physiography, land use and access characteristics (Figure 3.5).
- Within each element an assessment is made of the range of possible recreation uses appropriate to each element by virtue of physical, visual and location characteristics. Activities considered range from touring and scenic driving to motor bicycle pursuits.
- In each element, scores are recorded for the presence of or potential for each activity, reflecting extent of appeal, popularity and specialist interest together with facility and skill requirements.
- By adding all activity scores, a total score for each element is mapped.
- Scores of 100 points or more indicate a wide range of activities are possible; less than 50 points mean that a only a limited range of activities is possible.

The authors acknowledge that capability analysis can be only one component in producing a strategy for recreation and that whether the potential is actually taken up will depend on a number of factors including conflict with other activities and other practical considerations. The analysis must be seen as one element in the development of the Mourne

60

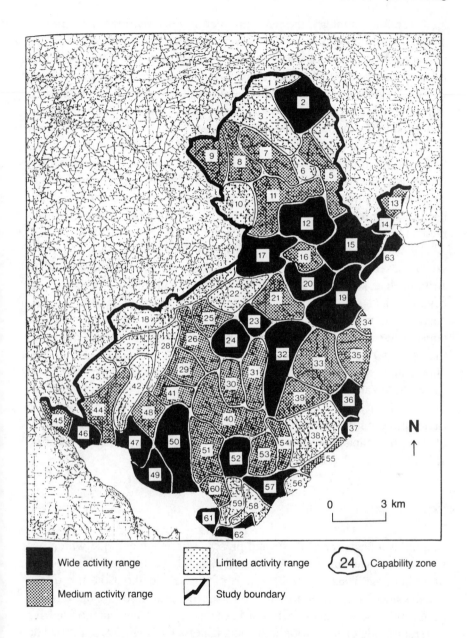

Figure 3.5   Mourne Area of Outstanding Natural Beauty: recreation capability analysis
Source: Greer and Murray (1988), p. 23

area recreation strategy, the main product of which was the definition of 14 zones within which different types of recreation policy would be pursued. As a planning tool, the approach appears able to provide a fuller understanding of the existing provision and potential opportunity for rural recreation. In particular, it assists in identifying the comparative advantages for different recreation activities across all elements of the countryside (Greer and Murray, 1988, p. 24).

A further observation is that there is a tendency in capability studies to focus on limiting factors for activities that are liable to cause conflicts. The Mourne studies are valuable in demonstrating the need to consider 'enhancing' factors, too. This may help to overcome the drawback of resource studies which pay insufficient attention to user requirements (Johnstone and Tivy, 1981, p. 95).

The Mourne studies also alight on the theme of capacity, a topic which has been of central concern to rural recreation researchers. In Britain, discussion has focused on ecological, physical and perceptual capacity, and the concept is examined more fully in relation to site design and management in Chapter 6. Area-wide application of the concept has been rare but where undertaken consideration is required of the type and number of visitors, activities undertaken, duration of use, choice and expectations of users and planning objectives. All these can fluctuate greatly and there are significant problems in indicating an innate capacity of an area of land or water (Owens, 1984, p. 167). In a rather more optimistic note, one commentator counters that the concept of carrying capacity remains as a basic management tool (Patmore, 1983, p. 232).

ZONING

Zoning as a basis for analysis and prescription is a technique which has survived the various waves of interest which have affected rural recreation planning. Thus, in 1990, as part of the debate about the use of the countryside for sport and recreation activities, the Sports Council suggested that the countryside might be zoned, with areas categorized for different kinds of recreation and sport (Sports Council, 1990, p. 9). The ability of the countryside to withstand pressures could be reflected in categories ranging from 'robust' and 'resilient', to 'stable' and 'sensitive'. Here, the concept of capacity would have a role to play in indicating what levels of use might be appropriate in different zones.

The value of zoning as a planning concept has also been stated in the Countryside Commission manual on the preparation of informal plans for community forests (Walshe, 1990, pp. 6–7):

- zoning allows complex issues to be broken down into units within which land use and management problems can be more readily handled;
- zoning can operate at several levels, with differing degrees of detail and flexibility;
- it allows prescriptions for land use change and management for distinct geographical areas.

In applying the recommended zoning approach in the Thames Chase community forest plan, zoning divisions were based on character zones which reflected different elements in the landscape: woodland, farmland, wildlife and recreation (Thames Chase Team, 1992, p. 41). Prescriptions for change were then worked up within a general broad objective for the community forest as a whole.

Zoning approaches have also been recommended for the preparation of areas of outstanding natural beauty management plans where they would form the basis for defining area specific objectives, management proposals and arrangements for implementation of policies (Woolerton Truscott, 1992, p. 14).

Sieve map analysis techniques have been used in some zone-based plans in order to identify the extent to which different land uses might be accommodated in the countryside. Typically, mapped sheets of data showing constraints on different activities are superimposed one on another, and 'suitable' areas emerge where there would be least objection to development or increase in an activity.

The approach has been used extensively for natural resource planning, being demonstrated in particular by American researchers (McHarg, 1969; Ortolano, 1984). In Scotland sieve mapping has been used to identify the suitability of land for different activities (Highland Regional Council, 1989, p. 12). In a number of local authorities in Britain the development of comprehensive geographical information systems enables ready analysis of the suitability of land for different uses. However, data tend to be for themes such as wildlife conservation areas or mineral reserves and it is still rare to find data specifically relating to rural recreation.

Sieve map techniques can be criticized on the grounds that they have been used mainly to filter out areas which are unsuitable for particular activities, rather than in emphasizing the requirements for recreational activities themselves.

STANDARDS

Standards have been widely used as a basis for recreational planning in Britain. Most widespread have been approaches based on the National Playing Fields Association 1926 standard of 6 acres of open space per 1 000 population. Veal records that an important advantage of the use of standards is the fact that they are generally easy to understand and they avoid unnecessary research by providers. Amongst their disadvantages are the questionable methods used to derive them and the failure of standards to take account of local conditions (Veal, 1982, pp. 6–7). In a rural context, the concept of standards has not been used widely. However, the STARPS studies attempted to identify standards of provision per 1 000 population (Dartington Amenity Research Trust, 1977, p. 68). The standards were based on nationally obtained data on:

- estimates of the percentage of population, resident or tourist, who will wish to take part in an activity;
- the expected average frequency of participation within an appropriate period of time;
- the capacity standard of the matching activity outlet for the same period of time.

Included in a schedule outlining standards of provision for per 1 000 resident and tourist population are: 2.15 parking spaces for visiting lowland countryside; 1.4 ha of nature reserves; 3.2 km of hill-walking routes; and 8.7 parking spaces for visiting beaches. A caveat to the standards reminds that they will need adapting to local conditions (Dartington Amenity Research Trust, 1977, p. 68). In more recent years, the use of standards has been most widely advocated in relation to provision of golf courses (Royal and Ancient Golf Club of Saint Andrews, 1989). Guidance from government in England and Wales would

Plate 3.1   Forecasts for golf based on standards suggested a need for almost 700 new courses between 1989 and 2000. Private golf course under construction on farmland at Tabley, Cheshire, 1990

appear to underline the value of using standards as a measure for provision of open space. *Planning Policy Guidance 17*, for example, draws reminders that the National Playing Fields Association standards and the Greater London Development Plan (GLDP) standards may provide a basis on which to consider provision at a local level (Department of the Environment, 1991e, pp. 4–5).

MATRICES

The use of matrices (or grids) as checklists can be valuable analytical tools. Veal, for example, suggests the following (Veal, 1986, pp. 10–11).

- They offer a schema for providing an overall assessment of leisure services.
- The approach can be used with minimal data to provide a broad-based assessment.
- They can be used to show the extent to which policies are catering

for particular groups of users: for example, physically disabled groups.

● For the practitioner with limited research resources, then matrices can quite clearly be valuable tools to assist in development of policy.

Matrices have been widely used to record the extent to which recreation is compatible with particular landscapes or other activities. They have been used to assess how far requirements for specific types of recreation pursuit or target groups are currently being met (Figure 3.6). Attempts might be made to apply scores to extent to which particular requirements are being met in different parts of a plan area or by different user groups as shown in Figure 3.6 and Table 3.2.

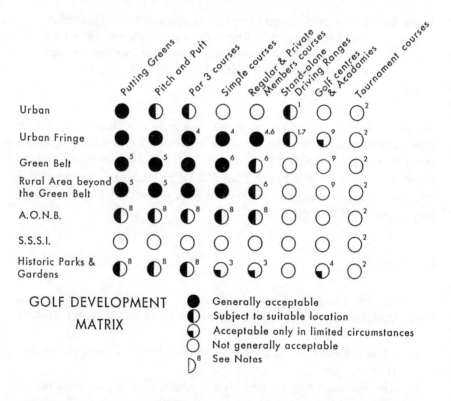

Figure 3.6   The matrix approach as used in recording information on rural recreation

Source: North Hertfordshire District Council (1991)

'SPATIAL' APPROACHES

Another technique adopted in plan-making acknowledges that, for particular pursuits, leisure facilities have catchment areas with measurable visit rates. Knowledge of visit rates should provide guidance on the level of use of new facilities which might be provided, unserved areas where latent demand for recreation exists, offering a 'spatial' route to provision (Veal, 1982, p. 22). Such an approach would acknowledge that catchments for different types of activity vary greatly and that for major rural attractions such as theme parks, appeal may be region-wide. The technique is probably most appropriate at the local scale where 'deficiency' areas of provision might be identified. Catchments will vary greatly for one type of user compared with another. For those dependent on walking, cycling or public transport, catchment areas are likely to be much smaller than for those who are more mobile. In addition, the approach might also be used to relate the location of facilities to the concentrations of priority groups in a locality and to provide policy guidance on shortfalls (Duffield and Long, 1984, pp. 165–170).

The spatial approach has received attention in the county of Cleveland, where most rural recreation sites are located in the south of the county. The county's countryside recreation strategy aims to rectify this uneven distribution of countryside recreation opportunities by channelling new schemes to the deficiency areas (Cleveland County Council, 1991, p. 24).

In his review of recreation plan-making techniques, Veal links the 'spatial' approach to provision planned on the basis of a hierarchy of facilities, ranging from local open spaces with very limited catchments to major parks with appeal over a whole region (Veal, 1982, p. 24). The Greater London Development Plan (GLDP) recommended that open space provision should be based on such a hierarchy: from local parks to linear open spaces and regional parks, linked to metropolitan open land and green belt corridors (London Planning Advisory Committee, 1988, p. 54). Study of recreational plans and studies suggests that the 'green corridor' or linear open space concept has been widely adopted by planners and landscape designers as a basis for open-space planning (Groome, 1990, p. 383). As a planning tool, its value in shaping urban form has been recognized, but for rural recreation, its value lies in providing town–country links in which people can travel in relative safety from home to the countryside.

67

Table 3.2   The matrix approach

Disability grouping / Landscape provision	(a) Semi-ambulant	(b) Wheelchair users	(c) Sensory handicap	(d) Mental handicap	(e) Disabled children	(f) Geriatric/elderly
Easy level access	2	2	2	1	1	2
Even footpath	1	2	1	0	0–1	2
Varied footpath	0	–	2	2	2	–
Level diversity	0	0	2	2	2	0
Steps	1	–	1	1	2	–
Ramps	0	2	1	0	0	1
Sheltered paths	2	1	0	0	0	2
Sheltered areas	2	2	1	0	0–1	2
Shading	0	1	0	2	1	2
Sunny aspect	1	1	0	2	2	2
Views to landscape	2	2	0	2	1	2
Views to outside	1	1	0	1	1	2
Raised planters	2	2	2	1	1	2
Ground beds	–	–	0	1	1	–
Horti-therapy	2	2	1	2	1	2
Toilets for disabled	1	2	0	0–1	1	2
Quiet areas	0	0	2	2	1	2
Car parking	2	2	0	0	0	2

Key: – = unsuitable
　　　0 = no value
　　　1 = moderate value/requirement
　　　2 = greatest value/requirement

Source: Rowson and Thoday (1985), p. 64

As a way of deflecting visitor pressures from national parks, the concept of a hierarchy of rural recreation spaces ranging from local country parks to regional parks and national parks has also had its adherents. Broom, for example, cites the examples of the Llyn Padarn Country Park which it is argued helps absorb pressures from visitors to the Snowdonia National Park; and a further instance of a country park in Leicestershire which seeks to deflect pressure from Charnwood Forest (Broom, 1991, p. 15).

COMMENT

This chapter has demonstrated that a range of techniques are available to planners in analysing and prescribing future patterns of rural recreation. Techniques have often been adapted from other branches of planning and other disciplines but interest in the application of techniques has tended to be more clearly expressed by researchers than by practitioners. In addition, interest has tended to be inspired at national and regional agency level rather than at a local planning authority level. Nevertheless, areas of common interest exist between researchers and practitioners, notably in recording and analysing data on natural resources where systematic studies of agriculture, forestry and wildlife conservation have also involved consideration of recreation. Unlike the former activities, it has proved much more difficult to develop reliable techniques of recording, analysing and prescribing action for recreation.

Within Britain, few examples exist of planning techniques being used to consider rural recreation provision in a comprehensive manner. Constraints on undertaking such studies have included the problem of justifying the use of limited resources to carry out necessary surveys and analyses. As a reflection of the limited powers of the planner in a rural context, there has been rather more evidence of the use of techniques to plan single activities or projects. Imperfect as such techniques might be, they can be of value in testing the feasibility of particular public- or private-sector recreation schemes.

Changes in administrative regimes in the 1980s and the 1990s are resulting in a greater emphasis being placed on accurate information bases on which to plan future recreation policies. The adoption of strategic approaches to the planning of rural recreation and a requirement to quantify benefits in precise terms are likely to result in increasing em-

69

phasis being placed on using planning techniques which can stand up to scrutiny.

Separate consideration is given in Chapter 6 to other tools which might be used by planners in the more detailed design and management of recreation sites where different issues arise from those discussed in this chapter.

Chapter 4

Rural recreation and statutory planning

A central concern of this book is the extent to which central and local government has shown a commitment to plan for rural recreation. The role of land-use plans in the development of policies for rural recreation is now considered under two headings: firstly, rural recreation as it has emerged as a policy theme in statutory development plans; and secondly, the approach to rural recreational planning which has been adopted in non-statutory policies and plans.

PRE-WAR AND WARTIME STUDIES

The pre-war period in Britain was dominated by concern with future military conflict, economic depression, unemployment and social deprivation. This meant that preservation of the countryside was seen to be of only secondary importance (Sheail, 1981, p. 195). Although rapid urban expansion was taking place, the approach by government was essentially 'gradualist' with a reluctance to impose total prohibition on development in the countryside. Instead, 'the aim was to provide as many citizens as possible with the chance to live in a rural setting. The challenge was somehow to accommodate greater numbers of people in the countryside and at the same time to preserve the countryside as *country*' (Sheail, 1981, p. 229).

Even in the absence of comprehensive planning machinery, advisory zoning plans drawn up in the inter-war period identified areas for public enjoyment. In part these were to separate satellite towns and other areas of urban growth, but they could also perform the role of open space corridors with pedestrian routes. Study of pre-war advisory planning schemes drawn up under the Town and Country Planning Act 1932 reveals concern with the need to prevent urban 'sprawl' but also shows attempts to identify sites for outdoor recreation. Such plans proved to do little more than express the hopes of their designers, largely because there were only very limited mechanisms to enforce effectively any proposals that might be made, and local authorities feared that claims for compensation would be made if constraints were rigorously enforced.

The need to plan positively for rural recreation was articulated during the period of social reconstruction in Britain after the Second World War. In quoting John Dower, Sheail, for example, fairly summarizes the views of many at the time: 'One way to alleviate the problem was to adopt a comprehensive planning strategy. Most holiday-makers wanted the noise, crowds and amusements of a popular resort, holiday camp or bungalow village and Dower asserted that it would be "ostrich-like folly" to ignore the great demand' (Sheail, 1981, p. 195). Plans which addressed the problem of countryside recreation included the Greater London Plan prepared by Patrick Abercrombie in 1944. The Plan included proposals for the creation of accessible countryside and the development of footpath networks, easy access by public transport from urban areas (Abercrombie, 1945, pp. 97–111).

Overall, though, review of early rural plans and studies shows that recreation was most often subsumed as a planning topic within the general heading of landscape or amenity, with unclear references as to how the competing interests might be accommodated within coherent policies.

DEVELOPMENT PLANS

The Town and Country Planning Act 1947 introduced a comprehensive system of controls over the use of land in Britain. Through development control, local planning authorities could determine whether or not a wide range of activities would be permitted in particular localities. The framework for decision-making included centrally determined regulations and orders, with local interpretation being achieved through development plans which took a long-term perspective on future development in a planning authority's area. A system of controls and stimuli for change evolved. Greatest focus was on controlling urban development. However, legislation with a sharper rural focus and which was concerned

72

with achieving landscape and nature conservation and public enjoyment was contained in the National Parks and Access to the Countryside Act 1949. It was this Act, with further legislation in the form of the Countryside Act 1968 and the Wildlife and Countryside Act 1981, which provided the context within which most rural recreation planning in England and Wales has been undertaken.

The development plans produced under the 1947 Act treated rural issues on two levels. Firstly, they included proposals for control of development of towns and villages, often categorizing settlements where different rates of growth might be expected. Secondly, they identified broad policies for rural areas as a whole, indicating different degrees of protection from development by means of such designations as 'white land' or 'areas of great landscape value'. Since the 1947 Act had excluded most rural land uses from planning control, including agriculture and forestry, development plans were able to make only the broadest of assertions about the ways in which these activities were to be undertaken. However, within this general picture, rather more detailed treatment of rural recreation issues was to be found in some plans. For example, the *Report and Analysis of Survey* of the Peak District Development Plan draws attention to the problems affecting tourist attractions and holiday provision (Peak District National Park, 1955, p. 91).

Despite the great importance attached to the creation of the planning system in the 1940s, the changes did not result in the adoption of national policies or plans for either the countryside or for recreation. The emphasis was on broad policy guidelines issued by government rather than on clearly identified policies and priorities which might be expected in a national plan for recreation (Palmer and Bradley, 1974, p. 288).

Besides the 1947 and 1949 Acts, other policy guidance directed at different strands of rural recreation has emerged from government. In a 1955 circular, local planning authorities were encouraged to create green belts (Ministry of Housing, 1955). The 1967 and 1968 Countryside Acts in Scotland and in England and Wales introduced clear new levels of national policy-making, notably for encouraging the provision for recreation in the countryside. Policy guidance has emerged via a series of other ministerial statements, circulars, advice and guidance notes. Of great importance in offering an indication of national policy towards planning issues have been ministerial decisions on planning appeals where balance has been sought between local and national interests (Gregory, 1970).

73

Table 4.1   The main statutes affecting rural recreational planning

National measures	Main features
Town and Country Planning Act 1947	Development plans, development control
National Parks and Access to the Countryside Act 1949	Countryside designations, open country surveys, public rights of way
Green Belt Circular 42/55 1955	Local authorities encouraged to designate green belts
Town and Country Planning Act 1968	Structure/local plans introduced
Countryside Act 1968	Wide range of enabling powers introduced
Town and Country Planning Act 1971	Consolidating Act
Local Government Act 1972	Re-organization of local government; provision for national park plans
Wildlife and Countryside Act 1981	Wide range of measures on mechanisms for designation of protected areas and for access to countryside
Town and Country Planning Act 1990	Consolidating Act, provisions for changes in form of local plans
Planning and Compensation Act 1991	New emphasis on the role of the development plan as planning consideration

RURAL RECREATION AND THE DEVELOPMENT PLAN SYSTEM – POST-1968

For over 20 years, the 1947-style development plans provided the main statutory framework within which consideration could be given to rural recreation. However, reference to recreation tended to be incidental to the more central thrust of rural policy which was to contain urban areas, ensuring that the countryside was largely retained for rural land uses, including, of course, potential uses such as outdoor recreation.

The report of the Planning Advisory Group (PAG) in 1965 recognized shortcomings in the planning system at that time (Ministry of Housing, 1965). Problems associated with the development plan system included the time-consuming nature of plan preparation and the failure of plans effectively to separate matters of strategy from local importance. Amongst the proposals made in the PAG report was a hierarchy of plans ranging from 'action' plans at a very local level, to local plans which could take a number of different forms, through to structure plans. The degree of detailed treatment in each type of plan would vary considerably. Very broad treatment would be offered in structure plans with general statements of policy, drawing on national and regional guidance from government, undertaken at county level and extending over a 10-year period. Translation of broad policy to detailed local interpretation, specific proposals for land use and guidance on day-to-day planning would be provided via the different forms of local plans.

The *Development Plans* manual which outlined the new provisions indicated that local plans could take a variety of forms: besides action plans and local plans which could cover a wide range of topics, there was also scope for the use of subject plans which could focus on particular themes, such as minerals or recreation (Ministry of Housing, 1970). The Town and Country Planning Acts of 1968 and 1971 incorporated the PAG proposals, and structure and local plans became the principal statutory plans produced by local planning authorities.

Structure plans

Guidance on the preparation of development plans is provided by central government from time to time. Advice is given on arrangements for the preparation of reports of survey about a plan area: the drawing up of draft plans with a requirement for there to be formal public participation, concluding with a submitted draft plan which itself is the subject of an 'examination in public'. At the examination in public, a panel would consider the draft plan and make recommendations to the Secretary of State on whether the structure plan should be approved with or without modifications.

A 1984 *Memorandum on Structure and Local Plans* (Department of the Environment, 1984, para 4.38), envisaged that structure plans would identify in broad terms:

- those areas where facilities for recreation and tourism would be provided;
- criteria for the provision for leisure facilities as a guide for development control;
- general proposals for major developments such as country parks, long-distance footpaths and major indoor and water sports facilities and policies for caravans and camping.

A case study in Wales indicates the approach adopted in one particular structure plan.

Draft Gwynedd Structure Plan (1989)

Gwynedd comprises the former counties of Caernarfon, Anglesey and Meirionydd. It covers an area approximately 90 by 80 km, two thirds of which is designated as national park or area of outstanding natural beauty. Structure plans for the formerly separate units of local government were produced in the 1970s, culminating in their approval by the Secretary of State in 1977. Just over half of the county falls within the Snowdonia National Park which operates development control and local plan-making functions and prepares a National Park Plan which concentrates on land management rather than planning issues.

The county has long been popular with visitors, with several seaside and inland resorts. However, since 1978 there has been a decline in visitors to Gwynedd. The completion of a major new highway, the A55 North Wales Coast Expressway, is likely to have an impact on tourism, putting the area well within a day trip for substantial numbers of visitors from northwest England.

The overall aims of the structure plan (Gwynedd County Council, 1989, p. 5) are to:

76

- enhance employment opportunities and reduce population loss;
- have material regard to the Welsh language in all planning actions;
- ensure land is made available for housing and other needs;
- conserve the natural and built environment;
- maximize benefits of tourism and recreation, but minimize adverse effects;
- assist and encourage development of education, health, community and commercial services;
- ensure levels of mobility which meet needs of local population, industry, commerce and, where appropriate, the tourist population.

Recreation objectives are indicated with the strategic aim of seeking to 'influence the development of tourism and recreation activity in such a way as to maximize the associated benefits to the county while at the same time minimizing any adverse impacts'. Policy themes indicated in the structure plan include the need to foster the development of high-quality holiday accommodation with the upgrading of existing holiday accommodation; provision for static and touring caravans and tents; development of visitor attractions including countryside recreation facilities; addressing problems associated with boating facilities and noisy sports; and developing recreation routes.

The plan indicates three categories of area where different strategic policies should apply (Gwynedd County Council, 1989, pp. 30–31):

A   areas within which by reason of location, accessibility, natural resources, infrastructure and the capacity of the local community to absorb growth could provide suitable opportunities for development;
B   areas which by virtue of the sensitivity of their environment, their community life or their culture would not be capable of absorbing development without unacceptable social, financial or environmental costs;
C   areas which do not fall into either of the two above categories in which proposals for tourism development will be assessed in terms of their impact on the host community and environment and the need for parallel management measures.

On implementation of policy, the draft structure plan was to be principally concerned with 'guiding private and public sector development

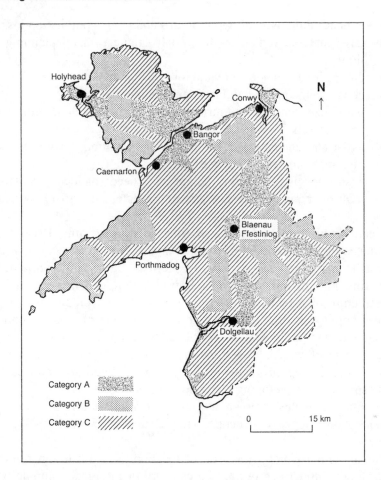

**Figure 4.1   Gwynedd Draft Structure Plan: recreation and tourism
zones**

Source: Gwynedd County Council (1989). (This approach to zoning was not
subsequently developed in the February 1991 submitted version of the Gwynedd Structure Plan.)

investment to the most appropriate locations'. However, the plan indicated that it would be a matter for the district councils to determine
through local plans where this development actually took place. The role
of the structure plan therefore was seen as providing a context for the
coordination of investment and affording a clear brief for development
guidance to the private and public sectors.

In many respects, the Gwynedd plan resembles other structure plans in its coverage of rural recreation issues in confining itself to strategic rather than local issues. However, of interest is the importance attached to the need to ensure that the benefits to a local community should outweigh any adverse impact of development in terms of environmental, linguistic and community costs. The Gwynedd Structure Plan incorporates explicit social and cultural objectives as elements of policy. Government has been at pains to remind planning authorities that they should confine statutory plans solely to land-use matters. It is surprising to find, therefore, from the Gwynedd experience that government ministers 'have confirmed in reply to parliamentary questions that the protection of the character, way of life and communities is a proper aim of statutory planning and language can be a component of that aim' (Gwynedd County Council, 1989, p. 7). Welsh Office Circular 54/88 underlines the importance of social, cultural and linguistic factors and emphasizes that these can be material considerations in considering planning applications. At the same time it stresses that material considerations 'must be genuine planning considerations, that is, they must be related to the purpose of planning legislation which is to regulate the development and use of land' (Welsh Office, 1988).

Study of other structure plans provides an indication of different approaches to rural recreation planning. In the case of Cornwall, then like Gwynedd, rural recreation policy is bound up closely with tourism development. In the Cornwall Structure Plan, the emphasis is again on restraint with the identification of 'tourism pressure areas' within which prospects for expansion of self-catering accommodation will be quite limited (Cornwall County Council, 1988, pp. 138–139).

The notion of zoning of recreation areas has been adapted and refined in structure plans produced for the Peak District National Park (Table 4.2). Here development proposals are judged against the suitability of the park to accommodate different types of recreation (Peak Park Joint Planning Board, 1991b, pp. 64–65). In other areas subject to less pressure, different stances have been adopted. In Cheshire, for example, the structure plan contains proposals for the encouragement of development for recreation purposes (Cheshire County Council, 1990, pp. 105–111). Policy TR4 explicitly states that there will be 'a presumption in favour of new major visitor attractions' in the Mersey Belt, River Weaver and other locations in the county. The general tenor of the plan is to adopt an

Table 4.2
Peak District National Park: Structure Plan recreation zones, 1991

Zone	*Appropriate form of recreation*
Zone 1	Footpaths, wildlife hides or similar provisions where they cannot be provided in other zones nearby
Zone 2	Low-impact recreation may be acceptable where necessary to service activities in zone 1; backpack campsites, camping barns, farmhouse accommodation
Zone 3	Modest-scale development: small car parks, small farm-based caravan sites, of facilities linked to walking, riding, cycling
Zone 4	Car parks, picnic sites linked to informal recreation, some overnight accommodation
Zone 5	Higher intensities of recreation use, major visitor facilities, car parks, information centres and related facilities

Source: based on Peak Park Joint Planning Board (1991b), p. 64

encouraging approach which recognizes the value of tourism and recreation to the quality of life, the economic benefits that they bring, the need to widen access opportunities and the need to protect existing recreational facilities.

A review of an earlier generation of structure plans in England and Wales undertaken in 1986 reveals a number of shortcomings in their treatment of recreational issues (Curry and Comley, 1986a). The investigation recorded a lack of systematically undertaken surveys or analyses and the plans surveyed sought to restrict recreational developments in high-value landscapes and encourage them in ordinary and derelict landscapes. Recreation was thus seen as being able to solve other land-use problems, including those associated with derelict land.

Given government attitudes towards the inclusion of non-land-use planning issues in structure plans, it is not surprising to find that most plans reviewed in the investigation gave only very limited treatment to the social aims of recreation policy. Rather, plans emphasized the need to minimize resource costs, shifting the incidence of financial burden from the public to the private and voluntary sectors.

LOCAL PLANS

The procedure for the preparation of local plans emerged from the PAG study in the same way as did the preparation of structure plans. Advice on procedure from central government required several stages to be followed in the production of a local plan: drawing up reports of survey, preparation of draft plans and with provision for public participation at a number of stages of preparation, culminating normally in a public local inquiry.

At a public local inquiry, an inspector appointed by the appropriate Secretary of State would consider the relevant information presented by supporters and objectors to the plan. He or she would then make a recommendation on the plan's proposals to the planning authority. The latter would then decide whether to modify the plan or adopt the plan without modifications.

Although by 1980 structure plans had been produced for the whole of England and Wales, by 1988 only a small part of Britain had local plan coverage. Outside Greater London, only about 20 per cent of England and Wales (by population) was covered by local plans (Department of the Environment, 1989c, p. 4). Only 54 of 333 non-metropolitan districts had local plans which fully covered their areas. Leaving aside subject plans, 70 districts had no local plans at all and the remainder frequently had local plans for only a small part of their areas. Despite its limited adoption by local authorities, the local plan has been valued as an important mechanism for framing planning policy, whether in the form of a comprehensive plan covering a district or part of a district, or as 'subject' plan focusing on one particular theme or issue such as minerals or recreation, possibly extending over a whole county.

A case study based in Greater Manchester considers more detailed aspects of one of the small number of countryside recreation subject local plans to have been produced in Britain.

The Mersey Valley Local Plan (1985)

A distinctive feature of Greater Manchester is the network of river valleys which thread their way through the county. Local plans for several such river valleys were produced during the 1970s until the mid-1980s. The plans were 'subject' local plans dealing specifically with programmes of environmental improvement and recreation provision

81

which were being undertaken by the County Council and the ten constituent district councils of Greater Manchester (Maund, 1982, p. 83).

The Mersey Valley in Greater Manchester runs for about 20 km from Stockport to the former steel-making town of Irlam. In width the Valley varies from 1 km to over 6 km. The Mersey Valley has been subject to much pressure for development over the years, being used for landfill sites, a route for overhead power lines and a major motorway, the M63 which forms part of the Greater Manchester Outer Ring Road. However, parts of the Valley contain attractive stretches of countryside, there is an extensive network of public rights of way and several sites have been in recreational use for long periods (Greater Manchester Council, 1985b, p. 4).

Early stages in the preparation of the local plan were undertaken in the late 1970s and early 1980s with a public local inquiry into the provisions of the Deposited Plan being held in 1985.

The plan contained two main components: overall valley-wide policies, and detailed proposals for some 148 specific projects which it was intended to implement over a 15-year period. The valley-wide policies drew strongly on the approved Structure Plan for Greater Manchester which aimed to maintain the river valleys as open features. The objectives of the local plan are summarized in Table 4.3. The plan proposed extensive tree planting, the creation of informal open space, footpaths, bridleways and cycle paths and restoration of landfill sites. The plan included a programme for implementation in three phases over a 15-year period.

Some of the plan's proposals would require planning permission and could rightly be expected to be offered for scrutiny at a local plan inquiry. However, many of the proposals were of a kind which might be expected to be excluded from consideration by a planning inspector, yet evidence indicates that they were discussed at length at the local plan inquiry held in 1985 (Greater Manchester Council, 1985a).

From the findings of one review of countryside local plans three themes appear to be of particular interest for the present study (Hill and Healey, 1985, pp. 48–56).

- Rural recreation as a topic has featured quite prominently in county-wide subject plans, possibly because of the land-extensive nature

Table 4.3   Mersey Valley Local Plan: objectives, 1985

Theme	Objective
Conservation	Retain the Valley as an area of significant open land within the urban area of Greater Manchester; improve the landscape as an entity, re-establishing a rural or semi-rural environment; conserve and improve features of wildlife, historical or architectural interest
Outdoor recreation	Make the best use of the Valley's potential for outdoor recreation; improve accessibility for walkers, riders and cyclists, keeping vehicle access where possible on the fringes; resolve conflict between recreation users
Environmental improvement	Remove dereliction, environmental pollution, eyesores and, where appropriate, non-conforming industries
Agriculture	Take account of the needs of farming and recognize its value in maintaining the rural character of the landscape
Public awareness	Increase awareness of the Valley's attraction for recreation; encourage public involvement
Development	Ensure that development in or near the Valley conforms to the visual and environmental objectives for the area.

Source: based on Greater Manchester Council (1985b), p. 6

of rural recreation and because counties had budgets to spend on recreation and environmental improvement.
- The contents of local plans have been clearly prescribed by central government, limiting the range of issues that local authorities were able to address in their local plans. Hence, in relation to agriculture and forestry, only those matters which could be con-

83

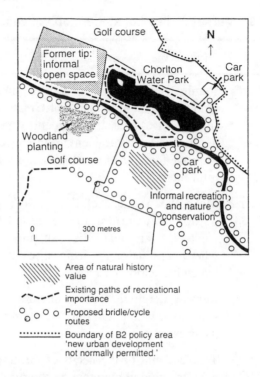

Area of natural history value

Existing paths of recreational importance

Proposed bridle/cycle routes

Boundary of B2 policy area 'new urban development not normally permitted.'

Figure 4.2   Mersey Valley Local Plan: recreation (extract)
Source: Greater Manchester Council (1985b)

trolled by the planning system could be included in a local plan. Situations have occurred where central government has struck out management programmes which local authorities have sought to include in local plans.

● The implications of this for recreation policies – access for example – could be considerable. Access has both a land-use and management dimension and allocation on a plan of land for public access is by itself insufficient. Unless an indication is also given of arrangements for subsequent management, policies would be likely to fail.

Within the framework offered by the statutory planning system, coordination of rural and recreational policies can be beset with difficulties. The example of the Mersey Valley local plan illustrates one attempt to overcome those difficulties and in a sense the plan is hybrid, incorporating both statutory and non-statutory planning provisions.

The approach to local plan preparation evolved considerably during the late 1980s. Government now requires comprehensive local plans which are intended to cover the whole of a district's administrative area. Such plans may include more detailed 'inset' plans. It is intended that the plans will be relevant for 10 years and will include a written statement and specific land-use proposals on a map base (Department of the Environment, 1992b). Provisions of the Planning and Compensation Act 1991 place a greater emphasis than previously on the role of the development plan. The Act stresses the need for determinations to be made in accordance with the plan unless material considerations indicate otherwise. Assuming that such determinations are confined to land-use planning issues only, then it is likely that there will be little scope for consideration of non-statutory matters including issues relating to rural recreation. The legislation provides for plans to be supported by supplementary planning guidance and there is a possibility that this could treat recreation and other topics in more detail than is possible in the local plan itself.

UNITARY DEVELOPMENT PLANS

Metropolitan districts in England and Wales sometimes contain substantial areas of open land. For example, about a third of the County of Greater Manchester comprises countryside. In the 36 metropolitan districts and 33 London boroughs, the abolition of the county councils in 1986 called for the use of new-style district-wide development plans, known as unitary development plans (UDP). These are designed to be all-embracing development plans for their areas whose essential function is to provide the necessary framework for development control and land-use planning (Department of the Environment, 1988f, p. 1). They are intended to provide a written statement of general policies for development and use of land together with a written statement spelling out policies in much more detail. During the existence of the metropolitan county councils and the Greater London Council, district planning policies evolved alongside county-wide structure plans. In the absence of county-wide authorities, Schedule 1 of the Local Government Act 1985 indicated that strategic guidance for unitary development plans was to be provided through the Department of the Environment. An example of the operation of this mechanism can be seen in the Strategic Guidance for Merseyside. Dated 1988, it was intended to provide a framework for UDP preparation for the five Merseyside metropolitan district authorities (Department of the Environment, 1988c). The guidance was produced following a conference of local authority planning officers in 1987. The strategic guidance on recreation and tourism extends to 20 lines of text, 15 of which are devoted to assertions about the value of tourism to the local economy. The section devoted to recreation itself is minimal, pointing out that 'Provision for sport, recreation and leisure not only enhances the quality of life for residents and encourages new housing investment but is good for the economy. The Councils should work with the Regional Council for Sport and Recreation who are reviewing their Regional Recreation Strategy to ensure that UDPs and other related plans are mutually supportive.'

In a section headed 'Green belt, agricultural land, countryside', general support is given to the notion of checking urban sprawl and safeguarding valuable countryside. In addition it is suggested that councils might want to foster diversification of the rural economy so as to increase employment opportunities, with farm tourism and recreation warranting special attention.

Strategic guidance as practised is based essentially on the district authorities' perceptions of what might be appropriately considered at a sub-regional or county level. The guidance is expressed in extremely broad terms and scope exists for wide interpretation in individual unitary development plans. As a vehicle for considering provision of regional parks, major tourist projects, community forests, long-distance trails and other rural recreation measures, strategic guidance would appear to have extremely limited value. The results of five or six individually produced unitary development plans cannot be said to offer the same overview or vision of strategic planning issues as might be covered in a structure plan.

The treatment of countryside planning in unitary development plans and district local plans, together with non-statutory measures, has also been the subject of guidance produced by the Countryside Commission (Countryside Commission, 1987c).

INFORMAL PLANS AND STRATEGIES

In a 1985 study of planning policy and implementation, it was found that structure and local plans were only two of a number of forms of policy guidance used by local planning authorities to implement environmental policies (Healey *et al.*, 1985, p. 90). Thus, in the case of the reclamation of derelict land, qualification for central government grant meant that local authorities had to draw up plans which indicated sites, costed schemes and indicated a programme of implementation. Such arrangements also apply in the case of rural recreation provision. Here, the grant-making agencies are different but their requirements have provided the impetus for the production of programmes of implementation and informal plans and policies for countryside recreation.

An example of this central influence is seen in the operation of the Countryside Commission's 1987 *Recreation 2000/Enjoying the Countryside* initiative which introduced a greater emphasis on increasing access to the countryside and on raising people's awareness of the opportunities available to them (Countryside Commission, 1989c, p. 5). A component of the new policies was the requirement for grant seeking bodies to produce their own strategies for countryside recreation. Such strategies could be expected to accord with Commission policies and the *Enjoying the Countryside* policies in particular.

Informal plans: a county countryside recreation strategy

A response to the *Enjoying the Countryside* policies of the Countryside Commission is seen in this strategy (Lancashire County Council, 1989). Lancashire is a county which has had considerable experience in the promotion of recreation in the countryside. One of the first country parks to be designated in Britain was in 1968 at Beacon Fell near Preston. The planning authority was centrally involved in the preparation of a comprehensive local plan in the West Pennine Moors (Lancashire County Council, 1980). The county contains a large number of industrial settlements as well as extensive areas of open countryside including two areas of outstanding natural beauty.

The strategy records the progress of the Council's policies over the previous 20 years: provision for car-based recreation (country parks, picnic sites); development of recreational routes (trails, cycleway); countryside management service; heightened public awareness of coun-

Table 4.4
Lancashire County Council: rural recreation strategy, 1989

Theme	Specific issues
Countryside management scheme areas	Development of countryside management scheme areas, producing overall plan for each with project officer appointed
Other areas	Low-key use of access network
Access network	Increase availability of network Signposting, waymarking, access maps, co-ordinate public transport/access network, introduce path hierarchy with local, regional and national paths/trails
Improvement of access network	Local networks, circular routes environmental/educational trails, needs of riders, cyclists, disabled, linking town/countryside/Open Country Access Forum/access areas Set standards of provision, e.g. path surfaces, barriers etc
Sport and active leisure	Encourage diversity and provision through country parks, use of derelict land, access to open country, long-distance walking, riding, cycling, special needs, water sports
Information	Raise awareness of opportunities for countryside recreation; countryside information centres, guided walks, countryside shop
Increasing accessibility	Pay particular attention to needs of those who find it difficult to enjoy leisure opportunities in the countryside Develop participation programmes Provide facilities near to towns, public transport
Assisting rural economy	To assist rural economy including diversification, rural tourism Stimulation of rural economy, working with private sector, expand low-cost accommodation, interpretation of heritage, car trails
Working with others	Integration of Council's activities with other bodies, public/private/voluntary

Source: based on Lancashire County Council (1989)

tryside and partnerships with local authorities and other bodies in the private and voluntary sectors. The strategy itself contains several separate strands and is illustrated in Table 4.4.

Of interest in the Lancashire example is the emphasis which is placed on social objectives in widening opportunities for enjoyment of the countryside and in developing access policies over extensive stretches of countryside. A second observation is that two elements of the strategy stress the interconnected nature of recreation with other policy areas. For example, the strategy emphasizes the way in which rural recreation and tourism can benefit the local economy. In addition, the strategy recognizes that the County Council will be unable itself to implement all the measures outlined in the strategy. Implementation of the strategy will be dependent on forging partnerships with other agencies including, for example, water companies. Stress is also placed on the role of voluntary organizations and on the part played by the Lancashire Access Forum on which sit representatives of a wide range of access and landowning interests.

A 1989 review of Welsh local authority countryside recreation strategies suggested a wide range of approaches to informal strategy development but acknowledged that certain key themes emerged (Peter Scott Planning Services, 1989, pp. 120–121):

- recognition of the value of the countryside for its tourism and recreation potential, notably the particular opportunities which are to be found in the areas which are strategically important to the main centres of population;
- the importance of defining recreational routes in coastal areas, river paths and themed heritage paths;
- using upland area commons, forests, national parks and areas of outstanding natural beauty for open country access opportunities;
- provision of recreation opportunities in coastal areas;
- development of existing recreation provision, including use of 5-year programmes for development of country parks, visitor centres and other facilities;
- provision of information and interpretation opportunities.

The strategies examined in this study were amongst the earliest of their kind produced in England and Wales and should be seen as being of an initial, exploratory nature. However, the investigation revealed that as

89

plan-making documents, the proposals contained in the strategies tended to be based on intuitive local knowledge of demand, rather than in obtaining and using fuller and more detailed information on participation rates, patterns and trends.

Informal plans: regional strategies for sport and recreation

As in other aspects of environmental planning, a regional standpoint can throw a different perspective on provision for rural recreation than that obtained at local or county level. Yet the history of regional guidance and strategies for rural recreation reflects the same mixed fortunes as regional planning generally in Britain. Tension and contradictions can often develop between central government policy guidance on the one hand and explicit policies which might seem most appropriate at the local or county level (Cross and Bristow, 1983, p. 235). Attempts at regional policy-making were undertaken in Britain during the 1960s and early 1970s when a series of regional plans were produced which provided a context for the preparation of structure plans. In the Regional Strategy for the North West, 1974, for example, the major regional recreation resources were identified and proposals made for broad priority areas within which investment in countryside recreation should be concentrated (Department of the Environment, 1974, p. 203). Such plans are now largely forgotten. However, in the late 1980s and early 1990s there was a revival of interest in the regional dimension in planning. Indeed, as has already been noted for unitary development plans in metropolitan counties, then some limited regional guidance is now offered by government as for planning issues which apply on a wider geographical basis than a single county or district (Department of the Environment, 1989c, p. 7; 1992b, p. 5).

In the search for a regional dimension to rural recreation provision, non-statutory recreational strategies for sport and recreation have been produced by regional councils for sport and recreation. Circular 73/77 required the ten regional sports councils in England and Wales to produce 'long-term proposals for the planned provision of sport and recreation facilities on a region-wide basis (a "regional recreational strategy"). It is then intended that these should be carried through into statutory planning at the structure and local plan levels' (Department of the Environment, 1977a, p. 1).

90

The North West Council for Sport and Recreation is a forum for sport and recreation interests. It has no executive powers but seeks to influence sport and recreation policy-making amongst its members who include local authorities, governing bodies of sport and other interested organizations. Guidance from strategies produced by such regional councils is seen by central government as having a role to play in the preparation of land-use plans at a local level. Planning Policy Guidance 11 issued in 1988, for example, underlines the importance of regional recreational strategies in local plan preparation (Department of the Environment, 1988c, p. 2).

In its 1989–1993 *Strategy for Sport and Recreation*, the expressed intention of the North West Council for Sport and Recreation was to:

- encourage the provision of improved opportunities for participation in sport and recreation;
- highlight policies and priorities for action;
- outline the role which member bodies and partner agencies might play in implementing the strategy;
- guide financial investment in sport and recreation in the region. (North West Council for Sport and Recreation, 1989, p. 5)

Besides indicating future directions for countryside recreation, the strategy emphasizes the importance of three main strands of policy-making:

- increasing participation in sport and recreation, particularly amongst target groups such as women and the rural population;
- promoting higher levels of performance and excellence;
- meeting shortfalls in provision of facilities including tourism related developments.

The treatment of countryside recreation in the strategy is summarized in Table 4.5. The strategy places particular emphasis on the role played by public agencies as providers, but also in their role as 'enablers'. In that latter role and through joint working arrangements with the private and voluntary sector, they can play an important role in widening opportunities and removing barriers rather than in simply providing facilities. No attempt is made to translate the requirements identified in the strategy into a physical land-use map or diagram.

Table 4.5   North West Strategy for Sport and Recreation: countryside recreation themes, 1989

Theme	Specific issues
Informal recreation	Use of managed sites important, but access to unmanaged locations can cause major problems; support for countryside management schemes
Information, understanding	Need to safeguard resources, increase understanding of countryside, achieve effective working with Nature Conservancy Council and other partners
Public/private provision	Notes increasing role of private sector but concerned about policy areas where no financial return can be expected
Access/demonstration projects	Value in developing informal outdoor recreation in urban areas or fringes relieving pressure on overused areas
Water recreation	Big demands for facilities, but need to safeguard resources particularly in light of water industry privatization; also need for more information on availability of water resources
Influencing provision and retention of facilities	Seek consultation status on sport and recreation provision, especially statutory plans, planning applications and appeals

Source: based on North West Council for Sport and Recreation (1989)

NATIONAL PARK PLANS

Another policy tool, the national park plan has sought to tackle the problems of land management which are normally outside the scope of statutory land-use plans. Introduced under the Local Government Act 1972, the plans exclude specific reference to such matters as education, commerce, industry and shopping which are treated in structure and local plans, and concentrate on land-management issues that arise, particularly in the fields of wildlife and landscape conservation, access and recreation.

National park plans are statutory documents although they do not form part of the development plan system. They are prepared by national park authorities and are submitted to the Secretaries of State for the Environment or for Wales for information but are not subject to approval. A 1988 advisory note records the following points.

- National park plans should both indicate the policy of the national park authority and reflect the policies of other bodies, too.
- Plans should be a way of involving local people in achieving national park purposes, especially the landowning and farming interests.
- There is a need to identify the relationship between statutory planning responsibilities and the national park plan. 'It is important for each type of plan to influence the content of the others' (Countryside Commission, 1988b, p. 4).

Specifically in regard to recreation, the national park plan is expected to show how the national park authorities intend to promote opportunities for recreation and access which are compatible with park purposes. Plans are expected to focus on a core list of policy areas of which the following are a selection: access and rights of way; rangers and their role in informing, educating and assisting; recreational pursuits with specific policies on location, access, relations with landowners; outdoor activity centres; military training areas; caravans and camping; holiday accommodation.

These are themes which are to be found in many informal plans. However, a feature of the national park plan is that each plan is required to be accompanied by a programme of action specifying objectives, timescales and measures of output and performance. Functional Strategies which are produced on an annual basis allow such programmes and costings to be monitored. As a 'hybrid' plan, there is a considerable overlap between the content of the national park plan and statutory development plans. That there would be overlap was accepted by the provisions of the Local Government Act 1972, and this is a reminder of the close relationship between countryside planning and management

93

(Countryside Commission, 1988, p. 4). The theme was explored in the Edwards Panel review of the national parks with a recommendation that the two types of plan be combined (National Parks Review Panel, 1991, p. 89).

REGIONAL PARKS

A concept which has received attention from time to time is that of the regional park. From the limited discussion that exists on regional parks, Travis (1985) notes a number of characteristics which might be taken by regional parks.

- Regional parks need to be at least 2000 acres in extent.
- They should have several extensive blocks of land which are available for public use and for a wide range of activities.
- They should be located within 10 or 15 miles of a city, although preferably nearer.
- They should be available to a wide range of users, and they should be subject to proper management.

Only part of the area of a regional park may actually be used exclusively for recreation; quite extensive areas could be used for other activities. Thus the setting for recreation within a regional park is likely to consist of agriculture, forestry, wildlife reserves or settlements. Regional parks may be expected to have more than local importance but the types of facilities available could determine the function of the park within the region.

Probably the best-known example of a regional park in Britain is that in the Lee Valley. Located in Greater London, it was designated in 1967. A special-purpose regional park authority was set up to coordinate efforts to develop the valley for recreation and to carry out environmental improvements. The park authority comprises representatives from six London boroughs and three shire districts and Hertfordshire and Essex County Councils (Limna, 1985, p. 25). The authority is able to levy a precept from the local authorities to cover the running costs of the park.

The authority produced a statutory plan in 1969 with a more detailed park plan following in 1974. Development control is undertaken by constituent member local authorities. From owning no land at all in 1967, the park authority is now a major landowner, with over 1 250 ha of

94

land or around 30 per cent of the total park area in 1986 (Lee Valley Regional Park Authority, 1986, p. 100).

The park authority has been criticized because of the emphasis it placed on indoor sports facilities rather than on the creation of landscaped open spaces that might be expected in a regional park (Turner, 1988, p. 33). However, in recent years there has been a change of emphasis from provision of formal facilities to environmental and open land improvements and creation of routeways, information and countryside management services (Davies, 1989). The problems faced by the authority in some ways are no different from those faced by other recreation providers. For example, it is concerned about the increasing revenue costs, particularly in respect of newly landscaped and improved landscape areas (Lea Valley Regional Park Authority, 1986, p. 101). What distinguishes the park from other recreational bodies is perhaps its ability to act like a local authority, purchasing land for park purposes, and using compulsory powers of acquisition if necessary. Even so, because the park authority's statutory powers are largely limited to the field of leisure and environmental improvements, implementation of its own programme is frequently dependent on other agencies' own commitments. In addition, although the precept on constituent local authorities has great potential value, only some 45 per cent of the maximum sum it could demand is actually raised. This reflected the influence of local pressure to keep down local rate demands. In 1988/89, the precept was £6 153 000 (Lee Valley Regional Park Authority, 1989, p. 15).

In commenting on the achievements of the Lee Valley Regional Park, Elson records how the park's activities have been pursued largely unheralded and how they appeared to generate hostility from the constituent local authorities (Elson, 1986, p. 206). Park officials themselves have been conscious of the limitations of achievements: 'In the public eye, rightly or wrongly, all development has been seen to be piecemeal and far too concentrated on constructing buildings with not enough effort and resources put into conservation and landscaping' (Limna, 1985, p. 28).

A second example of the regional park concept finding its way on to the statute books is to be found in Scotland. A strategy for a park system for Scotland was devised in 1974 (Countryside Commission for Scotland, 1974, pp. 20–25). The system features a hierarchy of recreational areas ranging from urban parks and country parks to regional and 'special' parks.

The Scottish regional parks have statutory status through section 8 of the Countryside (Scotland) Act 1981. Regional councils can designate regional parks and manage as a single administrative unit any parts of a park which are in their control. Orders for creating regional parks have to be confirmed by the Secretary of State. Public inquiries into designations can be held and they can, of course, be the scene for debate about both the principle of designating a park as well as providing opportunities for questioning details of specific boundary lines.

Progress in developing a regional park system in Scotland has been slow (Dickinson, 1988, p. 99). The reason for this appears to be not so much a lack of demand but the 'logistical problems in establishing such larger-scale parks and the costs involved in their development and management'. Dickinson feels that although the statutory framework now favours the development of regional parks, the problems of financial constraint amongst local authorities and the objections from landowners and users may restrict further development of regional parks in Scotland.

A commentator on the Clyde–Muirshill Regional Park also records the difficulties involved in implementing development proposals (Skelley, 1985, p. 20). Thus, without the use of compulsory powers, negotiation for land purchase can take long periods. Opportunism in the development of the regional park has proved more important than planning, taking advantage of opportunities when they occur.

There has been a reluctance to exploit fully the concept of regional parks in Britain. However, urban fringe recreation and management plans produced for metropolitan counties such as Greater Manchester, in function and forms of management have had many of the attributes of regional parks (Webster, 1985, p. 38). Equally, community forests currently being developed in Britain may also have regional park characteristics.

Rural recreation features in a number of other plans and strategies besides those which have been outlined in this chapter. They include countryside strategies, tourism development action plans, rural development strategies and others. A selection of the varied forms taken by these and other statutory and informed plans are indicated in Table 4.6.

COMMENT

In statutory planning terms, rural recreation may appear as being of only marginal interest. However, one of the major planks of planning in

Table 4.6 **Statutory and informal plans and strategies**

Type of plan	Institution/ agency	Time span	Land-use/ map based	Scope
Structure plan	County	10	Schematic	Indicates outline of development
District/local plan	District	10	Detailed map base	Provides detailed guide to development
Unitary development plan	Metropolitan district	10	Detailed map base	Provides detailed guide to development
National park plan	National park authority	5	Map base	Guide to countryside management; linked to grant system (DOE, CC)
Countryside recreation strategy	Counties/ districts	3	No	Proposals for recreation, basis for grant application (CC)
Regional strategy for sport and recreation	Sports councils	5	No	Main emphasis, urban sport, recreation. Influence on grants policy
Countryside strategy	Counties/ districts	–	No	Integrating policies for rural land uses and activities
Tourism development action plan	Tourism board/ districts	3	No	Integrating policies for rural tourism
Rural development programme	Counties	3	No	Basis for grant awards, investment
AONB management plan	Counties/ districts	–	No	Integrated approach to management of rural land

Britain, urban containment, has succeeded in retaining for future recreational use much open countryside within easy reach of towns and cities. As a recreation against the limited influence that statutory plans can exert on rural recreation, planning authorities have placed an emphasis on 'positive planning', stressing the value of partnerships with the voluntary and private sectors and demonstrating that countryside recreation can bring economic benefits. This has often involved the use of informal plans and policies.

Some types of plan and strategy have been introduced by local planning authorities in order to qualify for particular grants available from central government agencies for rural recreation, tourism and rural development. A possibility here is that plans may be produced to conform with a centrally designed formula rather than take account of particular local circumstances.

Running through the plans discussed is a distinction between planning for land uses and 'people' planning. At the one extreme, government has stressed the need for plans to confine themselves to land-use considerations only. At the other, social and cultural factors sometimes feature prominently in the informal plans considered in this chapter. This applies in particular to Countryside Commission and Sports Council inspired plans, where there is often a very strong 'people' dimension. Discussion of the Gwynedd Structure Plan revealed that in certain circumstances government is prepared to accept that social, cultural and linguistic factors can be material planning considerations. A point to emerge from the Gwynedd example and other plans considered in this chapter is that recreation and tourism can bring benefits to communities, but can also impose costs. The planning system is seen as an important mechanism for obtaining a balance between the two.

A feature of many plans which have been produced is the minimal attention given to survey and methodology. However, plans have made use of some of the well-established techniques for providing for rural recreation which were explored in Chapter 3. These have included the use of such concepts as zoning and channelling of demand. There has also been a tendency to adopt 'issues' approaches which have the advantage of being readily understood but offer no substitute for a more systematic analysis of the relationships between different policy issues.

Finally, there is evidence of overlap of objectives between certain types of plan. A reason for this is that the introduction of nationally inspired policies is often accompanied by a need to produce new types of action plan or programme specifically relating to those policies. Sudden surges of interest by government or by its agencies may mean that some types of plan are abandoned. The uncertainty which accompanies rapid changes in government policy-making places obstacles in the way of welding together conflicting policies for the use of the countryside for recreation.

Chapter 5

Development control and rural recreation

A central part of the 1947 Town and Country Planning Act was its provision for the control of development. The Act vested rights to the development of land in the State and, with certain exemptions in respect of agricultural and forestry operations and the activities of nationalized industries, planning permission was required for most forms of development.

In considering the relationship between development control and rural recreation, several issues can be considered. Firstly, there is the general role of the development control system in determining land-use policies, and recreation in particular, in the countryside. Secondly, there are particular site and policy issues which arise in the case of proposals for rural recreation, including the response of the development control system to new pressures for recreational development. Two other facets of development control which are of interest include the role of planning conditions and planning agreements as ways of achieving recreational planning objectives; and the special issues which arise as a result of environmental assessment requirements placed on developers for certain categories of project.

DEVELOPMENT CONTROL AND PLANNING POLICIES

Development control policies, guided by several kinds of development plan, have sought to reconcile conflicts between different and competing land uses. Underlying control policies has been the notion of regulation, restricting development to selected centres, safeguarding rural landscapes and protecting agricultural land. This has not meant that no development has taken place in rural areas, but it has succeeded in constraining development in the countryside to a considerable degree.

Some of the fullest accounts of the ways in which development control has responded to pressures for rural recreation are contained in investigations into land-use policies in green belts. Elson records that central government guidance on green belt policies would seem to indicate that, like agriculture, outdoor recreation could be seen in a sense as appropriate for areas so designated (Elson, 1986, p. xxix). He distinguishes 'appropriate' uses such as recreation from others, such as extraction of minerals, which would normally be considered only as 'acceptable' and where there might be greater reluctance to permit development.

Lack of hard-and-fast guidance from government on the 'acceptability' or 'appropriateness' of development has been seen as a way of allowing local government some degree of discretion in handling planning applications. What this has meant is that the attitudes by local authorities to recreational proposals have varied greatly. Writing in the early 1970s, Gregory, for example, notes the high rate of refusals for recreation developments in the West Midlands Green Belt (Gregory, 1970, pp. 49–53). Development control records indicated that there were relatively few refusals associated with proposals to satisfy local needs such as village playing fields. However, conflicts arose over leisure developments including, for example, a proposal for a recreation centre with swimming pools, tennis courts, bowling greens and a minature golf course; a boating marina; applications for three golf-driving ranges and for holiday caravan sites.

Other reviews of development control practice by local authorities confirm the low success rates for proposals for recreational schemes in green belts. Studies in Hertfordshire between 1974 and 1979 revealed a high success rate for minor changes for existing leisure uses. However, for applications with large surface areas the success rate was quite low with only 31 per cent of the land area applied for being approved (Elson, 1986, p. 196). As in Gregory's study, developments such as local village recreational facilities received favourable consideration; but there was marked resistance to developments such as golf courses, motor sports and other schemes which often involved a mix of leisure with retail and urban development.

Since the mid-1980s, there appears to have been some degree of relaxation towards recreational development in the countryside. For example, under the provisions of Circular 16/87, government encouraged

101

farmers to diversify their activities (Department of the Environment, 1987). Planning authorities were subsequently faced with significant increases in planning applications for tourist accommodation, farm shops, and other activities (Crowther, 1990, p. 94). Planning authorities have reacted cautiously to the new demands and, in the case of golf courses, they have drawn up guidelines which indicate where such developments might be most appropriate (Leicestershire County Council, 1991, pp. 8–9). Such policies have been drawn up against a background where planning authorities were expected to grant permission for a development proposal unless there was a sound and clearly stated reason for refusal (Department of the Environment, 1988b, p. 2). This meant that if permission was to be witheld, then the burden of proof would be with the local planning authority to demonstrate that the development was unacceptable.

The case for and against recreational developments in the countryside may often be extremely finely drawn and cases will tend to be considered on their individual merits. However, considerations that arise when planning applications are made for recreational developments appear to share a number of common characteristics. Study of inspectors' decisions on planning appeals suggest that applications can be considered at two levels (Planning Appeal Decisions, 1985, pp. 59–68). From Table 5.1 it will be seen that a first set of considerations relate directly to the characteristics of an individual site and the impact of the development on that site, including visual impacts, traffic and other factors. A second set of considerations relate to the extent to which a proposal conforms to wider planning policies. Here, a wide range of questions arise, including the ways in which a proposal conforms to national policy guidelines; the degree of conformity to local and subregional policies expressed in statutory plans. Of particular significance will be the extent to which a proposal might be seen to be creating a precedent for further similar developments.

The two broad sets of considerations outlined here are comparable with those adopted in a 1986 study of the relationship between development plans, development control, and appeals. In that investigation a distinction was drawn between 'practical' planning considerations – amenity, arrangement, efficiency – and 'strategic' considerations – where, when and how much development should be permitted – (Davies *et al.*, 1986, pp. 17–18).

**Table 5.1 Factors which feature in appeal
decisions for rural recreational developments**

Factor	Example
Site qualities and impact of development	
Visual qualities of site and of proposed development	Intrusive design not in keeping with rural surrounds
Uniqueness of site	Availability of other sites
Access, traffic generation	Access unsuitable, danger to pedestrians
Disturbance to residents	Noise
Conflict with other recreation activities	Prevent continued use of site by existing participants
Physical site problems	Site unsuitable, drainage difficulties
Wider planning policies	
Structure and local plans	Extent to which proposed use conforms with provisions of plans
Green belt	Extent to which use conforms to appropriate green belt activities
Conformity to national policies	National policies to generally restrict development in rural areas
Precedence, ease of control	Difficulty of control once development has commenced

Source: based on analysis of planning inspectors' decisions in examples
listed in Planning Appeal Decisions (1985)

Recreational proposals can be as contentious as any other development in the countryside. Conflicts are most clearly demonstrated in the
case of recreation and tourism developments in national parks. Comments
made by the Council for National Parks in respect of timeshare developments could apply equally to other projects: 'Many of these leisure
developments are little different from a residential housing development. Yet if a developer sought permission to build a new village on
most of these sites, it is unlikely that permission would be granted'
(Council for National Parks, 1989, p. 9). In other words, the criteria

which apply to many other kinds of development can also apply to recreation schemes.

In resolving conflicts at the local level, the development control system is able to handle the vast majority of applications for permission for development by means of decisions made by council committees. However, there are limits to what can be agreed and resort to central arbitration may be necessary. This can happen when a development involves conflict over interpreting what is of local and what is of national interest (Gregory, 1971). The issues which can arise in these circumstances are now considered in relation to a proposal to develop a goldmine as a tourist attraction in the Snowdonia National Park in Wales. The example highlights the way in which access, scale and appearance of a proposal, traffic generation, and noise can influence the outcome of a planning application. In addition, the example illustrates the way in which national and local interests can conflict over tourism and recreation developments, and the role of the planning inquiry as a mechanism for conflict resolution.

The Clogau goldmine planning inquiry

The developer, Snowdonia Leisure plc, proposed the construction of a cable car, car park and associated buildings including an interpretive centre at Bonddu, on the Mawddach Estuary in Wales (Welsh Office, 1989). The proposal aimed to turn the Clogau goldmine into a tourist attraction which would draw some 250 000 visitors a year. The developer originally envisaged providing a private sewage works to service the proposal, but it later emerged that he intended to make a contribution to a proposed new village sewage treatment plant.

The planning authority, the Snowdonia National Park Authority, had considered the proposal and a number of earlier schemes for the site. It offered qualified support for the scheme, subject to the imposition of agreements imposing stringent planning control on the proposals. The authority stressed that although the site was in the national park, it would not be unduly conspicuous and would be valuable in terms of local employment generation (60 employees, half of them full-time). Tourism was a vital lifeline in the area.

A number of organizations opposed the scheme, including the Countryside Commission. Grounds for objection included the fact that the proposal ran counter to established zones indicated in national park policies which sought to concentrate tourism and recreation schemes to

104

a limited number of established sites. In addition, the scheme was inappropriate in scale to the locality. The latter was felt to be incapable of satisfactorily absorbing the physical intrusion and impact that would result from the proposal. The planning application was called in by the Secretary of State for Wales and a planning inquiry subsequently held to enable all relevant aspects of the proposal to be considered.

The inspector's report on the inquiry throws considerable light on the considerations which can help determine the outcome of proposals for development of tourism and recreation in the countryside. The Inspector considered the proposal under three headings (Welsh Office, 1989, pp. 20–24).

- Dealing with the immediate scene at Bonddu, it was evident that there would be disturbance caused to people living in the village because of the need to provide car parking. In addition, there would be loss of solitude, the scheme would represent an incongruous extension to the existing tourist facilities, and it would have an impact on a small, Welsh-speaking community.
- In considering the wider area of the Mawddach Estuary, the inspector felt that visual considerations were central to the arguments. A landscape assessment which had been undertaken confirmed this; the cable cars would be visible and the development would result in a prominent vertical gash in the hillside.
- In respect of the relevant planning policies, the proposal was in fundamental conflict with the national policies which sought to conserve the landscapes of national parks. The proposal ran contrary to structure plan policies which sought to channel development to a limited number of sites. 'The advantage of one form of tourism would be to the disadvantage of another.'

An important issue considered by the Inspector was whether there were any circumstances which were compelling enough to justify the development in a national park. On the employment issue, the Inspector acknowledged that jobs would be generated, although he was sceptical whether they would be on the scale envisaged by the developer. National guidelines issued by government on rural development and enterprise indicated that whilst employment opportunities should be encouraged, this should not be done at the expense of changing policies for conserving and protecting national parks.

105

The Inspector concluded that planning permission be refused for the application.

It will be evident from this and from earlier discussion that development control is an essential corollary to the preparation of development plans. In the case of the Bonddu proposal, much debate revolved around ways in which the particular scheme related to the implementation of the statutory plan objectives.

Other aspects of the operation of the development control system are now considered.

DEVELOPMENT CONTROL AS A MEANS OF IMPLEMENTING RECREATION POLICY

Besides its traditional regulatory role, the development control system can also be used in a 'positive' manner to achieve recreational policies. In particular, the granting of a planning permission which is subject to conditions can be seen as an important tool in the hands of the planning authority. The issues which arise in the use of planning conditions to achieve recreation policies can be seen in the implementation of the Cotswold Water Park, a major rural recreation facility which has evolved over a 25-year period.

The Cotswold Water Park (Figure 5.1) is situated in the upper Thames Valley between Swindon and Cirencester, covering an area of about 5 700 ha. The area contains extensive areas of workable gravel, and exhausted workings have been put to recreational use. The water table rises to within a metre of the ground surface and there is a complex pattern of watercourses and around 100 lakes of varying sizes throughout north Wiltshire and south Gloucestershire.

In the light of the land-use problems which were expected to arise from continued exploitation of the mineral reserves, a Cotswold Water Park Joint Committee was created in the late 1960s. The Committee included representatives of the two county councils involved and other local authorities. Early in the proceedings of the committee it was recognized that development control would play a significant role in achieving a rational pattern in the development of the water park (Cotswold Water Park Joint Committee, 1969, p. 6).

A plan for the park outlined the key features of the area. It was well located in relation to regional recreational needs, being close to the na-

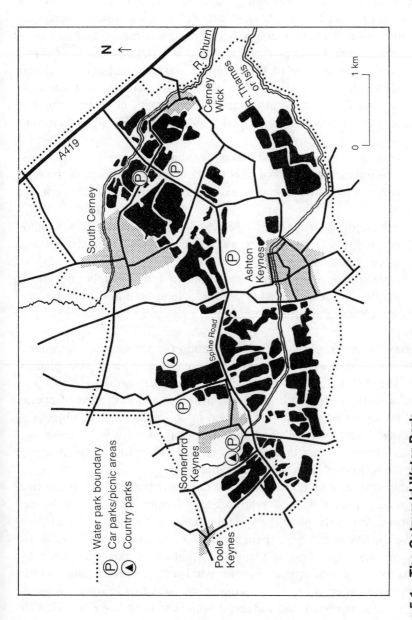

Figure 5.1   The Cotswold Water Park
Source: based on information contained in Gloucestershire County Council (1985)

tional motorway network; part of the area was being used for recreational activities at the time; and areas to be used for mineral workings were criss-crossed by an extensive network of footpaths. In respect of implementation of the recreational schemes, it was recognized that some public investment would be required, but it was felt that much would be achieved through the use of the system of development control. It was asserted that the county councils, in consultation with the district councils and other interests, would control development in such a way that the water park proposals were properly achieved. Specifically, this meant:

- ensuring the orderly and rational working of gravel;
- relating the extension of workings to the improvement of the road network and the eventual exclusion of gravel traffic from the villages;
- enhancing the after-use for recreation of worked-out pits by landscaping, retention of trees, and grading the pit edges to create a more gradual shore line;
- replacing, by alternative routes, public footpaths lost through gravel working, to retain an adequate footpath system in the Park (Cotswold Water Park Joint Committee, 1969, p. 6).

A review of progress in 1983 drew attention to the need to consider a number of issues which had emerged since the original park plan of 1969. The review focused in particular on progress on implementation, the roles of interested authorities and agencies and the forms of operational management which were needed to co-ordinate future objectives of the park (Cotswold Water Park Joint Committee, 1983). From the review, it became clear that the roles of the main actors were emerging along the following lines set out in Table 5.2.

In due course, a large proportion of the water park was included in a local subject plan (Gloucestershire County Council, 1985). The framework provided by the planning system has resulted in many of the 100 or so lakes in the water park being used for recreation, particularly by means of the imposition of planning conditions. Lakes are leased by owners to a variety of private clubs for windsurfing, sailboarding, sailing, fishing, and water skiing. Accommodation is available in the form of static holiday caravans and lodges. A spine road has been provided by the developers and the area has developed into a major recreational resource for water-based activities. Public provision includes two country

Table 5.2
Cotswold Water Park: roles in the development control process

Local authority role/joint committee	Developer role
General policy framework	Land acquisition, exploitation of mineral resources
Devise planning conditions	Undertake landscaping and restoration of worked out sites Provide infrastructure: e.g. spine road
Undertake limited recreation provision: country park, nature reserves	Lease sites; develop sites for recreation; liaise with user groups (water ski) Provide commercial leisure facilities (holiday village)
Countryside management, footpath maintenance	

Source: based on Cotswold Water Park Joint Committee (1983)

parks, nature conservation areas, car parks, development of the access infrastructure including the footpath and bridleway network and information services. Local authority provision of recreation facilities has therefore been undertaken, probably in a far more prominent way than was anticipated in 1969. Despite financial constraints there is visible evidence of both controlled site and area-wide management.

Besides these achievements in the development of the water park there have been problems associated with an approach which is very dependent on the uncertainties of the market and of the interest of developers. The problems of implementing the park scheme through development control were highlighted in evidence presented at a public inquiry held in 1989/90 into the development of an area of land within the water park for a holiday village. In reports produced during the inquiry, a review of the record of achievement stressed the absence of any feeling of 'unity' about the park and the indifferent quality or absence altogether of landscaping having been carried out (Cotswold District Council, 1989, p. 8).

Like the Clogau proposal, the holiday village scheme also generated strong feelings for and against the scheme. The proposal was felt by the local planning authority to be in accordance with the approved structure plan, although it did not accord exactly with proposals contained in the local plan for the area. Most, but not all, of the local authorities and other public bodies supported the proposal. However, residents in existing settlements in the area objected to the scheme because of the disturbance which it would cause and launched a campaign to oppose the proposal. The Cotswold Water Park Villages Society sought to protect the water park from development which they felt had the hallmarks of a holiday camp or fun fair (Figure 5.2). Despite the opposition to the scheme, it was approved by the Secretary of State for the Environment (Department of the Environment, 1991a).

Figure 5.2 Cotswold Water Park: local response to proposal for holiday village, 1990

The Cotswold Water Park example reminds us that private group initiatives and enterprise have a role to play in rural recreation provision. Such initiatives should be contrasted with publicly funded schemes which might be confined simply to those measures which benefit large cross-sections of society (Parker and Penning Rowsell, 1983, p. 187). In the Cotswold Water Park, local authorities provide assistance for the general public for activities which show little financial return, whilst the market caters for other activities. A problem which seems likely to persist is that of coordinating the efforts of bodies who have competing interests in the use of water spaces when the role of the planning authority is essentially reactive rather than proactive.

PLANNING GAIN

The development control system lends itself to other ways of ensuring that land is used in a particular manner. Under section 106 of the Town and Country Planning Act 1990, planning agreements can involve provision of such facilities as roads, access and car parking spaces as part of a planning permission. In the case of planning permission being granted for mineral extraction, a sum might be held in bond until the workings are completed, the site is restored and the planning conditions have been met. This particular situation has been one where in the past it has often proved difficult to obtain compliance with a planning permission.

Government has sought to limit the extent to which planning gain is used by planning authorities. It has attempted to ensure that there is a close relationship between planning gain and the land for which planning permission is being sought. If there is not a close link, then the planning gain can be seen as the 'price of planning permission.'

The use of planning agreements involving conservation measures has been explored in a study of proposals in southeast England (Elson, 1990). In a number of commercial developments planning gain was able to offer opportunities for creating open space for use by the public. A number of advantages were associated with such schemes but a cautionary note has to be struck on two counts. Constrained local authorities may well find it more acceptable to accept lower environmental standards for a proposal, particularly if a much-needed area of open space or leisure facility is provided along with the development. In addition, identification of the really important issues associated with a project

111

may become confused, with planning gain acting as a distraction from the 'real issues'. Despite these reservations, a number of schemes have now been implemented and they seem set to diversify the mechanisms for providing rural recreation facilities. In exploring mechanisms for implementing the community forest initiative, it has been suggested that planning gain may be one of the most important ways of achieving policies in urban fringe areas, notably in areas where complexities of land ownership are likely to be a major constraint on developing land for forests and recreation (Bishop, 1991, p. 8).

Clarification of the issues involved in planning gain was provided by government in a 1991 circular (Department of the Environment, 1991d). In the circular, the term 'planning obligation' was used to cover agreements made between a developer and a local authority and unilateral undertakings made by a developer as a result of a planning application having gone to appeal. The circular recognized the value of planning obligations as a mechanism for achieving planning goals but, as with earlier pronouncements, stressed the need for any obligation to be directly relevant to planning and the development concerned. It acknowledges the ways in which obligations can be used to offset the loss of or impact on an amenity or resource on a site prior to development. In addition, it welcomes schemes where nature conservation and tree planting have been provided by developers as part of planning obligations. As one of a series of 'tests' for assessing planning obligations, proposals should be fairly and reasonably related in scale and kind to the development. In addition, the costs of subsequent maintenance and other recurrent expenditure should be borne by the body in which the asset is vested. Paragraph B10 indicates that attempts should not be made to impose commuted maintenance sums when considering the planning aspects of the development, 'although exceptions can be made in the case of small areas of open space or landscaping principally of benefit to the development itself rather than to the wider public'.

An example of planning gain in operation is provided by Astbury Mere Country Park at Congleton in Cheshire. The site comprised worked-out silica sand workings, land awaiting development and had a long and complex planning history. Controversy over various proposals for use for industry or housing, from 1985, included the launch of a campaign by local residents to retain the site for recreational purposes. As a part of an approval for outline planning permission to build housing on part of a former quarry site, Hepworth Minerals and Chemicals Ltd agreed to

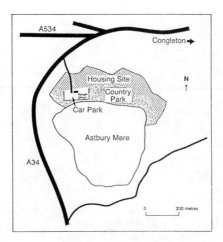

Figure 5.3   Congleton, Cheshire: country park resulting from planning gain – Astbury Mere Country Park
Source: information provided by Astbury Mere Trust, 1991

develop a country park (Figure 5.3) on the southwest side of the town (Cheshire County Council, 1989, p. 1).

The site is well located for easy access from Congleton with nearby roads and a network of footpaths and a bridleway. It conforms well to the location criteria usually considered when developing a recreational facility in an urban fringe location. The company duly completed the country park with footpaths, information centre, car park, toilets and landscaping. The mechanism for establishing the country park involved the company transferring the ownership of the land to a trust together with an endowment of £200 000. After a period during which the company maintained the country park it was transferred in 1991 to the Astbury Mere Trust. The site extends for 10 ha but at present does not include the extensive areas of water and land which adjoin the site to the south and which are in private ownership.

ENVIRONMENTAL ASSESSMENT

A significant addition to the powers given to planning authorities to scrutinize proposed developments has been through the introduction of

113

Plate 5.1   A country park created as a result of planning gain. Astbury Mere at Congleton, Cheshire is owned by a trust with site management contracted to Cheshire County Council, 1991

environmental assessment procedures. Environmental impact assessment (EIA) originated in the USA as a mechanism designed to measure systematically the effects of major developments on the environment. The approach was seen to also be applicable in western Europe and a 1985 directive required member states of the European Community to devise machinery to undertake EIAs of certain classes of project (Commission of the European Communities, 1985). A feature of the directive was that it identified major developments where preparation of an EIA would be obligatory (Annex 1) and other developments where an assessment might also be appropriate, depending on local circumstances in individual member states (Annex II). Into the first category would come developments such as open cast coal mines, oil and gas extraction; into the second would be included land drainage measures, afforestation and tourist villages.

There was considerable reluctance on the part of government in Britain to translate the directive's proposals into a local context. A view stated was that there was already an excellent system of controls over development and the introduction of another series of regulations was unnecessary. Despite a certain reluctance in Britain to adopt the directive,

114

it nevertheless became operative in 1988 although the terminology actually adopted was that of environmental assessment (EA) (Department of the Environment, 1988d).

The operation of EA procedures in England and Wales was outlined in a Department of the Environment circular which, as required in the directive, indicates (in Schedule 1) those projects where EA will be mandatory (Department of the Environment, 1988a). In Schedule 2 are listed projects where an EA may be required. Individual need for an EA may depend on the scale of the proposed development, its location, whether or not it was in a designated or protected landscape and whether the project would cause particularly difficult problems, including pollution.

In Britain, most projects requiring environmental assessment do so under the provisions of the Town and Country Planning Acts. Developments in connection with forestry, land drainage, highways, harbours, electricity and pipelines and fish farming are dealt with generally under separate statutes. Although a number of projects would under normal circumstances require planning permission, several do not. For example, forestry, land drainage and pipelines would not normally require permission. Thus, although local planning authorities might be involved in considering some proposals for development, separate systems of adjudication apply for others. A further point to note is that the only specific reference to the requirement for recreation projects to require an EA, relates to holiday villages. However, other categories of project in Schedule 2 might also include a significant recreation or leisure component.

The environmental assessment process

Guidance in undertaking an EA indicates a process with a number of clear stages, as shown in Figure 5.4 (Department of the Environment, 1989a). The operation and extent of various aspects of EA procedures have been fully explored in a number of publications and fuller reference can be obtained from those sources (Department of the Environment, 1989a; Wathern, 1988; Lee and Colley, 1990). From these various sources, the rural recreation perspective on EA can be viewed in three ways. Firstly, there is the environmental impact of certain major recreational developments. As indicated, these are likely to affect only the largest of recreational schemes, including the Cotswold Water Park Holi-

115

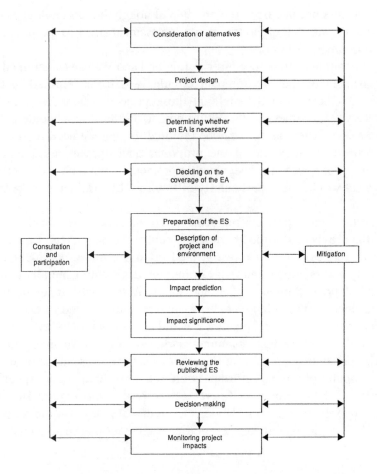

Figure 5.4   Stages involved in the environmental assessment process
Source: Jones *et al.* (1991), p. 2

day Village proposal for which an EA was produced (Cobham Resource Consultants, 1989). The impact of such a scheme is likely to be on a similar scale to other major residential or commercial developments. Secondly, consideration can be given to the impact of a project upon the existing and potential use of land or water for recreation. Such impacts could have only a very marginal effect, or they could result in major disruption to rural recreation sites or activities. Thirdly, the secondary or after-use of a site used for one activity requiring an environmental assessment, such as a large mineral extraction, may itself provide for recreational pursuits.

Reservations have been expressed about the quality of treatment of recreation and landscape issues in EAs (Countryside Commission, 1991a, p. 4). As experience is gained, it is likely that techniques will improve in quality. The value of the EA is that it can offer a systematic and rigorous approach to appreciating the effects of a development on its surrounds. For the developer it can provide a valuable framework for considering the relationship between a project design and environmental issues. For the policy-maker, EA can provide a better basis for decision-making and the implications of a new project are more thoroughly analysed before a planning application is made, enabling swifter decisions to be made (Department of the Environment, 1989a, pp. 3–4).

The use of the systematic approach required under EA legislation can be appreciated when consideration is given to the impacts of a project or development on rural recreation resources and activities (Table 5.3).

In the EA process, an important stage is the preparation of the environmental statement itself. This is undertaken by the developer and involves several steps. These include 'scoping', an exercise in which the key issues to be considered in the EA process are identified, and undertaking formal and informal consultations prior to submission of the statement to the appropriate agency: say, a planning authority. Another stage in the EA process concerns the review of the statement by the planning authority. The latter will be interested in establishing whether or not the statement meets acceptable criteria. In considering the issues that a person undertaking a review might seek to have answered, Lee and Colley (1990, pp. 37–43) offer a checklist under four headings:

- description of the development, the local environment and the baseline conditions;
- identification and evaluation of impacts;
- alternatives, mitigation and monitoring;
- communication of results.

Consideration is now given to how the review process might operate in the case of a proposal for development of mineral workings on urban fringe grazing land which is criss-crossed with an extensive network of

Table 5.3 Environmental assessment and rural recreation

Stage in EA process	Rural recreational considerations
'Scoping'	Informal consultations to establish key environmental/recreational issues, e.g. contact with local water sports users affected by project
Project description	Description of salient features of project; appearance, layout, materials, form, in construction, operational and decommissioning stages
Description of environment affected by project	Record rural recreation resources and activities; levels of use; recreation inventory; type of management (formal/informal); land ownership; potential recreational uses; e.g. urban fringe area popular for riding and walking
Magnitude of impacts	Statement of likely influence of proposed development on existing or future recreation, whether reversible or irreversible, e.g. indication of land area subject to access agreement which is lost
Significance of impacts	Importance of losses (or enhancement), e.g. fragmentation of footpath network, loss of regionally important coastal access point
Alternatives and mitigation	Extent to which project can be modified to take account of impacts: e.g. alteration of site boundary to allow continued use of footpath; or provision of alternative routeway
Review of environmental statement (ES)	Decision-maker's consideration on basis of environmental statement submitted by developer
Consultation and participation	Developer undertakes formal and informal consultations, exhibitions, sale of ES to public
Inspections by monitoring authority	Monitoring, testing of accuracy of predictions in ES: e.g. reinstatement of rights of way

Source: based on Countryside Commission (1991a)

rights of way. In these circumstances, the reviewer might expect the EA to provide answers to the following questions.

- Does the environmental statement provide a full description of the present-day recreational use of the site?
- Have site surveys of formal or informal activities been undertaken?
- What effect would the development have on the use of the road and rights of way network for walkers, cyclists and riders?
- Is that effect likely to be experienced during the constructional, operational or completed phases of development, or all three?
- What is likely to be the scale (significance) of the development on the network (severing a regional recreational route or national trail)?
- What measures might be undertaken to mitigate the adverse impacts of the development (temporary, permanent diversion of routes; choice of alternative site, alteration of site boundary)?
- How well is the information communicated? Can it be assimilated easily? Is information provided without bias? Does the document contain a non-technical summary with conclusions about alternatives?

Copies of the ES are required to be provided to consultees and to the public. If not satisfied with the contents of the document, the planning or other authority can require the developer to supply further information.

A CHANGING CONTEXT FOR DEVELOPMENT CONTROL

The ability of the development control system to handle conflict in the countryside has been tested by two significant developments during the 1980s. A first influence has been the reduction in central support for agriculture and the creation of substantial surpluses of productive land. This had led agriculturalists to explore alternative uses for agricultural land, the possibilities for which have brought them into close contact with the planning system.

A second influence has been the sometimes confusing changes in government attitude to the traditional regulatory role of planning in Britain. Government attitudes to control of development have been char-

119

acterized by a general attempt to 'lift the burden' placed by the planning system on the developer and on the landowner (Trade and Industry, 1988). A feature of this philosophy was a general desire by government to change the presumption in development control to be in favour of development rather than against it (Department of the Environment, 1988b, p. 2).

Perhaps the most significant indication of this change in policy direction was Circular 16/87 which encouraged farmers to seek alternative uses for agricultural land (Department of the Environment, 1987). The circular introduced new arrangements for the release of agricultural land for development. Although the best and most versatile land (grades 1, 2 and 3a) would be subject to measures of protection, safeguarding other land from development could no longer be assumed simply because it was agricultural land. If a proposal for development in the countryside was to be refused planning permission, then local planning authorities would have to rely much more on the need to safeguard rural landscapes in their own right rather than because of their agricultural value.

The circular was released at a time when the agricultural community was being urged to diversify its activities into woodland planting, leisure and tourism or to set aside land from agricultural use (Ministry of Agriculture, 1987). It was followed by other measures which sought to encourage change in agriculture. These included proposals contained in a consultation paper to increase the range of developments in the countryside for which planning permission was not normally required under provisions of the General Development Order (Department of the Environment, 1989b). The document predictably drew considerable opposition from amenity groups (Council for the Protection of Rural England, 1989). In the event the proposals to increase permitted development rights (PDRs) along the lines suggested in the consultation document were not pursued. However, since that time, the effects of diversification and increased fragmentation of farm holdings have become apparent.

A consultant's report records the considerable difficulties faced by planning authorities in controlling permitted development often associated with leisure and recreation (Department of the Environment, 1991c). The PDR report describes growing 'suburbanization' of some areas of countryside through the sale of 'leisure plots' in urban fringe areas and horse keeping with land subdivided as pony paddocks. Examples are cited of the misuse of permitted development rights and of the time-consuming and complex process involved in carrying out enforcement procedures.

The investigation leads to consideration of a number of aspects of development control policies including expectations of what they can achieve as well as the limitations placed on their use.

Firstly, considerable powers are available to local authorities to bring unauthorized development under planning control. Breach of planning law is regarded as a regulatory offence, although discretion to take action on any breach is bestowed on the enforcement agency itself (Jowell and Millichap, 1987, p. 175). In deciding whether to proceed with an enforcement action and with serving an enforcement notice a local authority needs to decide whether it is 'expedient' to do so and, whether enforcement is necessary.

Despite the existence of such powers, dissatisfaction with arrangements for enforcement has been expressed from time to time and a widely held view is that it is a neglected aspect of planning activity. The Planning and Compensation Act 1991 tightened up a number of matters, providing, for example, for increased fines for offences and revised forms of 'stop' notices which can be issued to prohibit an unauthorized activity where it has been carried out for up to 4 years instead of one year previously (Mynors, 1991, pp. 10–11). However, there are limits to which the procedures can be put and within the planning profession itself, the situation is still not regarded as satisfactory. In commenting on a Department of the Environment draft guidance note on enforcement, the Royal Town Planning Institute considered that the government appeared to suggest that local authorities should go out of their way to avoid upsetting small businesses (anon, 1991, p. 4).

A second theme concerns the extent to which permitted development rights might be brought under planning control. The authors of the PDR study argued for the use of such powers in the form of 'Article 4' directions which have to be confirmed by central government under the General Development Order 1988. They are seen to have a 'vital role to play in controlling the increasing proliferation of temporary structures associated with land fragmentation (Department of the Environment, 1991c, p. 50). However, in explaining the operation of the General Development Order, Circular 22/88 stressed that permitted development rights should be withdrawn locally only in exceptional circumstances (Department of the Environment, 1988e).

A further issue to consider in relation to development control is its ability to safeguard recreation resources. Some possibilities were explored earlier in this chapter in the case of the Cotswold Water Park and

121

Plate 5.2 Statutory local plans supported by strict development control and highway policies can safeguard town–country links: cyclepath/footpath link between Wythenshawe and the Bollin Valley, south of Manchester, 1992

procedures for carrying out environmental assessments. Although development control may be expected rightly to safeguard existing recreation areas subject to development pressure, in the case of land with *potential* recreation value the task may be much more difficult. If we take as an example the case of disused railway lines or canals with potential use as 'greenways' or recreational routeways, development control is likely to play a vital role in safeguarding that resource. Protection may be achieved through formal and informal policies but the problems involved in actually safeguarding such routes through development control can be summarized as follows:

- pressure has often been exerted by neighbouring landowners to incorporate potential recreational routeways for development;
- there has been often vociferous opposition to a route being safe-guarded for recreational uses by residents of nearby properties who perceive security problems;
- internal pressure has been exerted by other local authority departments who value the land for other purposes and whose internal lobbying is more effective than that of recreational interests;
- problems have occurred in demonstrating the true potential of land for recreation, notably in cases where schemes are unlikely to be undertaken for several years. This has applied in particular to major road schemes where a local authority may be in a weak position to argue for crossings for recreational routes which may be several years from implementation.

A fourth consideration which could affect the part played by development control in dealing with recreational issues, concerns the changing role of the development plan framework within which decisions are made and to which reference was made earlier. In 1992 the government reissued a 1988 planning policy guidance note indicating the general principles behind the statutory planning system (Department of the Environment, 1988b; 1992a). This appeared to greatly strengthen the role of the development plan in the planning system and stressed the need for development proposals to be in accordance with its provisions. This has been interpreted as a significant change to the advice offered in the 1988 version of this guidance note which asserted that there should be a general presumption in favour of development. The implications of the guidance for development control are not entirely clear. Certainly the measures seem likely to reduce the discretion of local planning authorities in making decisions on planning applications. On the other hand, they may strengthen the hand of the authority in adhering to long-term objectives, including those of safeguarding land intended for recreational use in the long term.

COMMENT

The development control system in Britain is faced with the task of responding to marked increases in pressures for change in the countryside, particularly for proposals involving outdoor recreation. From agriculture being the dominant rural activity, in some areas it is rapidly taking the role as a backcloth against which other pursuits, including recreation, can take place. There seems little doubt that in areas such as national parks and other protected areas the pressures for development will receive the same degree of detailed scrutiny as they have for many years. In other areas, however, a more flexible approach to regulation of change will occur and significant changes to the rural landscape are likely to be experienced. Two important questions arise from these various developments. Firstly, how resilient will the system of development control be to such pressures? Secondly, what type of landscape will emerge as a result of the break-up of traditional farming landscapes? So far, it seems clear that major development schemes, consuming extensive areas of land and generating quite significant amounts of traffic, are receiving a great deal of publicity and concern. However, rather less is known about the effect on the countryside of the many small-scale proposals for change carried out under the heading of 'agricultural diversification'. The effects of such changes could threaten the well-established objectives of the planning system which for 40 years has sought to maintain a clear distinction between urban and rural environments. Of particular interest will be the influence of European Community directives on future control of development. The Community's EA directive is one of the more important measures to have an effect on development control in Britain in recent years, but future policy may well be shaped further from that source.

Lastly, development control has a central role to play in ensuring that a long-term view is taken of land needs for recreation. It has been shown that conditions can be imposed to achieve recreational goals, but the pressures to which planning authorities are subject have resulted in there being many examples of lost recreational opportunities throughout Britain.

Chapter 6

Countryside management and rural recreation

Given the limitations of developing a strong recreational dimension to statutory plans, planning authorities have used alternative mechanisms in order to implement rural recreation policies. Of particular importance has been the adoption of techniques of rural recreational management.

Rural recreational management cannot be separated from consideration of the wider management and conservation of the countryside. In a paper advocating the adoption of a coordinated approach to the management of rural land, Hookway expressed concern about the deterioration in landscape quality because of rapidly evolving technology in agriculture and expansion of forestry (Hookway, 1967, p. 63). In his argument he also drew out the need for more controls and management of outdoor recreation: 'the evidence of the last decade has been the dramatic increase in the already large numbers of car-borne visitors probing every by-way and ungated field throughout the summer, and on Sundays throughout the year' (Hookway, 1967, p. 69).

Hookway then went on to outline ways in which the problems of catering for recreation and other rural land uses ought to be tackled. In particular he placed great emphasis on:

- the influence that individual land managers could have on the appearance of the countryside;
- the role played by public policies, particularly for agriculture, water resources, forestry and recreation;
- the part that could be played by management agreements and management plans as ways of achieving better uses and better appearance of publicly owned land.

In resolving the conflicts in the use of rural land, the late 1960s and the 1970s saw several attempts at managing rural land by the use of informal (non-statutory) mechanisms. The East Hampshire Area of Outstanding Natural Beauty conservation study is of interest in its approach to managing the use of the countryside (Hampshire County Council, 1968). The study established the principle of collective agreement as being the basis for resolving conflicts and for preparing management plans within discrete areas of countryside. With hindsight the involvement of public agencies only in the study (local authorities and representatives from the Ministry of Agriculture, Forestry Commission, Nature Conservancy and National Parks Commission) can be seen as a drawback in the investigation. Similarly, some of the methods of analysis might now be considered difficult to justify and adopt on a large scale. However, as a first exploration of concepts and techniques which were to be later refined in other investigations, the study must be viewed as a landmark.

In the East Hampshire study and in more recent investigations, a distinction has been drawn between the terms 'planning' and 'management' (Selman, 1987, p. 155). 'Planning' is normally taken to mean statutory planning, and the processes associated with the town and country planning system: the making of development plans, undertaking development control and providing a basis for policies with land-use implications which affect the physical, social and economic environment (Countryside Commission, 1974b, p. 1) The term 'management' can be taken to mean such activities as the provision of national park services, land acquisition, recreational development, land management, tree planting, clearance of eyesores, wardening, interpretation and information services, and traffic management (Countryside Commission, 1974b, p. 1)

A later definition places a greater emphasis on the public interest in countryside management, considering it to be a process by which 'the objectives of conservation, recreation and access are secured for public benefit in the management of both public and privately owned land' (Countryside Commission, 1981b, p. 1).

In discussing countryside and recreational management, it has been common to distinguish between 'area-wide' approaches extending possibly over many square kilometres and 'site-based' approaches which focus on smaller sites normally with discrete boundaries.

AREA-WIDE COUNTRYSIDE AND RECREATION MANAGEMENT

Encouraged by Hookway and by the recommendations for multiple land-use policies by the Ellison Committee in 1967, countryside management schemes have been adopted on a wide scale in Britain (Department of Education and Science, 1966; Hookway, 1977). The Countryside Commission sponsored experimental countryside management schemes in the Lake District and Snowdonia from 1969 onwards (Countryside Commission, 1976b, 1979b). An important objective of both of these experimental schemes was to resolve conflicts between visitors and landowners. A key feature of the schemes was the appointment of a project officer who liaised with different interest groups. The officer identified areas of agreement with the farming community and was able to offer limited financial support for projects such as the construction of stiles, signposting and path improvement.

In the years following the initiation of the Upland Management Experiments (UMEX), the practice of countryside management was extended to other areas. The countryside management experiment in the Bollin Valley (1972–75), south of Manchester, is of interest in being the first undertaken in the problematic urban/rural fringe areas around cities (Countryside Commission, 1976a). The Bollin Valley experiment proved a valuable testbed for implementing countryside management principles and was followed by the introduction of other urban fringe schemes in Hertfordshire/Barnet, Havering, Cleveland, Tyne and Wear and St Helens. The schemes can be regarded as successful in a number of respects, particularly in tackling problems of access, maximizing the opportunities provided by the existing rights of way, and developing small-scale recreational facilities. The valuable role of the project officer has been underlined thus: 'the farming community, being very pragmatic, found the project staff very helpful in dealing with specific problems, particularly those associated with public rights of way' (Lavery, 1982, p. 57).

Local authorities in other parts of Britain have created their own countryside management services. In Cheshire, for example, the first countryside officer outside a national park was appointed in 1969. Since that time a countryside management service has developed with a remit which focused initially on individual recreation site management, including several country parks, picnic areas and linear parks. Later, activities extended to other countryside issues, including access, conserva-

127

tion and landscape with an establishment of some 44 people including 35 countryside rangers (Smith, 1990, p. 5).

The scale of countryside management activities in Britain is considerable. One study showed that around a third of a sample of almost 200 local authorities were able to provide details of countryside management plans used by their authorities (Selman, 1987, p. 159). The findings demonstrated that most plans were concerned with 'amenity' and recreation issues such as access, site provision, wardening, tree planting, local traffic management and regulation of problem leisure pursuits. Policies also included matters (such as habitat management) too detailed for inclusion in statutory plans.

Despite undoubted success, there has been a danger of projects being undertaken in an opportunistic manner and local authorities may proceed

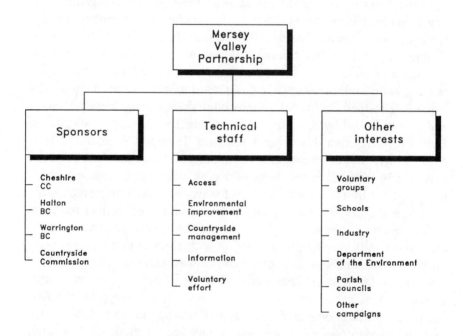

Figure 6.1 Mersey Valley Partnership: range of activities and participants
Source: based on Mersey Valley Partnership (1989)

with management programmes on a short-term, renewable, basis. The initial short life span of three years for urban fringe experiments meant that priority was placed on obtaining quick effective results. 'The whole emphasis was to demonstrate what could be achieved by joint working and cooperation, rather than on long-term maintenance measures' (Lavery, 1982, p. 55). Inevitably success depends greatly on the personal qualities of project officers or managers. Countryside management schemes face competition in bids for funding, but they are often able to undertake a wide range of countryside management activities, obtaining support from several sources (Figure 6.1; Mersey Valley Partnership, 1989).

SITE-BASED COUNTRYSIDE RECREATION MANAGEMENT

Besides management projects concerned with wider areas of country-side, management also takes place on 'controlled' sites which can be in public or private ownership. Like area-wide countryside management, a considerable amount of experience in site development and management has been accumulated in Britain over the last 25 years. There are several themes under which this development can be considered.

Acquisition and development of publicly owned sites may simply have taken place as a response to local problems of congestion: for example, at a beauty spot. Alternatively, a site such as Bolam Lake Country Park in Northumberland could have its origins as part of a scheme to improve former parkland which was in a degraded state (Laurie, 1983). Possible sites could also include woodland which might vary greatly in size and characteristics (Irving, 1985). Farmland, noticeably in connection with agricultural diversification schemes, might also be seen as having potential for recreational use, although this would be undertaken as part of other activities (Slee, 1989, p. 63). Lastly, land remaining from other activities including quarrying and coalmining together with disused railway lines might be used for rural recreation (Wells, 1987, p. 43; Andrew, 1988, p. 3).

For many local authorities, site selection has been opportunistic, taking advantage of land which was often made available in a fortuitous manner. In other instances, land has been acquired in a more systematic way. In the 1960s, for example, Durham County Council introduced a programme for the advance acquisition of land for recreation and conservation.

For the private provider, the site-selection process has generally fitted into wider financial appraisals, including the need for a financial return from revenue-generating activities and the availability of central or local government grants (Miles and Seabrooke, 1978, pp. 30, 91). In major recreational schemes, the process of site selection may take on a form similar to that for any other development, whether for shopping, industry or housing. For the private developer of Thorpe Park Water Park in Surrey, for example, the factors influencing exploitation of former mineral workings for recreation were as follows (Hartwright, 1985, pp. 58–64):

- location: proximity to centres of population, motorway networks (journey time determines the origins of visitors);
- local roads capability of handling high volumes of additional traffic;
- attractive surroundings and approaches and established tourist area with sympathetic local authority;
- size: suitable land for developing a leisure park, including parking (Thorpe Park is over 180 ha);
- site characteristics: attractive site with water present;
- services: capable of handling sudden surges in demand caused by large numbers of visitors.

Thorpe Park represents the larger scale of development of recreational projects. It nevertheless highlights the types of factors which are likely to influence both private and, arguably, public provision of rural recreation facilities. In particular, it reminds us of the influence that the statutory planning system can exert on the process of site selection.

RECREATION SITE-MANAGEMENT PLANS

In forestry and wildlife conservation it has long been the practice to produce working management plans. Such plans indicate in considerable detail the timing, form and scale of action needed to measure the proper production and use of resources. Thus a management plan for a nature reserve would identify practices needed in order to achieve stated goals and would include a schedule describing in detail when different tasks, such as grazing or planting, are required. Management plans for both

130

wildlife conservation and forestry have had the benefit of much accumulated scientific evidence to provide policy frameworks.

In rural recreation, the same traditions of practice do not exist. As a consequence, attempts to produce management plans have often been of an exploratory nature, indicating a few general principles only. This does not mean that recreation management *per se* is not practised, for much done under the heading of countryside management also involves a degree of recreational management. It is rather that such management often operates to an unwritten code of practice. This has the advantage of offering a considerable degree of flexibility to managers. However, in the absence of the regular and rigorous policy review and evaluation normally associated with a formally produced management plan, wider and perhaps more controversial long-term issues may not receive the attention they deserve. As was found in one study of common land management, policies tend to be reactive rather than prescriptive and to be concerned with short-term problems (Land Use Consultants, 1985, p. 52).

In looking for 'good practice' in recreation management plan preparation, examples tend to be found amongst agencies with a long tradition of rural land management. Such bodies might be expected to draft on to recreation management plans some of the established principles and practice under which they operate. Less well-developed forms of practice might be expected in, say, a local authority attempting to establish a country park or other recreational site. Here, a low-profile, tentative approach might be adopted, particularly if there is much internal competition for funds or if, for example, there is opposition to proposals from adjacent landowners or residents.

If it is decided that a management plan is desirable, what form might it actually take? In Britain, practitioners have been exposed for many years to overseas practice: for example, through studies of Dutch and American practice. Much guidance has been provided by the British Countryside Commissions as, for example, in the case of management plans for country parks (Countryside Commission, 1974a; Countryside Commission for Scotland, 1988). In addition a number of other sources are available to practitioners (Miles and Seabrooke, 1978; Green, 1985; Irving, 1985; Leay *et al.* 1986).

The preparation of recreation management plans might involve two main stages: description and prescription (Table 6.1). Planning briefs can be used to provide recreation site designers and managers with guidance

Table 6.1 Preparation of a recreation management plan

Theme	Content
Planning brief	Identification of external factors likely to influence site development
Description	Natural, semi-natural and other resources (topography, geology, water, soils, plants etc.)
	Land uses, neighbouring uses, populations
	Existing recreational uses
	Potential user characteristics, origins, mode of transport etc.
Objectives	Identification of primary and secondary objectives
Prescription	Broad management prescriptions related to different components of site
	Proposals for specific uses and activities (informal, formal, recreation; management of wildlife habitats; access, traffic, buildings, interpretation, publicity, charges, rental)
Implementation	Programme, priorities, costs
	Division of management responsibilities
Monitoring and review	Regular counts of visitors; monitoring of activities on habitats; and of conflicts between users

on the overall form of a project. A brief could be expected to indicate to a designer of a recreational site such information as: the appropriate scale and density of development; the relationship of the site to the wider context of land-use planning, traffic and circulation; the function of the site in relation to regional or subregional demands and needs for recreation and recreation strategies (if they exist); whether the site is expected to perform a 'social service' function used largely by visitors on foot, bicycle or public transport, or whether it is a 'gateway' tourism site which might be expected to pay a substantial part of its way. The management plan would be expected to reflect these possible roles.

The descriptive surveys undertaken will depend greatly on the physical characteristics of sites. A minimal checklist would require appropriate records of such information as site area and land uses, topography, soils, drainage, wildlife habitats and, possibly, historical associations. Information, too, which would be required would relate to legal constraints on the site including covenants, private and public rights of way. Having undertaken such an inventory, the plan designer would then be in a position to carry out an appraisal of the current forms of land management and changes taking place within it. This stocktaking would thus provide a record of both the site assets and liabilities.

On the basis of the inventory and appraisal, management objectives can then be specified within broad aims identified at the start of the design process (Leay *et al.*, 1986, p. 7). Objectives can, of course, be wide-ranging in form but they could seek to maximize access to the site for physically disabled visitors; or to focus visitor pressure on areas where vulnerable habitats can best stand heavy wear and tear.

In producing a plan, there may be few options available in relation to the objectives that have been set. However, it may emerge that there are several ways of achieving the objectives, each with different financial implications or with greater or lesser impacts on the site.

In the next stage of the plan-making process, prescription would be expected to outline ways of implementing the plan and its objectives. Prescription could take a number of forms indicating overall strategies and more precise indications of where and when specific projects or forms of management will take place.

Note would have to be made of staffing resource requirements (Bromley, 1990, pp. 153–156). For example, how many days of full-time staff labour will be required each year to maintain the surface quality of footpaths 'x' and 'y'? Financial management will feature prominently in the prescription, indicating total costs of inputs (labour, building development, capital and revenue) as well as outputs which could include incomes from charges for services, sales of produce or return from leasing land. On sites managed by land trusts or by private landowners it might be expected that each site would have its own profit and loss account (Sustrans Ltd, 1990, p. 9).

A feature of a recreational management plan would be a schedule which provided a clear set of instructions of tasks needed to be undertaken, and where and when. For the 59 ha Harrold-Odell Country Park, the management schedule is devised on the basis of six separate 'compartments' (Bedfordshire County Council, 1987). In this and other management plans, provision is made for review at regular intervals, possibly accompanied by annual reports.

Investigations into all the opportunities and constraints found at a site may well suggest a number of alternative solutions to the development of the site. To an extent the alternatives may be quite clearly constrained by the assumptions and objectives set out in a design brief. In other

Table 6.2
Alternative strategies available to the private woodland owner

Level of involvement	Activities	Management required
Minimal	Low-density informal: walking dog, walking, wildlife observation	Inspection, litter collection
Low involvement	Low-density informal: cycling, walking, picnicking, riding, guided walks	Minor path works, as above; also off-road inspections, litter collection
Medium involvement	Intensive informal: caravan site, BMX circuit, education	Increasing involvement owner/manager
High involvement	As above, also trim trail, fitness/adventure/ interpretation/shelter	Need for toilet, increased levels of maintenance and administration
Very high involvement	Specialist uses with higher levels of capital investment: equestrian woodland, large touring camp/caravan site, restaurant and chalet development	Landowner/developer schemes

Source: based on Irving (1985), pp. 74–79

cases, the range of options may be much greater, with available financial resources playing a particularly important role in determining what might be achieved. A number of possibilities have been outlined in the use of private woodland for recreation (Table 6.2).

A number of options might be pursued by the owner. They include a 'minimal involvement' arrangement whereby a site is run for private recreation at no cost to the owner. Or an option may involve a major joint scheme between a landowner and a developer. Although the schema is directed primarily to private owners, the range of options cited may be relevant to other types of owners, too.

An example of a recreation management plan with a strong conservation emphasis designed to protect attractive coastal landscape is the Seven Sisters Country Park. Its opening in 1974 was described as 'the culmination of 40 years of campaigning by the County Council to safeguard vulnerable parts of the East Sussex Coast and Downland' (East Sussex County Council, 1987). The site was purchased by East Sussex County Council in 1971 and was grant-aided by the Countryside Commission. The plan adopts a zoning approach to its policies for conservation and visitor services. Recreation uses are concentrated into an 'activity' zone. In a remote zone, conservation of the natural environment has overriding priority. For six main habitat types, specific types of management are prescribed, including vegetation management by means of sheep and programmed control of invasive or habitat-damaging species of plants and animals. The main means of management of visitors is by confining vehicles to two car parks. Besides the use of the zoning concept, the other principles of management are to spread the load of visitors outside weekend periods, a 'gradualist' approach to improvement or extension of facilities, and the maintenance of high standards of management. Paths, together with nature trails and riding trails, are used to focus use but, even so, controls are not obvious and people are able to walk over extensive parts of the country park (Gibbons, 1991, p. 231).

The plan records that 'the staffing and financial resources currently available to manage the Park are barely adequate to maintain existing services'. In this, the Park is probably no different from many other recreational sites. However, the plan outlines a number of ways of introducing and increasing revenue, including charging for car parking, leasing of land and buildings, and enhanced sales of goods.

DESIGN AND MANAGEMENT CONCEPTS

An important part of a management plan for a recreational site is the design of the layout for different land uses and activities. Detailed treatment of layout and design is likely to be a matter for specialists such as landscape designers and is not discussed in depth here. However, some of the issues that are likely to be of concern to the planner, particularly in drawing up a design brief, are now considered.

In drawing up detailed layouts for recreation sites, designs have generally sought to achieve a match between the requirements of particular recreational activities and the opportunities offered by the resources that are available on site. Important considerations are likely to be: the definition of appropriate objectives and levels of use; the desirable extent to which the site might be physically altered; the use of alternative types of treatment; and the amount of funding available for both revenue and capital expenditure.

Designers have used a variety of principles around which to frame their proposals. Some of the principles are explicitly stated in plans but, in other cases, they are perhaps less evident but still underlie designs produced for recreation sites.

The dominant principle which underlies most management plans is that of minimizing recreational impacts on the natural or semi natural environment. This approach is underlined in a major review as follows.

- Given the impact of recreation on soils and vegetation, the role of management (and design) should be to try to control the effects of recreation.
- Changes in ecosystem processes may be 'self-limiting'; once change has taken place, then the impacts of use are limited. For example, well-built trails deteriorate little over time.
- Behaviour on recreation sites is relatively predictable in terms of space and time, with use being concentrated at attractions and along linkages. Site designers can build on these behaviour patterns and ensure that impacts are confined to relatively small areas.
- Tolerance of different environments to recreational pressures can be considerable; recovery from pressure may be rapid or slow.
- Impacts are closely linked to the mode of travel of the user with major impacts when there is a great mix of different types of users

and where specific techniques of design and management might be used: for example, zoning.

- The different components of a site, including its resources and users, are closely interrelated. Measures to control use of one type of visitor in one location may affect or discriminate against visitors at that same location or elsewhere (Hammitt and Cole, 1987, pp. 195–198)

Such principles were considered in relation to 'wildland' sites in a North American context, rather than intensively used areas such as, say, country parks in urban fringe locations. Nevertheless, the principle of containing the environmental impacts of recreation underlies much recreation site design and management in Britain.

Matching user requirements with site characteristics

Besides the physical characteristics of a site, a further important consideration in site design is the specific siting requirements of different recreational activities. These factors include: space requirements (area or width and length of track for route-based activities); ground surface texture and local terrain, whether flat or undulating; slope tolerance including critical thresholds of slope angle; presence of water either for direct use (as for yachting) or as a setting for other activities (Hockin *et al.*, 1977, p. 4).

A key issue is the extent to which individual activities are able to take place satisfactorily alongside each other. To what extent are conflict and compatibility based on fear or upon reality? Or is the relationship between different uses based on managers' assumptions about the extent to which activities are compatible with each other? In their study of recreational sites Hockin *et al.* (1977, p. 45) considered that conflict was related to several factors:

- the nature of activity itself (creating noise or being dangerous);
- the way in which the activity is practised (by 'novices' as well as expert participants);
- the nature of the site (particularly on small or linear sites);
- where competitive activities make a site unusable for others, for example by disturbing ground surfaces so that they cannot be used.

137

In this study, 'inter-activity compatibility' was determined for 24 activities using a weighted scoring system based on the degree of compatibility between activities. High-score activities were those such as angling, rambling, orienteering and wildlife study; low-compatibility activities included, not surprisingly, motor cycle sports and field sports of various levels. Understanding the concept of compatibility is seen therefore to be central to site design. Matrices which identify degrees of conflict or compatibility between different types of use can be of assistance in focusing attention on activities which might of might not be accommodated alongside each other, or might be permitted subject to constraints.

**Plate 6.1   Pow Hill Country Park was developed on exposed
moorland at Derwent Reservoir from 1970 onwards.
Extensive tree planting was undertaken and 20 years
later the site takes on the enclosed appearance
intended by its designers, 1989**

Besides the requirements of individual activities, a further consideration is the extent to which sites might be modified to accommodate
different activities. Although the origins of sites may be extremely diverse,
the ability of a site to absorb visitors is likely to be influenced by the
presence of woodland or other 'mantle' cover. Important are the opportunities that woodland offers for the screening and seclusion and its
ability to absorb cars and caravans without noticeably disrupting the
appearance of the countryside.

However, woodland cover may not always be present and sites may
lack any established shelter at all. For example, Durham County Council's 18 ha Pow Hill Country Park was developed in the early 1970s on
the southern edge of the Derwent Reservoir on rough moorland (Derwent
Valley Advisory Committee, 1972, p. 11). The most important feature of
the design adopted for the site was for extensive planting and the creation of several enclosed spaces for picnicking. Twenty years after the
site was laid out, the mantle was beginning to take on the appearance
envisaged by its designers (as shown in Plate 6.1).

Capacity

The concept of capacity has been used to help determine the appropriate
balance between activities which might take place on a site and the
ability of that site to absorb those activities. Although frequently referred
to as a concept that can assist planners and designers, its application in a
systematic way in site design has been rather more limited. The concept
has been explored in a number of texts to which reference can be made
(Brotherton, 1973; Burton, 1974; Patmore, 1983, pp. 222–233; Green,
1985, pp. 186–187; Glyptis, 1991, pp. 148–152). Here it is sufficient to
record that physical capacity has been defined in its simplest form as the
maximum amount of use that can be recommended at a site. Most
typically, the notion of physical carrying capacity might be applied to a
car park where it would be possible to define a clear maximum number
of vehicles which might be accommodated there. Perceptual capacity is
seen as the level of use above which visitors experience a loss of enjoyment simply because of the presence of others. Although increases in
numbers of visitors will normally decrease enjoyment, the opposite may
also apply and presence of others may contribute to the enjoyment
experienced by a visitor. A third concept, ecological capacity, is based

on the extent to which levels of use can be sustained before the ecological value of a resource is measurably damaged.

It is argued that these concepts are only of value if the resource manager has been given a clear indication of the levels of use that are appropriate for the overall objectives set for the site. However, defining that level is fraught with difficulties. Much depends on there being a clear statement of management objectives and on recognizing that, even though capacity limits might be stated, they are nevertheless subjective (Glyptis, 1991, p. 152). At what point can it be said that the ecological carrying capacity of a site has been reached? 'In a country park, a ryegrass sward might be entirely acceptable but in a nature reserve the loss of even a single species might be regarded as too much to pay for that level of use!' (Green, 1985, p. 187). A further point is that carrying capacity may alter once it has been actually determined. This might occur, for example, because of the influence of wet weather on steep slopes hastening the effects of erosion.

Acknowledging difficulties in measurement of capacity, Green (1985, p. 187) outlines certain general principles which can help in understanding the notion of capacity:

- Productive vegetation has a higher carrying capacity than that to be found on poorer soils.
- The effects of trampling by visitors and vehicles can clearly have an impact with effects on vegetation, soil and fauna and subsequent loss of species which are most vulnerable to pressures.
- Other impacts which may be apparent include disturbance to animals, with some species being particularly sensitive to noise, rapid movements and proximity to visitors; pollution including sewage and oil from pleasure boats, erosion of river banks, fire and vandalism.

An analytical method which seeks to take account of both the requirements of visitors on a site and the constraints and characteristics of a site is the recreation opportunities spectrum (ROS). Adopted in the USA, it acknowledges that visitors enjoy recreation experiences in different settings which reflect a combination of physical, biological, social and managerial conditions. The opportunity spectrum ranges from primitive areas to substantially urbanized environments (Hammitt and Cole, 1987, p. 200). As an approach to matching demand with resources the concept can help identify diversity of opportunities, allowing separate strands of demand to be managed according to distinct objectives. Although acknowledging the value of ROS as a concept, critics have considered that it has a number of limitations (Jubenville *et al.*, 1987, pp. 24–25). In particular, it tends to play down the importance of the biophysical features of a site, particularly natural attractions, in acting as a draw to visitors.

Zoning

Another concept that has been very widely used by designers and managers as a way of resolving conflict is that of zoning recreational sites for particular types of activity. The origins of this approach, like many in the field of rural recreation, are probably to be found in management plans produced for wildlife conservation areas. In the latter, 'compartments' are identified where particular management techniques are to be used, supported by schedules specifying in some detail where, when and in what form practical measures will be undertaken. The zoning approach has been used extensively as part of the management of specific sites and wider areas of countryside (Sidaway, 1988, pp. 92–93).

At many reservoirs and lakes, zoning is used as a way of excluding users from wildlife habitats and of segregating water space users from each other. For example, Bewl Water in southeast England (Figure 6.2) is a pumped storage reservoir where zoning delimits areas for nature conservation, with little access to the banks of the reservoir. Other areas are set aside for angling, sailing and birdwatching, car parking and a 1 500 m rowing course extends across the southeastern end of the reservoir (Eachus Huckson Partnership, 1988, p. 19).

Such approaches to zoning commonly seek to ensure that access design minimizes disturbance to wildlife, recognizes tolerance distances, and acknowledges that damage can result from quite low levels of activity (Andrews, 1991, pp. 208–209). There is a suggestion that smaller zoning-control schemes on water spaces are less successful than larger ones since one interest tends to dominate at the expense of others. It is suggested, for example, that it is only on larger areas such as Rutland Water that enough space exists for different forms of recreation to take place alongside each other (Sidaway, 1988, p. 93).

Another concept that has been adopted is that of zoning by time. For example, close seasons exist for angling when fishing is restricted on

141

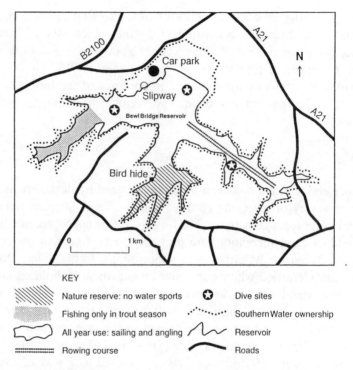

Figure 6.2   Bewl Water, Kent: zoning of recreation sites
Source: Eachus Huckson Partnership (1988), p. 19

water courses. In addition, attempts have been made to restrict movements of recreational craft on canals at certain times of the week, thus
allowing anglers undisturbed conditions for their pursuit (Owens, 1978,
pp. 139–141).

Zoning has thus been seen as a valuable way of solving problems
associated with incompatible recreational pursuits. However, a note of
caution on its use as a management technique has been offered: 'There
may be some debate on whether segregation is desirable as it enables
different interest groups to become possessive about their territory and
ignore the philosophies of multiple use' (Sidaway, 1988, p. 93). In
addition, of course, there can also be problems of enforcement of physical zoning of recreation activities on water, and regulations may be
ignored.

Channelling of visitor movement

This is another concept which has been widely adopted as a means to control visitor movements, particularly in deflecting pressure away from vulnerable wildlife areas or from areas where competition exists between different groups of visitors. In the New Forest in southern England, for example, it has proved to be an important means of excluding vehicles from vulnerable locations (New Forest Review Group, 1988, p. 38). The presence of an attractive, firm, well-maintained and dry track, rather than one which is rutted, poorly maintained and overgrown, can provide a focus for visitors' movements on site. A study of Tarn Howes in the English Lake District illustrates how the principles of channelling can be used to deflect pressure from vulnerable habitats (Brotherton et al., 1978). The investigation recorded problems caused by trampling on grassland and sought to assess acceptable levels of use for the site. The study findings suggested that visitor movements were greatly influenced by the extent to which people had a clear idea of what they wanted to do and the degree to which a 'goal' was visible. In addition, movement was found to be influenced by the weather, with wet weather discouraging the exploration of the more challenging terrain; and by the influence of the 'follow my leader' principle, with the uncommitted following those who already know of a route. The studies showed that the probability of a group's taking a particular route increased noticeably if people were visible ahead on that route. Closure of a car park, provision of alternative pathways, barriers and stiles resulted in the channelling of significant numbers of visitors away from more sensitive areas on the site.

An example of a comprehensive approach to the channelling of visitors is seen at Queen Elizabeth Country Park, Hampshire (Figure 6.3). The park comprises woodland and chalk downland measuring approximately 5 by 3 km, managed by the Forestry Commission and Hampshire County Council. The wooded area includes a network of tracks and paths which extend across the rolling countryside of the site. The country park attracts a wide range of users whose pursuits are channelled along particular routes. Routes have been designated for walking, educational groups, horse riding, motor vehicles, mountain bicycles, and disabled visitors, with areas zoned for other activities such as grass skiing, hang gliding and family orienteering. The site is traversed by a national trail, the South Downs Day. The concentration of such a wide range of activities into a relatively small area is a demonstration of how quite high

143

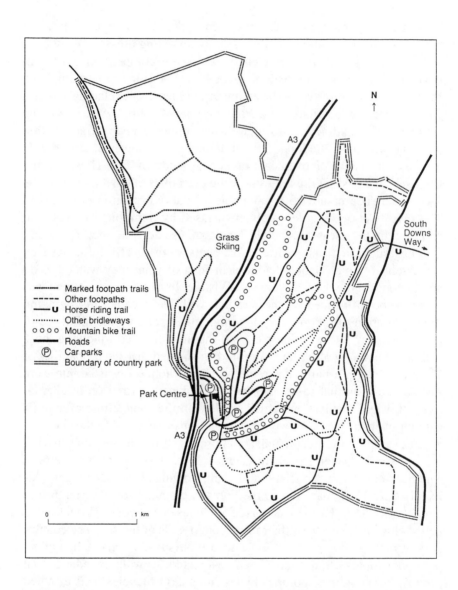

**Figure 6.3   Queen Elizabeth Country Park, Hampshire: channel-
ling of visitor movement**
Source: Hampshire County Council (undated pamphlet)

densities of recreational use can be accommodated within woodland areas by means of channelling techniques.

A further concept which has been used by designers is that of 'edge'. Designers have argued that potential uses within a site can be strongly influenced by the way in which the edges (boundaries) of the site are treated. The importance of edge in visitors' use of picnic or camp sites is seen in their being attracted to fringes that give a sense of enclosure: where there is a change in vegetation, for example, a break of slope, hedges, banks of streams or fringes of forests or woods (Beazley, 1969, p. 37). Empirical studies of picnic areas and rural car parks carried out by Heytze confirm the extent to which visitors are drawn to the perimeters of sites (Heytze, 1976, p. 10). 'Edge' can thus be used by designers as a device to alter the perimeter of a site and thus increase or decrease recreational opportunities. An example of the importance of edge for recreational sites is provided by the Wirral Way in Cheshire, a linear country park developed along the route of an abandoned railway line. The site is about 72 ha in extent, equivalent in area to a large urban park. As a compact, fairly regularly shaped site its edge or perimeter could be expected to measure some 3 or 4 km in length. Its configuration as a linear country park in fact increases the 'edge' length to around 38 km and extends catchments considerably (Cooper and Hull, 1978, p. 169).

Another form of boundary recognized as being an aid to design is water. It adds to the variety of sites, and designers have recognized its importance as an ingredient in attracting visitors. Besides being able to support a wide range of activities that require its presence, water is also able to provide a setting for other activities: it offers edge and acts as a lure to visitors and can provide a valuable focus for a site. 'Its very presence gives peace and sense of space far greater than that to which there is access. There is the endless fascination of watching the light shifting upon it' (Beazley, 1969, p. 37).

SITE DESIGN AND SPECIAL GROUP NEEDS

Consideration of the requirements of disabled groups has led to a number of trails and facilities which take their specific needs into account (Binks, 1973, 1987; Country Landowners Association, 1984; Royal National Institute for the Blind, 1986). Aside from the problems of actually getting from home to a recreational site, 'the topography, prevalence of

145

long-distance walks with no cut-back paths and the requirements for stock fencing and gates, all tend to *mitigate* against disabled people being able to make easy use of the countryside' (Rowson and Thoday, 1985, p. 47). A number of attempts have been made to adapt existing designs to the requirements of disabled people but many solutions are considered to be far from suitable for the majority of disabled people. In particular, detailed designs need to take into account such factors as access, condition of path surfaces, gradients of ramps, shelter, shading, aspect, handrails, seating and the provision of trails specifically for wheelchair users or the visually impaired.

A major review of disabled people's needs reminds us that at some stage of their lives much of the population is likely to find itself disabled, either physically or mentally or handicapped because of various impairments (Countryside Commission, 1981a, pp. 7–10). It records that the needs of disabled people vary greatly: ambulant disabled people, while not confined to a wheelchair, are nevertheless restricted because of their inability to walk over long distances or for prolonged lengths of time. For these users, stairs, kerbs or steep gradients present difficulties and firm surfaces are a requirement. Wheelchair users, however, can be extremely mobile, although those whose disability affects their arms may need to be pushed. Into a third category of users the review notes the needs of blind and partially sighted people. In designing for disabled people in the countryside, there is a need to create a 'barrier-free' environment so that 'a person in a wheelchair, a less active, elderly person or a blind person should be able to get to that site, travel through it, and leave it without meeting any unacceptable hazards or obstructions *en route.*'

Providers are therefore asked to adopt a 'disabled-friendly' approach to the layout of recreational sites from the early stages of drawing up the development brief to day-to-day management. Despite such exhortations, disabled groups argue for particular attention to be paid to the layouts of car parks, pedestrian access (seating at appropriate heights, ramped kerbs, shelters), paths (width, smooth, firm non-slip surfaces), boardwalks, handrails, gates and stiles, toilets, provision of information, signing and use of various interpretative media. The design of rural recreation for disabled people still does not meet the modest targets that might be expected. For example, the Fieldfare Trust has attempted to promote better designs of stiles and picnic tables for disabled people through a countryside access design competition (Fieldfare Trust, undated).

Rural recreational pursuits undertaken by disabled people are extremely varied (Croucher, 1981). Support for disabled people following recreational pursuits is highly dependent on help from private clubs or societies. However, public and private providers are increasingly becoming aware of their needs, and facilities increasingly attempt to meet the requirements of disabled people.

FINANCING OF RURAL RECREATION

In recent years there has been increasing interest in measuring the costs of providing rural recreation facilities. An important reason for this has been the realization that the considerable funding that was available to develop and support public recreation in the 1970s has now passed. This is primarily as a result of budgetary constraints imposed on the activities of local authorities. As a consequence, providers of rural recreation are expected increasingly to obtain a measure of 'return' on sites.

The element of the providers' gross costs covered by participants will vary greatly (Dartington Amenity Research Trust, 1982, p. 5). Thus informal recreation, particularly if it is the only or dominant use, tends to be heavily subsidized; sailing and angling activities which are often incidental to other activities such as water gathering are shown to bring in an income of between a quarter and a half of costs; golf is able to cover three quarters of costs and campsite costs are generally covered by income. Activities which demand more from the user in equipment or travel costs are generally those which are also able to cover a higher proportion of the costs of providing facilities.

Debate today focuses on whether it is better for revenue and development costs of recreational schemes to be paid for through general taxation policies or by the user. Increasingly, providers are being encouraged to charge the visitor for the use of facilities. However, there can be clear difficulties in raising income at rural recreation sites. Many sites are unfenced and it could be too expensive to restrict those who do not pay. In addition, charging could result in visitors' going to other possibly free or cheaper sites and increasing pressures there. The advantages of charging visitors for use of recreation sites have been recorded as follows (Bovaird *et al.*, 1984, pp. 2–3).

147

- Charging can provide managers with information on visitor preferences and point to factors which can influence demand.
- Charging can provide a valuable source of income and can assist in site development and protection from budget cuts.
- Charging can be used to limit demand to the available supply, with different levels of charges being set to ensure balance between supply and demand, reduce overcrowding and limit damage to sites.

The value of charging as a way of controlling site use has also been associated with attempts to make the user pay the full costs of a visit to the countryside on the 'polluter pays' principle. Several possibilities for charging visitors have been suggested (Broom, 1991, pp. 16–20).

- Charging for admission: this may be done directly, such as by charging an admission fee.
- Indirect charging for particular facilities such as car parks: income can be obtained in this way from visitors who are using the countryside for walking, climbing and fishing as well as visiting specific sites.
- Selling goods or services can augment incomes, possibly under licence, with retailing activities producing income for expenditure on wider management of sites.
- Voluntary donations from users or potential visitors can be of value: for example, at sites where there is free access but heavy demands on management. In addition, membership subscriptions can provide financial support for site management.
- Use of levies on complementary products, with setting aside of a portion of the purchase price of a good such as a publication which goes towards specific management tasks.
- Tourism taxes can be levied to raise money from visitors using areas subject to heavy management costs. In addition, tolls may be imposed for using roads offering access to countryside subject to visitor pressures.

Approaches such as these have been central to the activities of private and voluntary sector providers for a long time. Public providers now find themselves in a similar position and, in a way, can be seen to be competing for different strands of the rural recreation market. Charging

Plate 6.2   Charging for entry has long been accepted at commercial recreation developments as at the Landmark Centre, Carrbridge, Strathspey, 1991

visitors for the use of sites which have been funded by the population at large raises questions about the social objectives and functions of recreational site policy-making. Attention is increasingly being paid to measuring the costs and benefits associated with recreation provision but many of these are impossible to quantify. Various measures can be used in financial appraisals of sites, including resource cost per admission which allows comparisons between facilities (Coopers and Lybrand, 1979, p. 44): but such an approach inevitably represents an oversimplification of the issues involved.

INTERPRETATION

The role of interpretation in recreational management has been stressed on many occasions. Interpretation has been seen as a major tool in the hands of the recreational land manager (Miles and Seabrooke, 1977, p. 133). Also, 'the siting of interpretive facilities can be a valuable management tool in helping to reconcile public use with the maintenance of a natural resource' (Green, 1985, p. 189). Although such assertions as these might meet with widespread agreement, it is not surprising to find that interpretation has been perceived as performing other functions as well as being a management tool. It is clear that far from being a theme about which there are quite clear goals and readily identifiable outputs it is one where there is considerable debate about what is being interpreted, for whom, and by what means it is being done. Is it being undertaken for reasons of education, persuasion or enjoyment? (Lee, 1991, p. 17).

There seems general agreement that Freeman Tilden successfully contributed the first major work on interpretation, *Interpreting Our Heritage*. In this study, he defined interpretation as 'an educational activity which aims to explain meanings and relationships through the use of original objects, by first-hand experience and by illustrative media rather than simply to communicate factual information' (Tilden, 1967, p. 8).

Transferred to Britain from its American origins, interpretation has taken on a number of distinct characteristics. Firstly, it has been concerned with changing attitudes and opinions of visitors to the countryside. It has primarily focused on increasing visitor enjoyment in the belief that understanding of the countryside can increase pleasure obtained whilst visiting it. It has sought to increase public understanding and appreciation of the countryside, creating greater respect for it and awareness of the need for its conservation or development. Interpretation can thus play an important role in the management of a specific resource or area by influencing visitor movement (Countryside Commission, 1979a, p. 6). The value of interpretation and conservation of natural resources as a possible way of generating employment and business opportunities has been explored in Scotland's Highland Region (ASH Partnership *et al.*, 1991).

The process of preparing an interpretation programme can be marked by a series of investigations, studies and analyses which culminate in the production of an interpretive plan (Aldridge, 1975, p. 11). In preparing such a plan, consideration could be given to several factors, including:

- establishing the objectives of the plan;
- identifying the theme or resource which is to be interpreted (historic site, wildlife conservation area);
- whom the interpretive plan is designed for (age, special needs of visitors);
- how the interpretation programme is to be conveyed to the visitor (choice of media, designed for use by groups or individuals);

- implementation and management (costing, publicity/promotion, site maintenance);
- monitoring and review (achievement of objectives, visitor response, modification to programme).

There has been debate about the extent to which interpreters have succeeded in conveying ideas to visitors and users of environmental programmes. In particular there is a feeling that interpreters have failed to adapt interpretive methods to the needs of their audiences. Jenkinson considers that if providers wish to increase visitors' appreciation of the natural world then they need to popularize the theme in a way which people can relate to their everyday surroundings (Jenkinson, 1990, p. 10).

Plate 6.3   Explaining meanings and relationships through interpretation can increase the pleasure of visiting the countryside. Visitor eye's view of Stonehenge, Wiltshire, 1991

He feels that much interpretive effort fails to provide real experiences that people will cherish; interpretation tends to be directed largely at the converted and is not aimed at widening popular support. Reservations about the achievement of interpretive initiatives were recorded in a study of the effectiveness of visitor centres (Dartington Amenity Research Trust *et al.*, 1978, p. 65). It was found that although such centres succeeded in imparting short-term knowledge, there remained doubts about their ability to build up long-term additions to comprehension or understanding. Among the reasons for this was a feeling that centres failed to stimulate and create enjoyment among visitors. It was found that interpretation needed to relate to visitors' existing knowledge and interests. Much depended on the detailed layout, design and general atmosphere of centres.

A second issue that has been the subject of debate concerns the actual form and content of the message that has been presented in interpretive programmes. Countryside interpretation is often linked to the championship of heritage, concern with the past and with policies for tourism. Yet quite remarkable changes in settings of historic monuments and landscapes have themselves occurred as part of programmes to cherish and interpret the past (Lowenthal, 1985, pp. 275–282). Concern for the past requires careful handling: '...the past is no longer a finite entity, but a resource, sometimes the last resource. As such it is shaped and moulded to the needs of the present, and in the process filtered, polished and drained of meaning' (Hewison, 1987, p. 99). This is an issue which raises important questions about attitudes to change in Britain today, to the ways in which history is interpreted and protection is offered to natural and built environments.

The issue also arises in the relationship between interpretation programmes and recreational management policies. The tension that can sometimes exist between the two featured in an investigation into interpretive needs in the New Forest (Quinion and Glen, 1989, pp. 18–19). At stake here was the extent to which interpretive measures should be introduced to assist visitors to the Forest. Consultants stressed the need to make visitors feel welcome, in the belief that they would respond positively to the special nature of the Forest. However, the semi-natural state of the resource itself and the caution of the Forest management agencies meant that the implementation of an interpretive scheme would be difficult. There was for example a reluctance to construct permanent buildings on Crown Lands. The erection of wayside panels was opposed by some Commoners since it was felt that they would urbanize the landscape.

The problems of devising interpretation policies for recreation areas subject to high visitor pressures usefully remind us of the strong links that exist between site or area management and interpretation. Managers may wish to welcome visitors, but in order to maintain the present form of their resource they may be reluctant to encourage increased numbers. Managers can be torn between a 'do nothing' approach on the one hand and a perceived risk of 'overkill' on the other. Interpretive programmes may possibly be too successful. The programme itself could be more of an experience than the real thing: hence 'after interpretation, the reality is disappointing' (Green, 1985, p. 190).

COMMENT

Management policies for wider areas of countryside as well as discrete sites have sought to minimize the impact of recreation on the environment. This underlying theme has been reflected both in the objectives of management plans themselves and in prescriptions for action. In the early period of the development of recreation management, plans attempted to cater for a broadly defined range of users whose interests had either been clearly articulated and understood (for example, catering for anglers at reservoir sites) or, alternatively, could be catered for by relatively easily provided car parks and picnic areas or nature trails.

Today, the range of pursuits pursued in the countryside is on a much greater scale than, say, 20 years ago. The impact of this has been twofold. Firstly, changed demands for rural recreation mean that provision has now to be made for a wider range of active, rather than passive, pursuits. Secondly, the growth in pursuits where movement itself is an important part of the enjoyment gained from that activity has led to more attention being given to area-wide management and to creating routes which can be used by the walker, cyclist or rider. The effect of this has been to draw the attention of practitioners to the very varied needs of different classes of users, particularly the mobility-impaired.

A related issue concerns the extent to which management techniques are able to accommodate activities which are increasingly in conflict with each other. It raises questions about the actual design of sites managed for rural recreation as well as the limits to compatibility be-

153

tween activities. Providing physical barriers to segregate conflicting users may itself result in a highly managed site which might seem inappropriate in a rural location. For example, the introduction of formal path surfaces needed to handle large volumes of walkers may clash with beliefs that a path should have a rugged, rural character. Opposition to rural recreation projects is often effective notably in the case of proposals for noisy motorized sports, but other projects have also foundered for this reason.

In reviewing progress in rural recreation management over the last 20 or so years, two other factors enter into any evaluation. Firstly, since much provision has been grant-led by the Countryside Commissions, the funding bodies have been able to determine the form of sites and facilities to a considerable degree. Although much has evolved as a result of local innovation and experiment, the influence of the central agencies has been considerable. This has been particularly so in the case of promoting a strong conservation ethos behind countryside recreation management throughout the 1960s, 1970s and 1980s. Later years were marked by the adoption of policies with much stronger emphasis on access and social objectives in the late 1980s and 1990s.

Finally, the changed political and administrative climate from the early 1980s has resulted in a much increased awareness of the need to introduce a greater efficiency within recreation management services. The effects of this are likely to result in a rather more rigorous approach to management plan-making, with greater emphasis on review of performance. Reliance will be placed to an increasing extent on numbers of visitors as evidence of the 'return' on expenditure by public authorities on countryside recreation. This factor may be instrumental in changing the dominant conservation 'culture' which has characterized rural recreation management in Britain for a long time. The financial viability of a countryside recreation facility may well depend on achieving major entertainment 'draws' such as 'Legoland' exhibitions rather than on activities more closely related to the rural resources themselves.

Chapter 7

The access issue

A theme central to the development of countryside recreation policies has been that of access. Attention has focused in particular on the balance between rights assigned to property and the rights of people in the wider community. Holt reminds us that being able to walk on land which belongs to someone else as a matter of right cannot be separated from cultural, economic and political factors which are at the heart of the way that society works (Holt, 1989, p. 41).

In tracing the evolution of access as a policy issue, it is noticeable how it has been closely related to social, economic and institutional change in the countryside. The parliamentary enclosures of the eighteenth and nineteenth centuries resulted in people being deprived of access to previously uncultivated land. From 1865, the Commons, Open Spaces and Footpaths Preservation Society led movements against enclosures and the loss of London commons (Eversley, 1910, p. vi). Concern was expressed, too, at the ways in which private bills enabled landowners such as railway companies or corporation water authorities to encroach on common land. Threats also occurred in respect of public footpaths. These owed their origins largely to long, continued use by the public, normally without any formal act of dedication by the landowner. However, increasing use of footpaths led landowners to close rights of way to which the public previously had access. An account of an early footpath battle describes the attempts of a landowner in the 1820s to close a footpath at Flixton near Manchester (Lee, 1976, p. 8).

In time, measures were introduced to safeguard footpaths. For example, some protection was afforded by clauses in the Local Government Act 1894, which declared it to be the duty of district councils as highway authorities to maintain public rights of way.

THE CAMPAIGN FOR ACCESS TO THE MOUNTAINS

Stephenson records how the movement to gain access to the countryside gained momentum in the late nineteenth century. A series of parliamentary bills were introduced from 1884 onwards with the purpose of allowing the public to have access to uncultivated mountain or moor lands. Bryce introduced his Access to Mountains (Scotland) Bill in 1884 but like successor attempts, including a similar bill for Wales in 1888, this failed. Stephenson notes that between 1909 and 1939 no less than nine access bills were presented to Parliament (Stephenson, 1989, p. 142). The issues which emerged in debate at different stages in the progress of the various bills essentially revolved around the unwillingness of landowners to permit public access to land used largely for sport, particularly deer forests and grouse moors. In opposition to this view were those who recognized an increasing desire by urban populations to enjoy the countryside. In the Peak District, lack of public access was most serious on the upland grouse moors where in an area of 230 square miles there were only 2 footpaths of over 2 miles in length. The heather-clad moorlands were preserved for grouse, and unrestricted public access would affect breeding birds and killing them expeditiously (Sheail, 1981, p. 194).

Considerable internal debate took place within the open space societies themselves on the most appropriate course of action. Perhaps the action which led to greatest controversy within the outdoor movement was the 1932 Kinder Scout Mass Trespass. The trespass was organized by the British Workers Sports Federation, whose members came largely from the working class and who shared a different culture from members of the established rambling clubs. The latter tended to be middle-class professional people or specialist ramblers such as ornithologists, botanists and geologists (Rothman, 1982, p. 21). According to Stephenson, the Kinder trespass involved '...a brief scrap between some gamekeepers and ramblers and the imprisonment of five young demonstrators, was the most dramatic incident in the access to mountains campaign. Yet it contributed little, if anything, to it.' (Stephenson, 1989, p. 153). Although the importance of the trespass has been disputed, it can be seen as one of a number of initiatives which gave publicity to the access issue in the 1930s.

Eventually, an Access to the Mountains Act reached the statute book in 1939. However, for the English ramblers' groups, the Act contained only a watered-down reference to its principal objective of achieving

**Plate 7.1   The Kinder Trespass of 1932, as re-enacted in 1982.
Pressure continues for extending access to open
country in England and Wales**

access to open country. The costs of implementation of the Act would to
a large extent fall on ramblers themselves. Cherry records that '...the
Bill was in sharp contrast to the cardinal principle that people had a right
to wander freely over mountain and moorland. Moreover, the Bill itself
gave no access anywhere, merely machinery for obtaining.' In practice,
the legislation proved to be abortive, suffering the fate of an unsuccess-
ful compromise measure (Cherry, 1975, pp. 25–26).

The Second World War then intervened but the 1945 Dower report on
national parks in England and Wales stressed the need for access to
uncultivated mountain and moorland (Ministry of Town and Country
Planning, 1945, p. 35). The report of the Special Committee on Footpaths and Access to the Countryside in 1947 proposed machinery for
designating access land on uncultivated areas whether moorland,
downland, heath, mountain or cliff beach and shore (Ministry of Town
and Country Planning, 1947a, p. 31).

157

A major provision of the ensuing National Parks and Access to the Countryside Act 1949 was section 64 which dealt with access to open country. Under this provision, local planning and national park authorities could enter into access agreements or make orders allowing public access to mountain, moorland, heath, down, cliff or foreshore. Later, under section 59 of the Countryside Act 1968, woodland, rivers and riverbanks were included in the category of 'open country'. Agreements for access to open country involve payment of compensation to landowners for disturbance caused by allowing the public to use their land. In addition, the planning authority or local authority can manage the land for recreation, and conditions may mean, for example, closing the land to the public on days when shooting takes place.

The greatest use of agreements has been in the Peak District National Park. Between 1953 and 1979, the Board made 19 access agreements on an area of 76 square miles which included areas which featured prominently in the demonstrations of the 1930s (Peak Park Joint Planning Board, 1989, p. 87). However, even in the Peak District and to an extent in other national parks there is a prospect of less use being made of access agreements (R. Smith, 1990, p. 141). A problem now recorded is that pressure from greater visitor numbers is resulting in difficulties in renegotiating traditional forms of access agreement with landowners.

Elsewhere, the reluctance of local authorities to make access agreements suggests that in the early years at least they were vulnerable to local pressure, often dominated by the landowning class and unwilling to take on the task of providing for the recreation needs of urban residents living outside their areas (Shoard, 1987, p. 380). Despite these problems local authorities in Britain have succeeded in widening access using a variety of mechanisms (Wager, 1976; Bromley, 1990, pp. 297–302). Some local authorities have made widespread use of managing land under licence from landowners or have acquired leases on land. Of value are powers granted under section 39 of the Wildlife and Countryside Act 1981 (Bromley, 1990, p. 299). Under these, management agreements are made with landowners for recreation provision and enhancement of landscape features or natural history resources.

ACCESS AND ACCESSIBILITY: THE ACTORS

In a major study into access in the countryside for sport and recreation, a distinction has been drawn between 'access', which defines legal rights to the countryside, and 'accessibility', the processes of establishing and using rights and privileges of access (Centre for Leisure Research, 1986b, p. 6). Different groups of 'actors' can influence accessibility within the countryside including 'resource controllers', who frequently oppose demands for increased access. The controllers' opposition to increased access is based on a defence of private property rights and traditional access arrangements. However, other 'controllers' besides landowners might also oppose increased access. They include recreationists such as anglers, or shooting interests as well as conservationists. Such users might be keen to restrict access and safeguard the resources and facilities that they enjoy. Thus it is not unusual to find that resource controllers may join with others to form coalitions of interest to oppose others intent on widening access to the countryside.

In explaining the stances adopted by different actors, the study notes the differing values of the interest groups. These are identified as having their origins in either a 'non-market' or a 'market' perspective; with

Table 7.1   Access mechanisms and ideology

Access mechanisms	Ideology
De facto access	*Non-market*
Rights of way	Freedom to roam
Rights of navigation	Public rights over private land and water
Rights of open access	
Access agreements	*Market*
Management agreements	Public intervention in the market
Public ownership	Private rights of property
Property rights	
Sporting rights	
Permissive access	

Source: Centre for Leisure Research (1986b), p. 13

concern for 'aesthetic' considerations or with approaches which favour 'co-operative', 'instrumental' or 'participatory' stances (Table 7.1). Many different actors can therefore be involved in pursuing access policies. They include public, private and voluntary bodies who aquire buy or sell rights associated with land: property rights, shooting and fishing rights or rights of way, with a proliferation of organizations dealing with different forms of access (Thomson and Whitby, 1976, pp. 316–318). Such a state is seen as giving rise to diversity and the economic use of rural resources. However, it must be said, too, that it can lead to duplication of effort and the loss of potential complementary benefits.

WILDERNESS

When compared with the history of the access movement in England and Wales, quite different approaches to the issue have emerged elsewhere in Britain. In Scotland the same general range of actors is present but attempts to formalize arrangements for access to wilder areas of countryside have resulted in major divisions between different recreation and amenity interests. The issues were fully explored in the 1986 findings of a working group which reviewed the development of long-distance walking routes in Scotland (Countryside Commission for Scotland, 1986). One school of thought was concerned by attempts to formalize access arrangements by the creation of long-distance routes, and greatly valued the longstanding tradition of cross-country walking in Scotland. In upland areas this has meant that people can make their own way through the countryside unhindered and without the need to follow established tracks. Thus, although there might be a law of trespass in Scotland, 'access to wilder countryside is based upon a well-established mutual respect between the walker and landowner' (R. Smith, 1990, p. 152). Managed long-distance routes can thus be regarded as alien to the Scottish countryside. Their promotion runs the risk of walking opportunities being more restricted than at present and evidence for this fear is reflected in the appearance of signs indicating that 'walkers "should keep to the path", a directive which is anathema to the Scottish Hill gangrel' (R. Smith, 1990, p. 153).

In contrast, others in Scotland favour attempts to create formal access routes such as long-distance paths. They argue that routes can attract a wide range of walkers with different levels of experience. Long-distance

160

Plate 7.2   Scottish wildland, near Altnaharra, Highland Region, 1991

routes offer great opportunities for visitors to enjoy the countryside, as is demonstrated in the high levels of use of the West Highland Way.

That formal access arrangements might have the effect of restricting wider informal access was considered by the Long Distance Route Working Party. It recognized the need to protect free access to the countryside but saw that the provision of formal access facilities could help to reduce conflict between farming, forestry and sporting interests (Countryside Commission for Scotland, 1986, p. 15).

The wilderness debate was fully explored at a planning inquiry into a proposal to construct a bridge across a river in remote countryside at the Fords of Avon in Badenoch District in the Highlands of Scotland (Scottish Office Inquiry Reporters, 1988). Opposing the proposal was a coalition of interests including the Scottish Wild Land Group and the Mountaineering Council for Scotland. Supporting the proposal were various

161

organizations including the Ramblers Association (Scotland) and the Scottish Youth Hostels Association. The result of the inquiry was a ruling against the proposal, for reasons which included the intrusive effect of the proposal in a remote area of wild landscape.

Legal systems, physical terrains and countryside traditions differ from those found in England and Wales and they may account in part for the particular form of the access debate in Scotland. In England and Wales, lacking the same convention of free access to the countryside, the debate about 'wilderness' has been much more muted; indeed the term 'wilderness' is rarely used in connection with the English or Welsh countryside. Rather more, protection of formal, statutory rights of way including long-distance routes has been a central concern of Anglo-Welsh access lobbies. However, the Fords of Avon case and other debates about access raise fundamental questions about the extent to which the countryside should be opened up for recreation. Many people share anxiety about over-organization of the countryside and are reluctant to see yet more measures such as signing, route designations and zealous promotion (Lovett-Jones, 1988, p. 20).

PUBLIC RIGHTS OF WAY

Perhaps the greatest countryside recreation asset to be found in England and Wales is the public rights of way network (Table 7.2). The National Parks and Access to the Countryside Act 1949 required local authorities to prepare definitive maps which indicated rights of way on which the public had the right of access. The Act specified rights of way which were to be regarded as highways in exactly the same way as main roads or local roads. The provisions of the Act still stand and the main types of right of way specified in the legislation are:

- footpaths: highways on which the public can travel on foot only;
- bridleways which walkers, riders and, since 1968, cyclists have a right to use;
- roads used as public paths, which are highways other than public paths used mainly for the same purposes as footpaths and bridleways. This category is subject to review under part III of the Wildlife and Countryside Act 1981 and reclassification as footpaths, bridleways or 'byways open to all traffic'.

162

Table 7.2   England and Wales: estimated composition of the network of public rights of way, 1988

	Length (km)	Percentage
Footpaths	169 600	76
Bridleways	44 800	20
RUPPs/byways	9 600	4
Total	224 000	100

Source: Countryside Commission (1990b), p. 6

There are great differences in the characteristics, distribution and extent to which the 224 000 km rights of way system can actually be used by the public. The 1988 Countryside Commission survey found that although paths should be accessible, in practice many paths proved difficult, and in some cases impossible, to use. The reasons for these difficulties included ploughed surfaces, crops (particularly in arable regions), electric or other fences or barriers and impenetrable natural vegetation. Some 15 per cent of footpath 'links' or sections were found to be 'unusable' and a further 20 per cent were 'poor'. It was calculated that, on a 3 km walk, the chance of encountering an unusable section of footpath was 7 in 10 (Countryside Commission, 1990b, p. 16).

The findings of the survey reinforce the view that although rights of way form part of the highway network in England and Wales they are often poorly maintained. In addition, they can be difficult to use; inaccuracies exist in their recording; and only a third of paths are signposted from where they leave a metalled road. A 1985 study revealed the scale to which paths were disrupted by ploughing having taken place but with no attempt being made to restore paths (Joint Centre for Countryside and Land Development Studies, 1985, p. 78). The study found less evidence of ploughing of rights of way on arable land close to urban areas but disturbance was greatest in parishes located in more remote countryside. Local highway authorities often lacked resources to take remedial action. In addition, bias was revealed in the responses of local authorities and benches of justices to rights of way issues. Both tended to take greater account of the views of local interests rather than those from

163

outside, who were likely to be the people pressing for the use of the rights of way network.

Of some concern is the great variation in numbers of rights of way in different localities in England and Wales. An explanation is to be found under the provisions of the National Parks Act 1949, in which local authorities were required to prepare definitive maps indicating public rights of way. County councils in England and Wales sought suggestions from parish councils for paths that should be indicated on the definitive map. Shoard records that what many county councils did was send a blank map to parish councils asking them to mark on it the paths which they understood to be public rights of way (Shoard, 1987, p. 329). The principal influences on draft maps proved not to be recreationists but parish councils or parish meetings. These tended to be under-resourced, confused at times and claimed rights of way 'on the basis of intuition rather than any real criteria' (Shoard, 1987, p. 331). The influence of local landowners was often significant and, not surprisingly, parish councils dominated by such figures did not go out of their way to propose paths whose status was in doubt! The rights of way identified on definitive maps thus underestimate the true inherited legacy of public paths.

Long-distance paths

Interest in the concept of long-distance paths had existed in Britain prior to the Second World War. Tom Stephenson's efforts to create the Pennine Way were prompted by a letter that he had received from two Americans who queried whether there was a similar facility in Britain to the Appalachian Trail (Stephenson, 1989, p. 70). The long-distance path concept was taken up by the Special Committee on Footpaths and Access in the Countryside (Ministry of Town and Country Planning, 1947a, p. 26). Proposals were made for several long-distance paths including the Pennine Way and routes from Beachy Head in East Sussex to Winchester and along the River Thames.

An early task of the National Parks Commission was to approve the routes of the Pennine Way in 1951, the Cornish Coastal Path (1952 and 1954) and the Pembrokeshire Coast Path in 1953. In creating such paths, use was made of existing rights of way but new sections of right of way also had to be created, sometimes in the face of considerable opposition on the part of landowners. Manchester Corporation, for example,

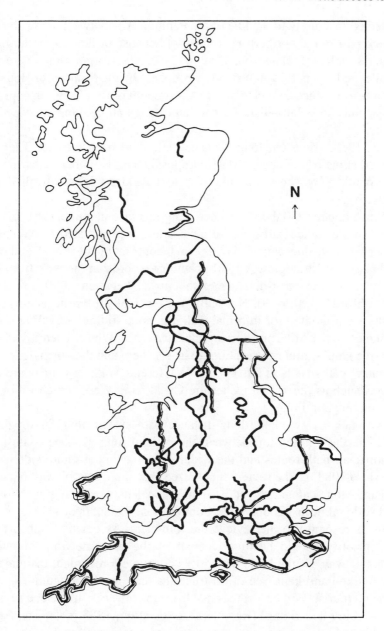

Figure 7.1 Great Britain: national trails and other recreational paths
Source: British Tourist Authority (undated), Walking in Britain

objected resolutely to the line of the Pennine Way between Crowden and Black Hill in the northern Peak District because of fears of pollution to water supplies (Stephenson, 1989, p. 110). The Corporation's case was challenged at a public inquiry but was upheld by the Minister of Housing. As a consequence of such disputes, the amount of time between approval of a route for a long-distance path and its actual opening exceeded 20 years.

By 1986, some ten long-distance paths had been created. They included some of the original 1947 proposals but also other paths such as the Wolds Way, the Cleveland Way and Peddar's Way/Norfolk Coast path (Figure 7.1).

Since about 1980 there has been a big increase in numbers of 'unofficial' long-distance paths. These have often been initiated by voluntary groups but in due course have been incorporated into local authority rights of way strategies. A 1990 inventory records an increase from 130 to over 300 in long-distance path entries between 1980 and 1990 (Blatchford, 1990, p. 9). Normally in excess of 30 km in length, such paths are promoted for informal walking, horse-riding or cycling (Long Distance Paths Advisory Service, undated). Many have been given distinctive names, route descriptions exist for them and they include 'cross-country' paths such as the 117 km Wayfarer's Walk in Hampshire and routes such as the 157 km Cheshire Canal Ring Walk, which follows a communication link.

A major review of the long-distance path system in 1988 sought to redefine the relationship between the official long-distance routes, the 'unofficial' path routes and the wider path network (Countryside Commission, 1988c). The review recognized that the rights of way network fell into four categories: parish paths, local networks, regional routes and national trails (Countryside Commission, 1988c, pp. 8–11).

In its response to the review, the Ramblers' Association felt that the first priority should be improvement of the basic network of public rights of way. 'If the basic network is adequately recorded, maintained, waymarked and kept free of obstructions then local communities, visitors and tourists will have a reasonable means of access to the countryside for walking and riding' (Ramblers' Association, 1988 p. 1). The Association had reservations about the proposed categorization of paths, fearing, amongst other things, that local authorities could well use it as a reason to promote some routes and neglect their statutory duty to maintain the basic network.

The Commission's responses to these and the views of other consultees appeared in a policy statement (Countryside Commission, 1989e). The statement proposed extensions to the national trail network, including the incorporation of established local authority and voluntary sector routes such as the Dales Way in northern England. In other cases, the proposals were a response to a perceived recreational need, notably in the case of the Pennine Bridleway. Creation of the latter was seen to go some way to meeting the shortage of national trails for horse-riders and cyclists. The policy statement also demonstrated how the national trails would relate to lower-tier paths categorized as regional routes, local and community paths. Most significantly, it indicated the Commission's intention to see all public rights of way in England and Wales legally defined, properly maintained and well-publicized by the year 2000 (Countryside Commission, 1989e, p. 5). Concern to achieve that target was reflected in Government making £3.75 million available over a three-year period as part of the 'parish paths partnership'. This initiative linked highway authorities, local councils (parish, town councils and parish meetings) and voluntary groups, and sought to improve the condition of rights of way through local initiatives at parish level (Countryside Commission, 1992b). However, some concern has been expressed with the danger of concentrating on footpath improvement rather than bridleways and byways, 'roads used as public paths' and other paths. The latter paths, suggested one commentator, 'in proportion to their mileage and attractiveness to the widest range of users, presently suffer the worst problems and will take the greatest resolve and investment to cure' (Anon, 1991, p. 33).

An important effect of the launch of the *Paths, routes and trails* initiative was to raise interest in the development of recreational trail networks. For example, walkers and cyclists proposed an east–west Trans-Pennine Trail from York to Southport. Public interest in the proposal was heightened by a mass walk and cycle ride in 1989 on a possible route. In due course, local authority interest was aroused and a consultants' feasibility study was undertaken (L & R plc *et al.*, 1990). Running in sections through urbanized areas, the proposed trail does not conform neatly to the criteria used for defining national trails but it must surely be seen as a possible candidate for that status.

Improving the rights of way procedures

The administration of the rights of way system has been described as '…byzantine in its complexity…' and an '…administrative and legal jungle' (MacEwen and MacEwen, 1987, p. 90). Dissatisfaction with the way in which the system is administered falls generally into two main headings.

Firstly, footpath and amenity groups feel that as well as pressing for the protection of the rights of way network, there is a vital need to create new rights of way. The measures available for doing this are relatively rarely used by highway authorities. One reason for a reluctance to undertake public path creation orders could be the large amount of time that is consumed in actually devising and implementing such an order (Figure 7.2). In one study of the process of making an order in the Frome Valley

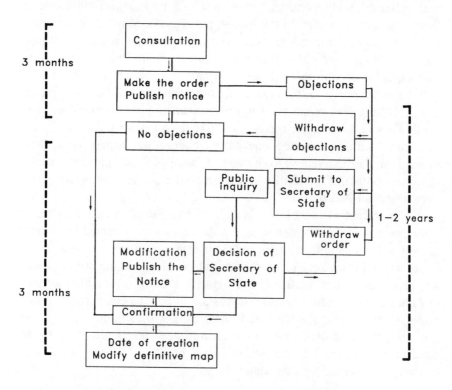

Figure 7.2 Stages in the creation of a right of way
Source: based on Dyke *et al.* (1986), p. 40

168

in Somerset a full three and a half years elapsed between the outline proposals being made and the opening of paths on the ground (Dyke *et al.*, 1986, p. 42). Footpath and amenity groups themselves have viewed moves to modify rights of way as attempts to water down the protection offered to the existing network. There is a feeling that only when highway authorities and landowners begin to take their responsibilities seriously will there be room for compromise. In practice, this means that many walking and amenity groups will object to orders to extinguish or divert public rights of way.

Secondly, landowning interests recognize the value of the rights of way resource but are aware of the inadequacies of the present system. Besides problems of damage to fences, hedges and walls caused by visitors, paths can disrupt agricultural operations and the anachronistic nature of many paths mean that they may be little used (Royal Institution of Chartered Surveyors, 1989, p. 7). There is a need many feel for rationalizing the existing system, a view which is shared by many local highway authorities faced with the problems of prioritizing competing claims for financial support.

The Countryside Commission sought to grapple with the rights of way issue in a consultation document which set out a number of possible changes in the statutory provisions. To ensure the best use of investment, the network was in urgent need of fine tuning so as to meet the varied needs of recreational users and those of the landowner or farmer (Countryside Commission, 1988a, p. 2).

A number of possible ways of improving the administrative arrangements for the rights of way network were outlined, including suggestions for 'changes on demand' for small-scale diversions. Following consultation, a policy statement issued by the Commission proposed a number of measures. These included: setting up advisory groups to help local authorities develop rights of way policies; production and promotion of codes of practice; exploring how far statutory notices might be made easier to understand and how existing procedures might be speeded up (Countryside Commission, 1989g, pp. 22–23). In addition, the policy sketched out a number of other changes that might be explored, including ways of determining disputed cases.

Some measures to improve present mechanisms were made in 1990. The Rights of Way Act of that year is seen as an important move to counter disruptions to footpaths and bridleways, amending obligations contained in the Highways Act 1980 (Barker, 1991, p. 3; Countryside

169

Plate 7.3   Reinstatement of right of way disturbed by agricultural operations: Wye, Kent, 1988

Commission, 1990a). The 1990 Act stipulates that when a field is ploughed, the farmer must make good the surface to a minimum width; when crops are grown they must not grow on to the minimum width of a footpath, bridleway or other right of way. In the case of ploughing, the surface must be made good within 14 days of the first disturbance for the crop or within 24 hours of a second or subsequent disturbance. Penalties on the occupier for failure to comply include prosecution; or a highway

170

authority can carry out the works that it thinks are necessary and recover costs from the occupier.

Ultimately, much will depend on the ability and willingness of the highway authority to carry out its monitoring role in an effective manner. In some cases, rights of way strategies have been prepared and local authorities are making concerted efforts to use the powers available to them. In Kent, for example, strategic policies have been adopted by the county council in order to achieve a network of high-quality and varied recreation routes (Kent County Council, 1990, pp. 3–4).

SHARED USE OF ROUTEWAYS

Greater participation in walking, cycling, riding and motor-based pursuits has placed increased pressure upon footpaths, bridleways and other rural routeways including ancient 'green lanes'. The latter are normally unmetalled rural tracks once used for vehicular traffic and locally important to rural communities. For these different classes of rural path, debate has arisen in recent years over their shared use by different categories of visitor. The main issues can be summarized as follows.

- The condition of many paths reflects a cycle of neglect, degeneration and lack of use, leading to over-use of those routes that remain accessible (Cairns, 1985, p. 6). On highly promoted paths, such as national trails, surfaces have proved incapable of handling the volumes of visitors experienced (Porter, 1991).
- In the case of bridleways, where walking, cycling and riding are permitted, deterioration from use by horse-riding can make conditions difficult for other users (New Forest Review Group, 1988, p. 46; Grimshaw, 1988, p. 49). In the period 1976 to 1986, it has been estimated that the total area of track subject to wear and tear by horse-riding in the New Forest increased from around 162 ha to almost 260 ha (Tubbs, 1987, p. 1).
- Increase in levels of vehicular use by trail bikes and four-wheel-drive vehicles as well as agricultural vehicles can result in rapid deterioration in the surface of rural byways including green lanes (Yorkshire Dales National Park Committee, 1988, p. 1).

An indication of the problems of shared use is provided by the example of the Ridgeway, an ancient routeway which runs for 135 km across south-

171

ern England. Opened as a long-distance path in 1973, it has been the focus for prolonged conflict between walkers and motor vehicles, particularly on a 55km byway section on which motor vehicles are allowed.

A user study of 3 600 visitors in 1988/9 provides a picture of people's perceptions of pedestrian/vehicular conflict on the Ridgeway (Survey Research Associates Ltd, 1989). The findings indicated that, at 10 per cent, motorized users were a relatively small proportion of all visitors. Most visitors came because of the Ridgeway's scenic attributes. However, around half of cross-country vehicle users cited the reason for their visit as the opportunities that the Ridgeway offered for bringing their own vehicle on to an off-highway path. The survey highlighted the concern of visitors towards motor vehicles with over 20 per cent of respondents referring to motor cycles as the most disliked vehicle encountered on the Ridgeway. As part of the effort to control motorized traffic, the Commission sought traffic regulation orders on summer Sundays and Bank Holidays. It failed to achieve imposition of the traffic order, but instead instituted a 'code of voluntary restraint' which sought the same restrictions.

The problems of controlling motorized traffic on byways have also been experienced in Surrey. As a result of reclassifying roads used as public paths (RUPPs) as byways open to all traffic (BOATs), local residents in all parts of the county have pressed for traffic regulation orders (TROs) to be introduced, prohibiting use of such routes by motorized vehicles (Surrey County Council, 1992). Yet, it is argued, TROs do not provide an easy answer to the long-term management of byways:

- procedures on making TROs are time consuming in respect of consultations and the legal process involved;
- the cost per order, allowing for advertising and signing is estimated at £5,000–6,000, excluding staff costs;
- there are ongoing costs for maintenance of signs and barriers;
- proposals to make a TRO can highlight the fact that vehicular rights exist over a route and this can increase interest and use;
- police are reluctant to support the making of orders because resources are not available to enforce orders.

In addition, proposals for TROs can themselves generate considerable opposition, with over 500 objections being made to an order in the Mole Valley.

The County Council's solution to this situation was to adopt a policy of making TROs only where there was significant danger to users or where physical conditions were unsuitable for vehicular use. Again, achieving successful shared use of rural routes will depend on voluntary restraint by user groups.

Conclusions from shared-use studies of rural routeways remind us not surprisingly that perceptions of discomfort caused by other users generally depend on the numbers of other participants, particularly for noisy activities. However, evidence from the findings of a shared-use study of the Leeds and Liverpool Canal towing path for walkers, cyclists and anglers suggest that there may be a less direct relationship between level of conflict and volume of users (Banister *et al.*, 1992, pp. 154–157). In this investigation it was found that, up to a certain point, increases of numbers of cyclists caused dissatisfaction to walkers and anglers. How-

Plate 7.4   User conflict on canal towing path: Leeds and Liverpool Canal, Wigan, 1989

173

Plate 7.5   Canal towing paths have been the subject of a number of shared-use experiments involving different types of visitor: Leeds and Liverpool Canal, Gathurst, Wigan, 1988

ever, annoyance seemed to plateau out once numbers of cyclists increased to certain levels.

There are a number of practical solutions to solving damage caused to routeways. In the case of horse-riding, then physical segregation may be possible by means of divided bridleroutes. However, the cost of construction and maintenance liability can be considerable if divided routes are provided over long distances. In the absence of divided routes, then other solutions have to be found to reduce damage to surfaces. Regular and hard use of bridleways by horse-riders can cause surfaces to break up. In such circumstances, the solution may be to seal surfaces fully with tarmac, even though this may be far from an ideal solution for riders.

A further approach might be to encourage use of off-road travel on land owned by public and private estates. The Forestry Commission, for example, permits rallying on certain forest roads. In addition, the Commission has been keen to encourage cycling routes in its woodlands, a policy which generally attempts to segregate cyclists from other users (Forestry Commission, 1984).

One of the fullest explorations of access problems at a local level has been the Neath Access Experiment. This project was undertaken from 1985 onwards in an area extending northeastwards from the town of Neath in South Wales. The area comprises built-up areas, land used formerly for industry, lowland valley, moorland, afforested areas and coastal dunes.

The access issues in the Vale of Neath included familiar problems such as fragmentation of the rights of way network, incomplete processing of claims for public rights of way status, trespass, overgrown paths, erosion caused by off-road motor vehicles, and objections to further recreational use of water areas and towing paths by anglers and canal owners. Finally, a feeling of disenfranchisement was felt by those who perceived themselves to be remote from decision-making about access issues (Countryside Commission, 1987d, pp. 10–14).

A central feature of the Neath experiment was the important role of a full-time project officer and the creation of a local access committee. The latter was seen to be the principal mechanism to implement access policies. It comprised representatives from recreational bodies, local authorities, voluntary groups and landowners. Implementation of schemes depended greatly on volunteers and on government employment-creation schemes. The schemes included improving access to a byway leading to a scenic area, public footpath improvements, opening up of permissive paths, waymarking and signing. There appear to have been clear advantages in channelling activities through the local access committee, which has been able to create a more favourable climate within which access issues can be tackled and awareness raised. Nevertheless, there proved to be clear limits to what could be achieved in terms of access for users such as motorcyclists and canoeists.

TRAFFIC AND ACCESS TO THE COUNTRYSIDE

In handling the car in the countryside, two main but related themes emerge: firstly, the safety of vulnerable groups such as walkers, cyclists and riders; and secondly, the methods which might be adopted to minimize the physical and visual impact of the car on the countryside. In dealing with the safety issue first, in many parts of Britain there are only very limited public rights of way networks and visitors may have no option but to resort to using country lanes used by motor vehicles. Tarmac and paved highways are used for recreation in the countryside to a surprisingly high degree. A survey of walking and type of surface used by visitors found that most people walked where they knew that they are able to do so, on roads and waymarked paths. No less than a third of walkers used country lanes and roads used by cars, pavements on sides of roads and roads through villages (Countryside Commission, 1989h, p. 4).

The conflict between use of the rural road network for recreation and for motor vehicles was tragically illustrated in 1976 in Northamptonshire. In the 'Kettering Accident' 28 members of Kettering Rambling Club were walking along a country road near Rushton. A Ford Cortina which suddenly appeared over the brow of a hill swerved to avoid an oncoming vehicle and crashed into the ramblers, killing five of them (Ramblers' Association, 1978, p. 1).

Measures can be introduced to provide alternative routes to walking on road carriageways but risks also relate to two other groups of vulnerable users: horse-riders and cyclists. For the latter, locations such as

Plate 7.6   A third of all walks undertaken by visitors in the countryside involve the use of pavements and tarmac surfaced roads: Sutton, near Macclesfield, 1991

176

Plate 7.7 Footpath separated from carriageway alongside busy road in the Lake District. The path links separate components of the rights of way network: Outgate, near Hawkshead, 1991

roundabouts are known to be particularly hazardous (Watkins, 1984, p. 70). However, quiet country lanes may pose equal danger. Current increases in recreational cycling may result in many more cyclists being exposed to potential danger on rural highways.

It is clear that volumes of traffic using country roads are going to continue to increase. 1989 forecasts of vehicle numbers on British roads suggested that between 1988 and the year 2025 there would be increases of between 83 and 142 per cent (Department of Transport, 1989, p. 1). Traffic flow figures for selected roads in the Peak District National Park show a steady increase over an 11-year period (Figure 7.3).

The need to control motorized traffic in the countryside was stressed in the Dower Report of 1945 and, in a more muted way, in the Hobhouse Committee Report of 1947 (Ministry of Town and Country Planning, 1945, p. 25; 1947b, p. 37). However, few measures were introduced in practice until the *Routes for People* scheme was launched in the Peak District National Park (Peak Park Planning Board/Derbyshire County Council, 1972). The scheme was implemented between 1973 and 1975 and still operates. The policy identified a number of roads in a part of the National Park where access would be limited to particular types of

177

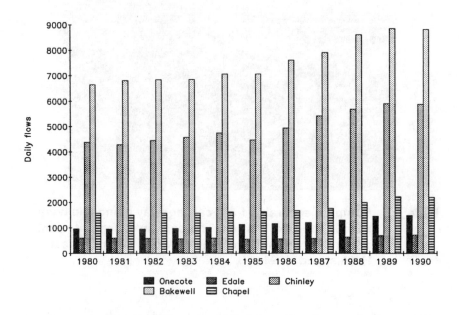

Figure 7.3   Peak District National Park: average daily traffic flows on selected roads, 1980–1990
Source: based on Peak Park Joint Planning Board (1991a), p. 28

vehicle. It involved constructing a new link road for heavy traffic; a major village bypass; weight restriction orders; visitor car parks; cycle paths; and waymarking of public paths. The scheme required major expenditure by the highway authority and is clearly unlikely to be re-peated on the same scale. However, the approach is used as a basis for traffic management elsewhere in the National Park (Peak Park Joint Planning Board, 1989, p. 110).

The various approaches available to handling rural traffic have been summarized under the three headings of formal traffic orders, informal traffic management and parking policy, as listed in Table 7.3 (North York Moors National Park Committee, 1982, p. 5). In 1977, Circular 118/77 drew on the recommendations of the Sandford Committee and explained how designation of road hierarchies could form the basis for

Table 7.3 Traffic management measures

Measure	Description
Formal measures	
Formal traffic orders	'Access' only for certain classes of vehicle Prohibitions based on weight Waiting restriction and clearway orders Speed restriction orders Use of chicanes, humps and other measures as deterrents to speed
Area traffic management	Comprehensive range of formal and informal measures to channel vehicular movement, within road hierarchy
Signing	Selective signing to channel vehicle movement, scenic routes
Informal measures	
Signing	'Persuasive' signing using advisory signs, e.g. 'gated road', provided signs are justified on highway criteria
Kerbing	Deterrent kerbing and verge treatment can deter use of highways
Road condition	Deliberate non-improvement of roads*
Road 'listing'	Constraints on developments which affect the amenity and historic value of country lanes
Parking controls	
Restrictions	Parking restrictions, verge treatment
Parking provision	Deliberate provision of new parking areas, either on or off the highway Closure of car parks

*Liability issue may arise in the case of vehicular damage caused by non-maintenance traffic management schemes in national parks with the use of advisory signing to discourage specific classes of vehicle from using certain roads (National Parks Policies Review Committee, 1974, p. 84; Department of the Environment/Department of Transport, 1977).

At the same time, the circular stresses the need for management measures to foster the free and safe flow of traffic. However, it also records that, after road safety, environmental quality is a major consideration in the design of road schemes. Outside the National Parks there is no similar guidance. The highway authority, it must be assumed, will be generally more tempted to place greatest emphasis on free flow and safety, rather than on environmental quality. Certain exceptions to this exist, including Essex County Council's procedures dating back to 1974 for 'listing' minor rural roads which have amenity or historical value (Essex County Council, 1991). The intention of this policy, which forms part of the approved structure plan for Essex, is to fit traffic volumes, weight and speed to the capacity of the protected lanes.

Traffic management in the Lake District National Park

The problems of controlling the motor vehicle have been described in several reviews of traffic policy in this national park (Wilson and Womersley, 1972; Lake District Special Planning Board, 1990; Friends of the Lake District, 1990). Since the designation of the national park in 1951, the planning and highway authorities have fostered a number of initiatives to reduce the impact of recreational traffic on the countryside. These have included small-scale traffic-management measures and fostering public transport services, including support for the 'Mountain Goat' coach service linking towns, villages and countryside. The problems of congestion caused by motor vehicles have clearly registered in the public's mind (Lake District Special Planning Board, 1976, p. 11). Public consultation undertaken as part of the preparation of the National Park Plan suggested that there was widespread public support for quiet enjoyment of the national park. Respondents felt that enjoyment could be achieved by limiting numbers of vehicles at car parks and adopting a traffic management approach rather than constructing new roads. However, responses in the same consultation exercise indicated strong resistance to the suggestions for actually restricting vehicular movement, even in sensitive areas, and an unwillingness to accept closure of roads to private cars. 'Even hints of traffic management, such as might be applied at Haweswater, have met with considerable opposition from the public...' (Lake District Special Planning Board, 1990, p. 27).

The dilemma facing the National Park authority is that desirable as traffic management schemes might be, there is liable to be opposition to any measures to restrict the movement of traffic. The authority's 1990 *New Policies* report outlines a number of ways of tackling the problems caused by recreational traffic (Lake District Special Planning Board, 1990, p. 28). However, the report recognizes that virtually all of these could themselves help to generate further problems.

The intractable difficulties of actually implementing restraint policies can be seen in proposals for handling the problems of congestion caused by visitor traffic in the Borrowdale area, south of Keswick. Board minutes record that the scheme sought to 'test the degree to which visitors could be persuaded to use public transport in preference to their cars by means of a well-publicized frequent and cheap bus service on the one hand and relatively high parking charges on the other' (Lake District Special Planning Board, 1991). Clearly, the scheme could make a contribution to reducing congestion and, in theory at least, could be seen to go some way to meeting anxiety about adverse effects of congestion and difficulties of car parking which affected visitors to the Lake District (Cumbria Tourist Board, 1991, p. 24). However, the scheme failed to attract the support of local interest groups. Although some criticism appeared to focus on the way in which local residents learned of the measures, there were objections to the principle of the scheme. The main fear was that the scheme would result in a reduction in numbers of visitors and would reduce income from tourism. In addition, the local parish council was not convinced that there was a serious traffic problem in Borrowdale. The scheme could also threaten the existing public bus service, which itself had been scaled down in operation in recent years.

The Lake District example demonstrates the way in which handling the problems of recreational traffic is intertwined with a complex pattern of planning, development and community-focused issues. It relates, in particular, to the willingness of people to pay for improvements to the physical environment.

Traffic management in the New Forest

A different example of an application of traffic management in a rural recreational area is to be found in the New Forest in Hampshire. The

history of the New Forest, its social traditions and physiography com-
bine to create an area with its own special attractiveness, but also problems. Many of the problems in the New Forest are associated with the
movement of vehicles, including recreational traffic such as camper
vehicles, towed caravans, day visitors and significant volumes of com-
muter and resident traffic. Volumes of traffic are too great for the narrow
highways of the Forest, resulting in encroachment on to verges. Traffic
speeds are often excessive for the road character and, despite fencing of
some roads, cattle and ponies which are reared on open land in the
Forest as part of a centuries-old tradition of husbandry, are regularly
killed by vehicles.

In 1971, following a study of recreational demands on the New Forest, a major initiative resulted in the banning of cars from extensive
areas of the Forest, including the creation of extensive 'car-free' zones
(New Forest Joint Steering Committee, 1971, p. 14). The scheme was
implemented in subsequent years and to a certain extent the 'off-highway'
problems were solved (New Forest Review Group, 1988, p. 15). However, problems still remained in respect of on-highway traffic and accidents and congestion persisted.

In the late 1980s, as part of a highway strategy for the New Forest,
Hampshire County Council considered a wide range of measures to help
reduce the impact of traffic on the Forest (Figure 7.4). Measures were
proposed which exhorted drivers to respect the special and unique quality of the area by means of 'gateway' signs at the entrance to the Forest;
speed limits which might help to reduce the average speeds of traffic to
levels appropriate for the highways concerned; the definition of a highway hierarchy which identified primary and secondary roads and byways, and could provide a framework within which to plan constraint
measures; and, finally, physical restrictions on speed introduced from
wide choice of measures, ranging from the creation of road bumps,
chicanes and 'rumble' areas to alterations to junctions, introduction of
traffic signs and road closures (Hampshire County Council, 1989, p. 32).

Public consultation on these different possibilities was undertaken,
after which certain possible measures were eliminated, including, for
example, proposals for some road closures. A six-month experimental
period started in March 1990 and featured several of the possibilities
which had been explored earlier.

The conclusions from the early stages of the experiment suggest that
the media campaign succeeded in stimulating interest but really needed

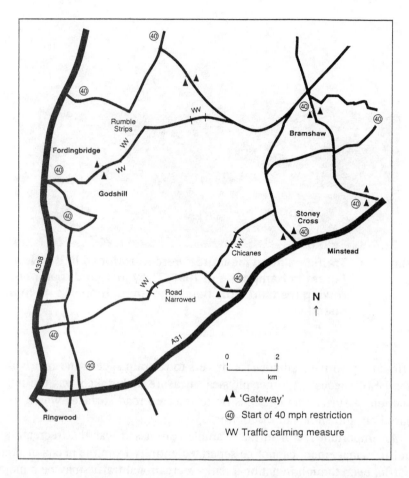

**Figure 7.4   The New Forest, Hampshire: traffic management
          measures, early 1991**
Source: derived from Hampshire County Council (1989)

to be seen as part of a much longer-term process of changing people's
attitudes to the way in which they and their vehicles made use of the
Forest (Hampshire County Council, 1991, p. 2). Secondly, the experimental 40 mph speed limits appeared to operate effectively at first, with
overall reductions in the speed of vehicles. However, in time, there was
a 'modest' recovery in vehicle speeds towards their former levels. The
third feature of the experiment involved the use of 'rumble strips' which

183

Plate 7.8   Traffic calming measures were introduced in the New Forest in Hampshire in 1990. They included road narrowing measures (as here) and imposition of a 40 mph speed limit

offered a positive reminder for drivers to restrain speed, and met with a degree of success. Another physical measure undertaken was the introduction of surface undulations on to selected road surfaces which were based on 'thresholds of discomfort'.

An important factor in the examples discussed was that recreational traffic management cannot be separated entirely from the needs of other traffic, even though in national parks recreational traffic may be a major concern of highway planning. Another issue concerns the conflict of objectives that can arise in traffic management and wider recreation and conservation policies. In the Peak District, for example, there has been a measure of disagreement over proposals to sign the National Park specifically as a designation from the surrounding motorway and trunk road network. Such signing would be likely to increase numbers of visitors, creating greater problems of visitor management than those already existing (Peak Park Joint Planning Board, 1989, p. 112).

Implementation of traffic-management strategies in the countryside depends on action primarily by highway authorities. However, their priorities and indeed philosophical outlook may differ from those contained in wider countryside policies. In working with highway authorities, arrangements between a park authority and the highway authority have sometimes worked well. However '...there have been difficulties in some instances in following policies into practice, and assessing the impact of highway design on the landscape is often a difficult matter of subjective judgement. Future consultations should take place at an early stage, before programmes have been designed and costed' (North Yorkshire Moors National Park Committee, 1990, p. 116).

The success of implementing traffic-management policies will also depend on demand management at different levels of transport policy-making. For major new developments, much consideration is likely to be given to the traffic generation implications of, say, a proposal for a theme park. It is likely that far less consideration will be given to the incremental growth of traffic as a result of smaller-scale schemes in connection with farm diversification, including rural tourism, livery or farm shops. Yet these developments can themselves result in the transformation of quiet rural road networks into relatively busy thoroughfares.

Public transport and traffic management

Measures to control vehicular traffic in the countryside have often included the promotion of public transport as a means of weaning visitors away from a dependence on the private motor vehicle (Groome and Tarrant, 1985, p. 82; Countryside Commission, 1987d, p. 4). National park authorities in particular have introduced a wide range of measures to foster public transport.

The opportunities for developing recreational public transport in pressured areas have been explored at length (Dartington Amenity Research Trust, 1976). From those investigations it was suggested that the opportunities for developing public transport systems could depend greatly on the location of facilities and their relationship with the origins of visitors.

The approaches to providing schemes appear to fall into two main categories. Firstly within quite clearly defined areas of countryside, recreational public transport has been provided as part of a total or partial ban on other motorized traffic. Examples to illustrate this approach include the Goyt Valley and Upper Derwent initiatives in the Peak District National Park (Countryside Commission, 1972; Peak Park Joint Planning Board, 1989, p. 175). In a second category, attempts have also been made to provide recreational transport services but without

185

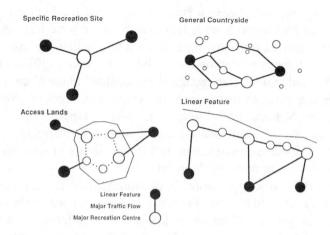

Figure 7.5   Provision of recreational transport in the countryside
Source: Dartington Amenity Research Trust (1977), pp. 7–8

significant changes being made to the existing pattern of traffic circulation. In this situation, public transport provision has had to compete with the private motor vehicle. An example of this category is to be found at the Ironbridge Gorge Museum at Telford where the several sites are served by a 'park and ride' scheme introduced to reduce the volumes of private vehicles travelling between different attractions and lessen the congestion and delay which they cause (Morris, 1989, pp. 16–17).

Evaluating the contribution of such schemes to the reduction of the impact of the car is not entirely straightforward. Certainly, the effects of the highly 'controlled' initiatives have been quite clearly demonstrated, most dramatically perhaps in the case of the Upper Derwent. Here, carefully provided car parks, minibuses, a cycle-hire scheme and marked routes have succeeded in removing all but essential vehicles from a valley which is extremely popular with visitors (Patmore, 1983, pp. 183–4).

In the case of the Ironbridge Gorge recreational transport services, studies revealed a gradual increase in numbers of visitors to the Gorge and Museum who patronized the park and ride scheme from 5 per cent in 1984, to 11 per cent in 1987 and 14 per cent in 1990. However, many visitors revealed a reluctance to be separated from their cars, stressing the greater convenience and flexibility of their own vehicles compared with the park and ride scheme.

186

The Ironbridge studies are of value in reminding us of the close relationship that exists between the driver and his or her car. Despite extensive promotion of park and ride, the total proportion of visitors who use the scheme remains small. For the traffic problems to be alleviated much stronger measures including bans outside the central area of Ironbridge would need to be entertained (Research Surveys, 1990, p. 4). In contrast to the situation in the Derwent Valley, controlling traffic movement in an area with a significant local resident population and many diverse land uses and ownerships could result in formidable problems of implementation

In concluding this discussion on traffic in the countryside, reference is again made to the revised traffic forecasts for the period to the year 2025 (Department of Transport, 1989). In 1991, an investigation suggested

Plate 7.9   Traffic levels in the countryside could rise by between 2 and 4 times by the year 2025: Horse Shoe Pass, Llangollen, Clwyd, 1991

187

that as a result of concern over the implications of the forecasts, a 'new realism' was beginning to emerge which recognized that there would be no possibility of increasing road supply to a level which met the expected growth rates in demand (Goodwin *et al.*, 1991). The hallmarks of new realism include improving the quality of public transport; use of traffic calming methods in order to reduce traffic speeds and tip the balance of advantage in favour of pedestrians and cyclists; the use of advanced traffic-management systems; exploring the role that road pricing might play; and only limited construction of new roads.

Some of the concepts explored in the new realism could also be applied to seeking solutions to solving the problem of handling the car in the countryside, too. For example, traffic calming may have a part to play and road pricing could also have an application. Regulation through the mechanism of parking charges, as proposed in Borrowdale and as currently practised at many recreational sites, is also a possible form of control. In respect of public transport then, both within the national parks and in other selected areas, there is scope for devising workable systems.

Concern about the effects of motor vehicular traffic in the countryside was shown to be fully justified in a 1992 study. The investigation into the trends in transport in the countryside demonstrated that vehicle use outside towns had increased much faster than in towns over the last 10 to 15 years; that based on current trends, traffic levels could rise broadly by between 2 and 4 times in the countryside generally, and to an even greater extent in certain rural locations (Stokes *et al.*, 1992, pp. 13–14).

COMMENT

The access issue has attracted attention from a wide range of interest groups and has involved continuing conflict between landowners and the access lobby. Policy debate tended initially to focus on access to open country and wilderness areas in Britain, but growing importance has also been attached to access to the wider countryside on statutory rights of way. The role of government has been central to access policy-making, with the former often being seen to resist intrusion on the rights of landowners. Within the limitations prescribed by legislation, agencies such as the Countryside Commission have sought to increase access opportunities, generally successfully, although not all of their policies have been accepted by the access lobby. The role of local government in promoting access has been criticized largely in terms of the low priority assigned to access issues and the ineffectiveness of policies. The access debate has highlighted the important role which can be played by local communities in extending opportunities for access, but it also reminds us that they can inhibit attempts to resolve access problems. They are important actors and their support has been necessary in order to implement policies.

Future access policies and the target of achieving a usable rights of way network in England and Wales by the year 2000 are likely to be influenced by sufficient public funding support and commitment, and by the attitudes of both the landowning and access lobbies to the use of the countryside for recreation. Conflict and competition for land and access, particularly involving the use of the motor vehicle in the countryside, suggest the need for radical solutions. However, the prospect of reduced involvement by financially constrained local authorities is likely to place a greater emphasis on other agencies' taking a lead in facilitating access to the countryside.

Traffic management as a tool for controlling visitor pressures has been applied only to a limited extent in the British countryside. An issue which continually arises in implementing traffic-management policies concerns the acceptability of schemes to people affected by the measures. In the case of lightly populated areas, where land might be within a single ownership, then it is likely that the room for experimentation might be considerable. The success of 'car-free' zones created in the New Forest can to a large extent be explained by much of the land being in one ownership. However, elsewhere in rural areas, disruption caused by traffic-management schemes is likely to generate both support and opposition. Traffic-management measures inevitably involve transferring costs, including inconvenience, from one group of a community to another.

Despite the advent of the new realism in transport policies, the agenda for recreational traffic policies will be dominated by arguments over the extent to which there should be unrestricted use of the motor vehicle in the countryside. This issue, of course, forms part of wider debate about attitudes in society to the private motor car. Whatever conclusions are reached, they will have a major influence on the future form of the countryside and the extent to which different user groups will be able to enjoy it.

Chapter 8

Widening opportunities for enjoyment of the countryside

A concern in recent years has been that of ensuring that rural recreation, when provided, is made available to as wide a section of the population as possible. Central to this concern has been the knowledge that rural recreation is pursued by only a limited section of the population. If public money is to be spent on rural recreation, then it is important that whatever is provided is not just used by those who are able to pay for it.

Recognition of the inequitable nature of access to rural recreation can be traced to several sources. For example, calls were made in 1971 for investigation into the needs of the underprivileged, in particular those on low incomes, without cars and often living in inner urban areas (Anfield, 1971, p. 21). The Cobham Committee report drew attention to the needs of those unable to take part in the expanding recreation provision of the time (House of Lords, 1973, p. xxv). The Government's 1975 white paper on *Sport and Recreation* cited the need to develop more recreational facilities in the urban fringe for use by people without access to private cars (Department of the Environment, 1975, p. 14). A similar message was contained in a review by the Countryside Review Committee in 1977. It urged a deliberate policy to assist a wider cross-section of the public to discover recreation in the countryside. This is an important social objective, particularly in relation to the underprivileged. The contribution, physical, mental and emotional, which countryside recreation can make to the quality of life is self-evident. Evidence... 'suggests a large unsatisfied demand for country leisure among those who have no access to personal transport' (Countryside Review Committee, 1977, p. 18).

In terms of the social groups who have been the subject of this concern, then one common characteristic is that they fall into the category of

190

the 'mobility deprived', without access to a motor car. This covers a wide range of groups within the population with different social characteristics. Hillman summarizes the situation:

Who are these people and what are their circumstances? In the first place it is important to note that they consist of groups in the population who often have more time and inclination to use their leisure in countryside recreational activity: children and teenagers, particularly during their long holidays, mothers with young children, the unemployed and poorer families who cannot afford to pay for their leisure and people over the age of retirement – groups that is who, in the main, cannot travel by car unless they are *'taken'*. (Hillman, 1984, p. 14).

This description can be refined, referring, for example, to the influence of physical disability as a constraint. In addition, participation can be related to specific neighbourhood types based on census enumeration districts, using for example the classification scheme which goes under the acronym of ACORN (Countryside Commission, 1985a, pp. 5–6).

In devising ways of overcoming the uneven opportunities for enjoyment of the countryside by different social groups, policy-makers have adopted a number of approaches. Underlying many of them is the notion of social equity.

SOCIAL EQUITY AND RURAL RECREATION

Provision of much rural recreation in Britain is highly dependent on public funding support, as records of local government financial statistics reveal. It is unusual for user charges to cover more than a small proportion of the capital or revenue costs of publicly provided recreational facilities (Department of the Environment, 1991b, pp. 66–67). Although public providers may intend to ensure a fair distribution of recreation opportunities, inevitably what is offered can be subject to pressure from a variety of influences. There can be pressure to adopt particular policies by different interest groups. Decision-makers' own 'culture' can exert a major influence in interpreting demands. In addition, the availability of grants or central support and the 'visibility' of measures which are adopted are likely to have strong influences on policies. The fairness of distribution of services is also likely to be reflected in the precise form of delivery of a service. Le Grand demonstrates that, in the case of a government function such as support for transport services, the form of the subsidies designed to benefit all who use those services often results in benefits going to the better-off rather than those in greatest need (Le Grand, 1982, pp. 117–118)

In the case of rural recreation, social objectives, where stated in policy, have aimed to reduce as many 'barriers' as possible by making the service free or available at a low cost. However, as in the case of transport cited above, the greatest use of such free services has tended to be by those who can afford to pay for them. Despite policy-makers' intentions, opportunities for access to recreation facilities or services might remain unequal. In the search for a more effective delivery of countryside recreation services, policy-makers have embarked on a

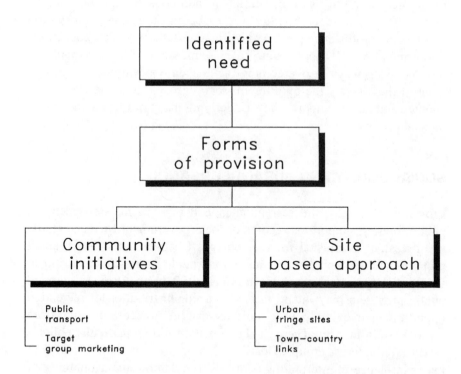

Figure 8.1 Ways of widening opportunities for enjoyment of the countryside

number of ways of ensuring a better match between expenditure (and subsidy) and need (Figure 8.1). Such approaches might be based on increasing the supply of the service in the expectation that those in need may make use of those services; or targeting subsidies through policies which are directed specifically at groups seen to be in need (Gratton and Taylor, 1985, pp. 211–214).

SITE-BASED APPROACHES

New opportunities for rural recreation have been created in Britain for some decades, but new building developments have swallowed up much open land which was once available to city dwellers (Shoard, 1979, p. 89). The spread of the built-up areas increased the distance that people had to travel in order to reach the countryside.

Attempts to recreate those opportunities for countryside have resulted in the development of recreation facilities in urban fringe. The general concern with the need to widen access opportunities was reflected in a change in emphasis in grant-making policy by the Countryside Commission (Countryside Commission, 1975, p. 10). In respect of sites policy, this resulted in priority being given to sites in green belts and in buffer areas between the main centres of population. Amongst the factors to be considered by agencies seeking grant support would be 'purpose, need, planning provision, management, design and public accessibility to the area by public and private transport.'

Policies which have sought to promote urban fringe sites include those of the former Greater Manchester Council and the districts of that county (Newman, 1981, p. 37). Although many projects were carried out with the aim of achieving improvements to the physical environment, an important objective, too, was to develop sites which were near to where potential visitors lived or could be easily reached by means of transport other than the private motor vehicle. By 1984, some 17 sites had been developed, principally along river valleys such as the Irk, Irwell, Medlock and Mersey. Visitor surveys carried out in 1984 confirmed that the location of inner urban fringe sites near to working-class areas of Greater Manchester had resulted in visits being made by such groups as unemployed people and public transport users who would not normally feature prominently in countryside visits (Pawson and Groome, 1987, p. 88).

193

Plate 8.1   Surveys remind of the importance of the local country-side as a venue for visitors: a railway path offers a traffic-free link between built-up areas and open space: Worsley, Salford, 1988

In a number of other locations in Britain, policies have also sought to provide sites near to where people live rather than in the deep country-side. However, despite this shift in policy-making, evidence suggests that the use of recreational opportunities in urban fringe areas by the mobility-disadvantaged is much less than might have been expected. For example, studies of the metropolitan green belt in 1978 revealed, firstly, that many recreation sites performed the role of local open spaces, not unlike urban parks, with a quite localized clientele. Secondly, relatively few people from disadvantaged areas actually used green belt sites (Harrison, 1983, p. 312).

PUBLIC TRANSPORT AND ACCESS TO THE COUNTRYSIDE

In the light of findings such as these, attention has focused on the scope that public transport might offer as means of reaching the countryside, including urban fringe sites. The decline in opportunities for using public transport to the countryside has been recorded thus:

> The bus to the country has been allowed to wither away because Britain lacks any strategy for ensuring that the countryside gives people what they want and need from it. Countryside recreation provision around London over the last ten years has been based on several unspoken but quite fallacious assumptions – for instance that only people who happen to own cars need be helped to find refreshment in rural surroundings (Shoard, 1979, p. 98).

The absence of public transport is clearly a major constraint on accessibility, but of equal importance too is the timing and frequency of services (Tanner, 1987, p. 195). Although at one time urban transport operators promoted services to surrounding countryside, the decline in recreational traffic has resulted in the loss of those services. In a West Midlands study, it was shown that a high proportion of country parks could not be reached by public transport without difficulty (involving a journey of three or four hours) or not at all (Williams and Tanner, 1982, p. 101).

Schemes to assist people to visit the countryside have varied greatly in scale, location and success of operation. Shoard cites the example of the Surrey Rambler bus which provided a circular route from Dorking to the surrounding countryside (Shoard, 1979, p. 99). The success of the scheme led to the suggestion that other towns in southeast England could provide similar services. However, other experimental schemes indicate that the potential for such services may be more limited. The Sunday Bus experiment in Gwent demonstrated the problems of providing a bus service from an urban area to recreation sites in the countryside (Greening and Slater, 1981, p. 23). A home interview survey of Newport residents suggested that there was a demonstrable need for such services. Four bus services were provided in 1977/78 but patronage for the services was low and fare revenue failed to cover costs. Extensive promotion of the services was undertaken but interview surveys suggested that although people may have originally indicated an interest in using public transport to visit the countryside, in practice, other factors proved to be barriers: 'did not have time', 'rarely or never make trips on a Sunday' or 'did not want to go'. These attitudes were separate from whether or not people felt that travelling by bus was uncomfortable. In other words, social factors proved to be a major constraint on the take-up of the services.

In a 1983 study, it was found that virtually no special-purpose public transport services covered their running costs (Groome and Tarrant, 1985, p. 83). An ability to cover 60 or 70 per cent of running costs was regarded by providers as a good rate of return. The study drew a distinction between promotional schemes based on special-purpose public transport services and those that made use of regular services. Of some 70 examples examined in the study in England and Wales, it was the special-purpose services that failed most of all to meet the providers' expectations. The findings from this and later studies suggest that the more 'successful' services are likely to be those in tourist areas and regular services that are subject to promotions targeted at specific market segments. The findings of this study suggested that the market for some services was not so much from the mobility-disadvantaged but from people who were likely to be car owners themselves but had selected to use public transport to get to the countryside.

A notable scheme for the promotion of recreational public transport was the Wayfarer project undertaken between 1981 and 1984 in the northwest of England, West Yorkshire and the Peak District National Park (Countryside Commission, 1985b, p. 10). The project involved a wide range of initiatives including the marketing of whole networks of public transport routes for their recreation potential, the provision of special-purpose recreational bus services, travel clubs for particular age groups with discounted fares, and simplified timetables. In its way, the project can be considered as a 'social service' and the benefits extended beyond simply extending opportunities for enjoying the countryside. For example, the travel clubs appeared to play a valuable social function for their members (Lumsdon, 1984, p. 112). It is clear that patronage increased on many services as a result of the scheme. Amongst several conclusions, the project demonstrated that the potential demand for little-used 'social' routes to the countryside may help to make such services viable. Also, the project stressed the importance of maintaining public transport routes as planned networks with good opportunities for transferring from one service to another (Countryside Commission, 1985b, p. 12). Regular bus services which have been subject to marketing and

**Plate 8.2   The 1980s saw the introduction of many special-
purpose recreational transport services: Tatton Park,
Cheshire, 1984**

promotion have also succeeded in generating recreation and tourism
traffic and have provided a valuable bonus to normal revenues. Dobbs,
for example, demonstrates the considerable cross-subsidization that has
occurred in Gwynedd in North Wales. Here, income from increased use
of regular bus and coach services by recreationists was used to underpin
losses made by services out of the tourist season (Dobbs, 1984, p. 29).

Since deregulation of public transport in Britain in October 1986, it
has become increasingly difficult to keep an accurate record of the
extent of recreational transport services. 'Commercial' services, registered with the Traffic Commissioners, may include an element of the
rural recreation market. Some tendered (i.e. subsidized) services may be
provided for recreational purposes, for example in national parks by a
park authority. However, in most areas, the situation is subject to con-

tinuing change and uncertainty surrounds bus networks. In an era when transport budgets are subject to severe constraints and cuts have to be made under special needs, education, evening urban or rural headings, then support for services with a primarily recreational function may be difficult to justify.

So far, discussion has focused on the use of bus and coach travel as means of influencing use of the private motor vehicle in countryside subject to heavy recreational pressures. In the case of rail services, too, several initiatives have featured in national park policies. Best-known of these perhaps has been the 'Dales Rail' scheme based in the Yorkshire Dales and using the scenic Settle/Carlisle railway line (Dartington Amenity Research Trust, 1979). Other lines that have been promoted include the Conwy Valley route in North Wales, which runs through part of the Snowdonia National Park, and the Esk Valley line in the Yorkshire

Plate 8.3   Recreational transport: Dales Rail, Yorkshire Dales National Park, 1990

Moors National Park. Valuable as these initiatives have been, the limited extent of rail services in national parks means that their contribution to the overall volume and distribution of visitors (and their vehicles) has, of necessity, been only on a small scale. Despite this general picture of uncertainty in the provision of recreational transport services, a number of additional experimental schemes continue to be undertaken. For example, attempts have been made to explore the market for cyclists using bus public transport to reach the countryside as an alternative to declining opportunities for reaching the countryside by rail travel. Experiments in Merseyside and Greater Manchester suggest that there may be scope for widening opportunities by this means of transport (Transport for Leisure *et al.*, 1991, p. 23). The Bike Bus scheme, undertaken over a 3

Plate 8.4   Declining opportunities for cyclists to use British Rail services led to the coach-based Cycle Transport Network Experiment: Merseybus service near Buxton in the Peak District, 1990

year period from 1990 to 1992, involved the use of buses with space to carry bicycles. At weekends during spring and summer, excursions were arranged from Merseyside and Greater Manchester to North Wales, the Peak District and the Yorkshire Dales. However, here as in other schemes discussed in this chapter, a degree of subsidy was needed because of the limited revenue raised through fares. One conclusion from the exercise was that the needs of cyclists in respect of public transport resembled those of disabled groups in requiring low loading access and space free from seating inside the vehicle. Unlike the situation in some other European countries, few bus and coach designs in Britain provide for wheelchair/cycle access as a matter of course. Yet modified regular service buses could make a contribution, albeit modest, to widening access to the countryside for these user groups.

A further example of an initiative to assist the non-car owner or user has been the 'Countrygoer' project. Launched in northwest England in 1990, the project features a campaign to encourage use of rural public transport. It was extended to the rest of Britain in 1992 and its sponsors included the Ramblers' Association (Countryside Commission, 1992a). The success of these and other schemes depends on effective definition of the market, selling the service and careful monitoring to see whether it is achieving its objectives (Countryside Commission, 1987d, pp. 3–5). In addition, most recreational transport schemes are often going to depend on support from public sources and at best will be able to cover marginal operating costs only (Dobbs, 1984, p. 31).

COMMUNITY-BASED INITIATIVES

Within the remit to widen opportunities for enjoyment of the countryside, other approaches besides providing public transport services alone have been undertaken. The findings of the Sunday bus experiment and other studies all seemed to indicate that simply providing public transport services did not necessarily result in people actually using those facilities to visit the countryside.

Besides problems caused by mobility disadvantage, other significant barriers included: a lack of knowledge of public transport; a lack of skill in the use of bus and train timetables; an unfamiliarity with places to go in the countryside; and a lack of money amongst some respondents who were struggling to clothe and feed their families (LeMottee, 1984, p. 2).

Attempts to rectify such recreational disadvantage have included local authority recreation policies with specific social objectives and target group approaches which identify those groups in the population who currently make little use of the countryside. Attempts to achieve more equitable access to rural recreation is illustrated by reference to schemes in Nottinghamshire and Greater Manchester. They usefully highlight both the desirability and feasibility of achieving more equitable access to rural recreation.

The first scheme, Operation Gateway, was launched in 1983 by Nottinghamshire County Council and sought to:

- investigate demand from special groups for recreation in the Nottinghamshire countryside;
- assist in the provision of appropriate services and facilities which would enable and encourage members of these groups to visit the countryside (Countryside Commission, 1989a, p. 21).

A 1989 review of the Project records that Nottinghamshire County Council was concerned about under-use of recreational facilities by unemployed people, skilled and unskilled manual workers and people of Afro-Caribbean or Asian ethnic origins (Countryside Commission, 1989a, p. 21). Using discussion group techniques, low-income and unemployed people in inner and outer Nottingham housing estates revealed the constraints and opportunities which influenced their use or lack of use of the countryside.

Project workers established contact with wardens of community neighbourhood centres in deprived areas of Nottingham, over-60s clubs and ethnic minority groups. They organized a series of day trips using hire coaches to local country parks, other recreation sites and farms. Self-help for the costs of the excursions themselves was expected, although on some trips there was an element of subsidy from Nottinghamshire County Council. During a 4 year period from 1985, project officers ensured that the Project expanded with no less than 119 'awareness' events, 68 visits to farms, 22 trips to country parks and 12 coach excursions to the wider countryside. A wide range of techniques were used to widen awareness of the opportunities for enjoying the countryside: a directory of trips encouraged self-help in planning trips using public transport; 'open afternoons', mailing lists of activities, suggested trips and events, host rangers at country parks all helped create 'fuller awareness of groups' special needs in terms of cultural and physical differences' (Countryside Commission, 1989a, p. 24). In 1989, the experimental status of the scheme was abandoned and a full-time member of staff was appointed by the county council to further the scheme.

Another approach has been undertaken under the guise of the Greater Manchester Countryside Recreation Information Project (Greater Manchester Countryside Unit, 1991). The project was set up in order to achieve the following:

- to improve people's awareness of the local countryside;
- to demonstrate what there is to see and do there;
- to test new methods of conveying information to the public.

The project was funded by the Countryside Commission and by the constituent ten local authorities of Greater Manchester. The several initiatives of the Project were targeted at three locations: Wythenshawe in South Manchester; North Marple in Stockport and Burnden in inner Bolton (Table 8.1).

The key feature of the exercise has been the appointment of a project officer who developed links with those involved in countryside management and with those working in the three target areas. A difference from Operation Gateway is that from the start the exercise attempted to raise the profile of countryside recreation across the whole of Greater Manchester itself as well as the three target areas. In addition, the target areas themselves were identified on the basis of market research to find out how far there was a hidden demand for trips to and information about the countryside.

The Gateway and Greater Manchester Projects have not been the only attempts to adopt a community-based approach to the provision of leisure from outside particular target areas. The approach is not without its problems, as was demonstrated in the Quality of Life experiments from 1973 to 1977 (Department of the Environment, 1977b). Although largely focused on urban leisure, the arts and education, in the experiments in Stoke on Trent, Clwyd, Sunderland and West Dumbartonshire rural recreation initiatives were also undertaken; for example, guided walks and cycle-hire schemes. As one review records, these particular experiments were considered to have limited benefits (Lawless, cited in Torkildsen, 1983, p. 271). They were able to demonstrate the potential for self-help amongst local communities. However, for sustaining the momentum

Table 8.1
Greater Manchester Countryside Recreation Information Project

Initiative	Scope
Countryside information pack	Resource file for information staff and ready reference for users of visitor centres
Countryside familiarization day	Visit to countryside sites for information centre staff
Senior citizens' outing	Use of scheduled public transport services to reach country park
Countryside treasure trail	Event to encourage use of local countryside
Equal opportunities in the countryside	Outings for minority communities in Burnden (Bolton) area to local country parks
Local information point	Use of local library in Wythenshawe for advisory service, activities
Great Countryside days out	Low-cost leaflets highlighting information on places to visit in neighbouring countryside

Source: based on information provided by the Greater Manchester Countryside Unit, Ashton under Lyne, 1991

generated by such experiments, much would depend on the availability of sustained leadership and effective voluntary organization. In addition, support for any programme would require a positive response from providers of facilities themselves.

In Nottingham's Gateway scheme and the Greater Manchester project, the test of the initiatives will be the extent to which they continue to receive support from the public. In Operation Gateway, a rather different and more distant involvement of county council staff has followed in the later stages of the project. In Greater Manchester, much will depend on the role of the county-wide countryside advisory service and on the extent to which individual local authorities follow up the initiative in their own rural recreation strategies.

The two examples cited above indicate possible forms for social recreation policies. To what extent might similar approaches be adopted elsewhere? In adopting a 'countryside for everyone' approach a number of steps can be followed (Countryside Commission, 1989a, p. 10):

- contacting those who might benefit from increased opportunities for enjoying the countryside ('defining and reaching the customers');
- providing assistance by working at a personal level with individual community groups, raising awareness through publicity events, exhibitions and the media; 'signposting', providing the mechanisms to enable users to help themselves;
- making things happen: ensuring that providers' arrangements for running a 'countryside for everyone' approach operate efficiently.

THE MARKETING APPROACH

Central to most of the initiatives explored in the 'countryside for everyone' concept is the use of marketing techniques. These emphasize the need to build up a thorough understanding of who and how many people are to be catered for and what they might be prepared to pay relative to what it costs to provide (Worth, 1984, p. 99). Promotional and marketing approaches have become closely associated with 'recreational welfare' policies which have sought to remove social barriers to participation (Coalter *et al.*, 1988, p. 66). The importance of marketing is stressed in Countryside Commission policies, including a consultation paper, *Visitors to the Countryside* (Countryside Commission, 1991b). Much emphasis is placed in the paper on improving access to information about the countryside, with better information about public transport, and on the need for recreation staff to have more training in 'customer care'. The latter, it is suggested, could be enhanced by means of 'visitor welcome' audits and by ensuring that action follows from the results. In addition, providers should target policies towards the needs of minority groups by featuring them in publicity, providing specifically designed events and activities and making sure that they are employed in recreation services.

204

For example, the consultation document argues that 2 per cent of 'first line' recreation staff should be of ethnic minority origin by the year 2000.

The paper also stressed the need for visitors to have the necessary skills and confidence in order to feel at ease in and to explore the countryside. To assist in building that confidence, it is suggested that countryside staff must give positive first impressions. In addition, countryside staff need to work in urban areas so that they can provide stimulus and interest through providing information and organizing events. Identifying potential areas of conflict between 'untutored' visitors and other users of the countryside, it stresses the need for visitors themselves to adopt 'green' attitudes.

The extent to which such approaches are being adopted by providers of rural recreation in Britain is not clear. Conservation principles underlie much countryside recreation management in Britain and practice is strongly resource- or site-based. For the 'countryside for everyone' approach to work, rather more of a 'people-based' approach will be required.

WALKING AND CYCLING AS MODES OF TRANSPORT TO REACH THE COUNTRYSIDE

Besides overall sites policy, public transport and community-based approaches to widening access to the countryside, a fourth approach is to consider improved provision for access by foot and bicycle. Although access to the local countryside is far from ideal in some areas, elsewhere networks of footpaths, bridleways and byways provide convenient access to the countryside.

An advantage of both walking and cycling is that they require minimal preparation for undertaking a visit to the countryside. They offer a high degree of independence without a need to rely on other modes of transport such as a bus or a car. In practical terms, therefore, they may well offer the key to a successful approach to the 'countryside for everyone' concept.

The requirements for both modes of transport are similar although the distance travelled by the majority of users in each category is likely to be different: for most walkers, a one-way distance of 3 km or so is likely to be the outer limit; for 'non-expert' cyclists, a distance of up to 5 or 6 km is more likely. In both cases, the mode of transport itself is likely to be a form of recreation, even if other pursuits such as fishing are pursued at the end of the journey. Again, although the 'goal' may well be an established recreational facility such as a country park, equally valued are likely to be the route networks themselves.

The likelihood of a walker or cyclist being able to travel with reasonable ease from town to countryside is often constrained by fragmented route networks. In the case of footpaths, the general comments about fragmented sections of path, linked only by busy roads, blockages and problems with using the network apply equally in the countryside around towns as in the deep countryside.

In the case of cycling, fear of traffic is likely to be a significant deterrent to using that mode of transport (Claxton and Dartington Amenity Research Trust, 1978, p. 32; Plowden and Hillman, 1984, p. 131). In both the 'deep' countryside and the urban fringe, several types of constraint may discourage travel by bicycle (Countryside Commission, 1989g, pp. 13–15). Volume and speed of traffic may lead to hazardous cycling conditions on main roads which might be the only links between town and countryside. It may be particularly difficult to cross a main road from one byway to another. The development of new road networks may turn quiet country lanes into cul-de-sacs and hence reduce town–country links. Physical development in the urban fringe for residential or commercial development can result in the loss of valuable links for both cyclists and walkers.

Site policies have generally paid the minimum of attention to access to countryside facilities by foot or bicycle. Where access is easy for those on foot or bicycle, then this tends to happen fortuitously rather than by design. The creation of town–country links may involve giving priority to improving and signing existing path and road networks and, where possible, agreeing the creation of permissive paths with landowners. A number of urban fringe management schemes have had this as a goal and town–country links have been created on the routes of abandoned canals, towing paths on operational canals and disused railway lines. In Strathclyde, the Forth and Clyde Canal, abandoned railways and riverside banks have been connected to create a 35 km link between the centre of Glasgow and Loch Lomond. In Derbyshire, a segregated town–country link follows the line of the old Derby Canal for a distance of 12 km from Derby to Melbourne (Figure 8.2; Countryside Commission, 1989g, p. 26).

206

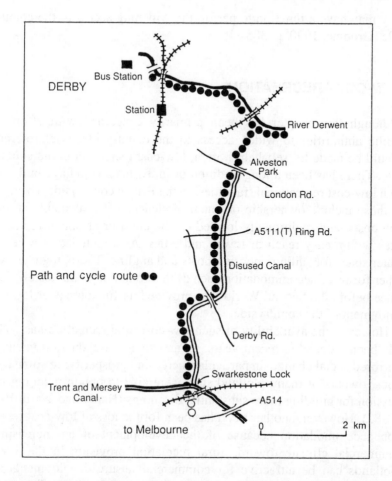

Figure 8.2   Town–country link: Derby to Melbourne footpath and cycle route
Source: Countryside Commission (1989g), p. 26

Of interest are the high levels of use that can be generated by the provision of such town–country links. From there being almost no use at all, estimates of some railway path conversions suggest levels of use of over one million visits a year on an individual route by walkers and cyclists (Sustrans Ltd, 1990, p. 3). Such linear routes may function as local open spaces with quite limited catchments. However, their other function in affording links between town and countryside suggests that they may have a function to perform in widening access to the countryside (Groome, 1990, p. 385).

LOW-COST RECREATION

Although this chapter has been primarily concerned with efforts by public authorities to widen access to the countryside, brief reference should be made to 'self-help', often, low-cost recreation in the countryside. There has been a long tradition of individuals who have built their own low-cost recreational 'facilities' in the British countryside. Examples of these include ownership or rental of chalets, often available at quite low costs, and traditionally located on the coast or at inland recreation sites within easy reach of towns and cities. Also included is access to water space for sailing, mooring boats and angling. These, together with other forms of accommodation such as that found in youth hostels, have since before the Second World War provided useful sources of low-cost enjoyment of the countryside.

However, the availability of such low-cost rural recreation has gradually been reduced in recent years. To an extent, the reduction in supply mirrored social change, in particular increasing prosperity; in some locations, owners of many plotland sites were able to obtain planning permission for building more substantial dwellings (Hardy and Ward, 1985, p. 282). However, another trend has been for the loss of low-cost recreation accommodation because of the development of an increasingly commercial climate towards rural recreation provision in the 1980s. Plotlands can be attractive for commercial leisure developments and chalet owners can find themselves displaced as a result of those pressures. A material consideration for planning authorities will be the effects of such developments on existing occupiers, but their ability to constrain schemes may be difficult, particularly if projects result in the tidying up of poorly serviced, unsightly buildings. In addition, concern was expressed about the possible loss of low-cost recreation opportunities, including access to water space as a result of privatization of the water industry in England and Wales in 1989 (Eardley, 1989, p. 9).

THE PROBLEM OF THE NON-PARTICIPANT

So far in this chapter, emphasis has been placed on public policies which have sought to encourage people to participate in rural recreation. Some researchers have criticized this assumption and have stressed the need for a distinction to be made between constraints and preferences as influences on visitors to the countryside. The importance of this distinction for policy-makers has been the subject of a critical review of countryside sites policy (Curry and Comley, 1986b, pp. 15–17). Issues raised in this review include the following.

- Unlike housing, clothing or food, countryside recreation is by no means an essential commodity. Some sections of the population have little interest at all in participating in countryside recreation. This applies to all social classes, although it seems that lack of interest is greatest amongst the less well-off.
- Although government policies have encouraged use of the countryside for recreation, they have been qualified by emphasizing that they should be developed in accordance with people's interest, choice and wishes.
- Social groups show differing degrees of interest in the types of recreation that can be offered by the countryside. For example, amongst less well-off groups there is a tendency to favour commercial 'performance' or 'showman' type activities.
- Cultural factors are suggested as an explanation for people's preferences for countryside recreation, but those factors themselves are closely related to the ability of people to actually participate.
- There can be dangers in developing supply-led policies which alter leisure preferences and can result in 'misplaced philanthropy'.

With reference to Operation Gateway, they record: 'Certainly such a policy may engender the interest of "disadvantaged" groups but it does seem inherently that policies designed to encourage people to do things in which they show little interest, have little application' (Curry and Comley, 1986, p. 23).

This is a valuable cautionary note. In developing the 'countryside for everyone' approach it should not be automatically assumed that everybody has an interest in the countryside. It would be equally wrong to underestimate that there is an underlying lack of interest in enjoyment of

209

the outdoors amongst less well-off social groups. Where there are minimal physical barriers between home and site, then countryside recreation can be enjoyed by groups from outer housing estates who are otherwise under-represented in most national surveys of countryside recreation. In addition, as the Gateway Project and a number of other studies have indicated, enjoyment of the outdoors can be valued by a wide range of social groups. In explaining its 'Countryside for everyone' policies, the Countryside Commission addresses the issue as follows:

> The issue is not about forcing people into the countryside against their will nor changing the lifestyle of everyone into frequent countryside users. It is about ensuring that everyone can make genuine choices for themselves about whether they wish to visit the countryside (Countryside Commission, 1989a, p. 5).

COMMENT

In reviewing challenges to 'demand-led' public policies for rural recreation, this chapter has recorded the performance of several initiatives which have sought to widen leisure and recreation access to all sections of the community. The projects have been launched under the heading of a 'countryside for everyone' or similar titles and can be seen as forms of recreational welfare. Implementation of the different schemes has presented a number of problems in ensuring that the service is provided to the consumer at whom it is targeted.

Marketing techniques involving market segmentation can help in enabling the service to be more carefully directed, but a difficulty concerns the ability of site-based management systems to adjust to fundamentally different approaches to the service that they currently provide. From experience with the Gateway Project, it was clear that the 'product' sought by visitors was very different from that provided by the managers of recreational sites. The commercial nature of many visitors' interests in the countryside reminds us of the role that the private provider can play in satisfying demands.

This chapter has recorded the existence of links between rural recreation policy and other policy areas. This is particularly so in the case of transport where the weakening of local authority influence means that attempts at coordinating countryside recreation initiatives will be increasingly difficult to achieve in the future.

In the light of the difficulties of removing barriers that discourage the non-car-owner from travelling to the countryside, a partial solution may lie in the reintroduction of 'countryside' into the city. The creation of linear parks, improvements to run-down and under-managed urban parks and events such as 'country fairs' can assist in providing a perspective on the countryside. Could it be that the problems of widening access to the countryside are to be found in the town rather than in the countryside itself?

Chapter 9

Rural tourism

It might be questioned whether rural tourism requires separate discussion from the other themes outlined in previous chapters. However, the existence of a body of analytical and prescriptive techniques, policies, agencies and literature, all specifically dealing with tourism in the countryside, suggests that there exists here a focus for planning activity.

A number of attempts have been made to define tourism and to distinguish it from leisure and recreation. A widely accepted definition is that a tourist is someone who is away from home for more than 24 hours for social, leisure or business purposes. However, it should be noted that the term has also been interpreted to include visitors passing through an area and visitors on leisure trips from home (English Tourist Board/Employment Department Group, 1991, p. 6).

Although these are terms which have been used widely by policy-makers, is there any refinement to the definition which can be applied to tourism in the countryside? A distinction drawn in one review is that whereas tourists have always paid for their services, recreationists in the countryside frequently have not (Slee, 1989, p. 78).

In another study, the question raised is whether rural tourism is simply tourism in a rural location or is it something that requires more subtle definition?

What are the features which rural tourism must possess to be truly rural? Smallness of scale is an obvious parameter. Closeness to nature, absence of crowds, quietness and a non-mechanized environment are clear necessities. Personal contact – the antithesis of urban anonymity must be important. A sense of continuity and stability, of long and living history is another contender for inclusion. The possibility of getting to know an area and its people well is a special quality of the rural environment. And for any rural community, retention of individual identity is important as also is local control by manor house, farm, business or local council (Lane, 1988, p. 62).

This view might well be contrasted with other perceptions of what might be included under the heading of rural tourism. For example, the 1988 *Development Strategy for Rural Tourism* includes in its coverage such developments as time-share schemes, themed leisure attractions, steam railways and Sherwood Forest's Center Parc (English Tourist Board, 1988b, p. 13).

Attitudes to use of the countryside for recreation and tourism have been subject to considerable change. Prior to the late eighteenth century, wilderness areas were shunned but the influence of writers such as Scott and Wordsworth generated a new and continuing interest in mountains and other areas of scenic beauty (Drabble, 1979, p. 173). Inland resorts such as Windermere in the English Lake District developed as a result of this interest by the better-off but tourism was dominated by the seaside holiday. Countryside within easy reach of towns saw some growth in recreation. For example, northeast Cheshire became popular in the early twentieth century for activities such as scouting, with the creation of camps on the edge of the Peak District (Shercliff, 1987, p. 68).

However, it is only relatively recently that the countryside has become fully recognized as a tourist resource in its own right rather than, for example, a place to go to for one day on a week or fortnight's holiday by the sea.

PRESENT PATTERNS OF RURAL TOURISM IN BRITAIN

In 1989, British people took 31.5 million domestic holidays of four nights or more, and spent around £3.8 billion. In addition, some 17.1 million visits to Britain were made by people from overseas (British Tourist Authority, 1990, pp. 6–7). Although significant numbers of Britons also took holidays overseas, tourism is considered to be of importance to the British economy. The dominant impression that tourism is urban-based is borne out by Table 9.1, although the rural dimension is, nevertheless, of some significance.

Rural tourism in England and Wales for both domestic and overseas visitors comprises around a quarter of all trips, or a rather higher proportion if trips involving visits to small towns are included. This proportion

Table 9.1
England and Wales: tourism trips by geographical locations, 1987

Tourist trips	Britain (%)	England (%)	Wales (%)
Seaside	23 (31)	23 (32)	27 (34)
Small towns	20 (18)	21 (18)	11 (8)
Large towns	19 (14)	17 (13)	17 (10)
London	12 (8)	15 (10)	0 0
Countryside	24 (27)	21 (24)	40 (43)
Unspecified	4 (5)	4 (5)	7 (7)

( ) figures include visitors from overseas
Source: English Tourist Board (1988b), p. 12

is repeated in respect of bed-nights and spending. The rural component of the tourist picture is substantially higher in Wales compared with England but the data include business visits which are more likely to take place in urban rather than rural areas.

It is estimated that around £850 million a year is spent by British people actually staying in the countryside out of a total of £3 000 million spent by all types of visitor to the countryside (English Tourist Board, 1988b, p. 4). Overseas visitors are estimated to have spent around £200 million while visiting or staying in the countryside. Spending on tourism in England and Wales reflects the importance of traditional areas such as the West Country and the Lake District in attracting visitors (Figure 9.1).

Central to discussion about planning for tourism is the way in which provision can be made for a wide range of overnight accommodation in the countryside. Accommodation can be considered under several headings: serviced hotels, guest houses, bed and breakfast; or self-catering accommodation, caravans, camping, holiday-let cottages. The division between these different headings varies considerably. In Wales, for example, division of bed spaces is as shown in Figure 9.2.

The picture is not static, with a number of trends occurring in provision of different types of accommodation. In the case of hotels, for example, there has been a general picture of decline of bed spaces in favour of self-service accommodation. However, this has been offset to

214

Figure 9.1   England: tourism expenditure in excess of £200 per resident, 1988
Source: England Tourist Board (1988b), p. 7

an extent by the tourist industry's building hotels in association with other large-scale leisure developments, targeted at a specific strand of the market, such as the business sector. Tourism schemes undertaken or proposed in national parks have attracted considerable adverse publicity where they have been developed as part of leisure complexes (Council for National Parks, 1988, p. 1). There has been a trend for static holiday caravan sites to be redeveloped with chalets and for the term 'holiday park' to be used for managed recreation sites used for caravans, chalets

215

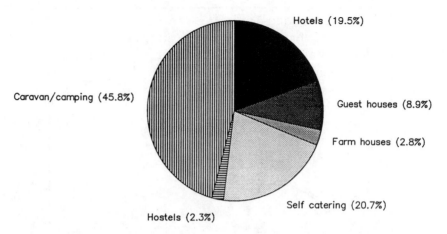

Hotels (19.5%)

Caravan/camping (45.8%)

Guest houses (8.9%)

Farm houses (2.8%)

Self catering (20.7%)

Hostels (2.3%)

Figure 9.2   Wales: tourist accommodation resources, 1990
Source: based on Wales Tourist Board (1990)

or tents (Woodman, 1985, p. 64). Although quite small in terms of overall scale of accommodation, growth of farm tourism has received attention as part of moves towards farm diversification (Slee, 1989, p. 63).

A trend which emerges from overviews of the tourism industry is that provision has moved 'up market', with developments such as the Sherwood Forest and Thetford Forest Center Parcs, themed attractions and the upgrading of holiday parks. However, these trends also remind us of the danger of the disappearance of traditional low-cost tourism which has been available in the countryside in the past.

The tourist component amongst total numbers of visitors to the countryside varies considerably. In the case of the national parks of England and Wales, then it is estimated that about a half of all visitor days are taken from home, about one third are from a holiday centre outside the national parks, and the remainder comprises people staying within the parks (National Parks Review Panel, 1991, p. 46). In some national parks, such as the Lake District and the Pembrokeshire coast, there is significant tourism accommodation within the park. At others, such as Dartmoor or Snowdonia, there is relatively little accommodation, although major coastal holiday resorts are to be found nearby. In the countryside, as in the city, there are a number of different strands of the

216

tourism market and tourists seeking enjoyment do not comprise a single group but include several different types who seek different things. However, a number of studies indicate that a common characteristic shared by many of them is an appreciation of the appearance of the countryside. Alongside other factors, the degree of 'natural endowment' of the countryside exerts a great influence on visitor levels (PA Cambridge Economic Consultants Ltd, 1987, p. 23).

THE COSTS AND BENEFITS OF TOURISM

Central to the promotion of tourism has been the notion that economic benefits accrue to its development. Government, for example, has stressed the industry's great potential for growth, job creation and enterprise and has sought ways of realizing opportunities for tourism (Cabinet Office, 1985, p. 2). In addition, up-beat promotional literature reminds us that: 'Tourism enterprise is thriving. Recent figures plot the growth in visitor numbers, tourist nights and visitor spending throughout the country. Most importantly, real jobs are being created at a rate of 1 000 each week, investment now exceeds £1 billion a year and the commitment of both public and private sectors has never been stronger' (English Tourist Board, 1988a, p. 1). Yet it is also regarded as an industry with high financial risks which is vulnerable to changes in the economic cycle. Commentators argue that claims for the benefits of tourism should be treated with a degree of caution and that the industry is not the panacea that some would seem to regard it (Shaw *et al.*, 1988, p. 5). Much attention has focused on the extent to which it is possible to estimate economic benefits from tourism using the concept of the multiplier, a measure of the impact of extra expenditure introduced into an economy as result of tourism investment. This extra expenditure can take the form of spending on goods and services by tourists visiting an area; investment by external sources; government spending; and export of goods stimulated by tourism. The difficulties of undertaking multiplier studies have been explored by several researchers and the literature includes a 1986 overview of the concept (Jackson, 1986). It points out the difficulties of identifying and isolating the tourist industry from other parts of the economy, mainly because the industry is so diffuse.

● It is not a well-defined industrial sector with a corresponding

217

activity heading in the UK Standard Industrial Classification nor in equivalent classifications elsewhere.

- It includes elements of the hotel and catering industries, transport, retailing, entertainment, information and recreational services.
- Few if any of the firms, individuals or public authorities engaged in these activities will be solely serving tourists, but will also be providing for local residents.

Despite the difficulties in assessment, multiplier analysis has provided a standard mechanism for measuring the economic benefits of tourism. Estimates of the scale of the multiplier effect have varied greatly, but the different approaches demonstrate concern with the extent to which the additional income generated by tourism 'leaks' out of or is withdrawn from the local economy. A typical example of leakage is illustrated if we take the case of a family spending a short break in a rural area, staying at a guest house. The amount of visitor expenditure generated by the visitors will depend on how much they spend and what proportion of that spend is directly attributable to items with a high local component. Self-catering accommodation, where visitors import most of their own food, would result in rather lower visitor expenditure than serviced facilities such as bed and breakfasts, guest houses or hotels. However, if self-service visitors go to several attractions in the area and if major spending is involved in entrance fees and purchases on site, then they may well be making a number of economic benefits to the local economy.

Table 9.2   Edinburgh:
total employment multipliers by type of accommodation

Serviced accommodation		Unserviced accommodation	
Hotel	0.19	Tent	0.12
Guest house	0.21	Caravan	0.11
Bed and breakfast	0.28	Friends and relatives	0.13
Halls of residence	0.33	Others	0.25
Weighted average	0.21		0.14

Source: Vaughan (1977), p. 34

Although the multiplier factors that have been adopted in research studies vary considerably it is clear that visitors generate different scales of multiplier. Jackson's review indicates a repeated pattern of serviced accommodation having high multipliers (bed and breakfasts) while unserviced accommodation such as tents and caravans had low multipliers. An example from one study is shown in Table 9.2.

JOBS GENERATED BY TOURISM

Studies carried out in five rural districts indicated the importance that employment in tourism can have locally (PA Cambridge Economic Consultants Ltd, 1988). For each area selected, studies were made of the following:

- composition of tourist facilities in the area, whether serviced, self-catering and camping/caravanning accommodation and attractions;
- estimates of direct employment at the facilities (comparisons were then made with estimates from the Census of Employment);
- estimates of employment in tourism, obtained by identifying local area supply linkages, short-term multipliers and visitors' other expenditure.

The contribution to the local economy of tourism was estimated as shown in Table 9.3. In Restormel, Ryedale and the western part of the Isle of Wight, tourist jobs account for around 10–12 per cent of total employment. The importance of tourism is emphasized further by row E, which records the support to the local economy offered by jobs indirectly related to tourism through supply linkages, off-site expenditure and multiplier effects. The study records the limitations that can restrict the impact of tourism on the local economy. The benefits might depend on the degree to which it is possible to fill the jobs generated through tourism. Clearly, if the jobs are filled by workers from outside, then the incomes paid are taken outside the area. However, if tourism results in people being taken off the unemployment register, then the benefits might be more visible.

The relationship between tourism and agriculture has been explored in a study of the Scilly Islands, where tourism has been shown to be an important support to the farming industry (Neate, 1987). Investigation

Table 9.3   England: jobs supported by tourism in rural areas, 1981

	Restormel	Rye	Tynedale	New Romney	Isle of Wight
A No of jobs	3 252	1 445	539	207	1 536
B Percentage of total employment	12.2	10.8	4.5	5.0	10.6
C Total direct and indirect jobs	10 008	5 276	1 476	596	5 456
D Ratio direct and indirect jobs	2.1	2.7	1.7	1.9	2.6
E Total direct and indirect tourist jobs as percentage of all jobs	37.6	39.5	12.3	14.4	37.5

Source: based on PA Cambridge Economic Consultants Ltd (1987), p. 57

showed that income from tourism subsidized losses incurred from farming – in some cases doubling household income. The studies also showed that not all farmers could share in the benefits from tourism to the same extent. On the larger farm holdings, tenants were more able to raise the capital needed for tourist developments such as chalets or conversions of dwellings. Other farmers would have nothing to do with tourism at all, preferring to 'eat limpets rather than resort to tourism to make money' (Neate, 1987, p. 18).

Table 9.4
Reasons given for providing farm-based accommodation

Reason given by respondent	%
To increase annual income	35
Enjoy the company	25
Falling income from farming	20
To use disused resources	16
To provide accommodation for potential family use later	3
A new interest	1

Source: Frater (1982), p. 14

Frater's (1982) study of farmers in Herefordshire is of interest in exploring motives of farmers and their families in opening tourist accommodation (Table 9.4). Although increased income was cited by respondents as being the main reason for providing accommodation, Frater stresses the importance of the social benefits and contacts that tourism can bring. The study emphasized the importance of women in running tourism enterprises, with the wife's or daughter's labour, which may be under-used, offering the impetus to cater for tourists. The tourism enterprise generates interest and income for the wife who would otherwise have little contact outside the farm, offering both income and employment while also being able to remain at home.

The investigation also showed that users of farm accommodation were seeking holidays *in* the countryside rather than farm holidays. Visitors sought the attractions of the countryside itself but, surprisingly, farm holidays did not appear to be particularly attractive for families with children. What many appear to value are the facilities that a farmer may be able to offer for horse-riding or fishing. Slee records a negative attitude on the part of some farmers towards tourism and 'townees' but notes that, amongst others, a '...positive desire to mix and meet people may lead to the provision of farm tourist accommodation for non-economic reasons' (Slee, 1989, p. 69).

An issue which often arises is the vehement opposition and support that tourism developments can generate. Development schemes, even of a minor nature, are able to generate both supporters and opponents to change. It can not always be assumed that local residents will always oppose tourism land-use changes and that business groups will be the greatest supporters of change (Roehl and Fesenmaier, 1987, p. 482). Nevertheless, within local communities, views can frequently polarize over the alleged benefits and costs of tourist initiatives.

THE ENVIRONMENTAL IMPACT OF TOURISM

The effects of tourism on the environment have been recorded by a number of researchers. They have categorized impacts as positive or negative, as changes to be feared or to be regarded as a positive force to channel change. Gunn notes the way in which prior to the introduction of tourism as a managed activity many sites were subject to considerable pressure and to degradation, and now provide financial support for na-

Table 9.5   The costs and benefits of tourism

Benefits of tourism	Costs, negative effects
Halts emigration and creates jobs	Produces one-sided, vulnerable economy
Generates income	Promotes lopsided, uncoordinated growth
Finances infrastructure	Undermines earning power
Improves living conditions	Squanders land
Supports agriculture, helps preserve landscape	Places burden on nature
Promotes self-confidence amongst local people	Puts local people at mercy of external decision-makers, decreasing independence Undermines uniqueness of local culture Aggravates imbalances Contains seeds of social tension

Source: based on Muller (1990), p. 16

tional parks (Gunn, 1988, p. 5). In addition, the experience of visiting national parks and other scenic areas can have the effect of increasing public awareness of the need for conservation. A benefit noted by a number of commentators is that tourism can result in the increase in protection for cultural assets (Pigram, 1983, p. 207; English Tourist Board and Employment Department Group, 1991, p. 10).

Despite the assertions about the benefits of tourism, major environmental problems can be caused by tourist pressure. Perhaps the issues are most clearly spelled out by Muller (1990), and Table 9.5 attempts to produce a checklist of costs that may accompany the benefits from tourism.

The issues involved in assessing the effects of tourism on local populations are outlined in a study of tourism in Badenoch and Strathspey in Scotland (Getz, 1982, p. 16). The investigation reminds us of the great difficulty in balancing evidence provided in the form of quantifiable criteria (such as the raising of personal and household incomes); and the evidence of much more subjective criteria such as a general concern about over-dependence on tourism.

The problems caused by rural tourism are also underlined in a more recent review of the environmental impact of tourism which identified several ways in which conflict could arise (English Tourist Board/Employment Department Group, 1991a, p. 16):

- overcrowding, when the numbers of people at a site exceed the capacity of the place to handle them;
- traffic congestion, resulting in disruption to local road users, damage to roads and verges and visual intrusion, noise and pollution;
- wear and tear, which is largely confined to a limited number of sensitive heavily used locations;
- inappropriate development, with visitor pressure leading the need for new development to serve them, ticket kiosks, toilets, signs, car parks and others;
- conflicts with the local community, which can arise as picturesque locations change in character as tea rooms and souvenir shops take over from local shops.

Many of these impacts will be associated with pressure for use of the countryside by both day visitors and the tourist. However, particular impacts are associated primarily with tourists and can often have a

223

longer-lasting effect on a locality compared with pressures from day visitors. Self-catering accommodation can have an adverse effect on local communities, introducing another element of competition into local housing markets. In addition, tourist numbers can exceed local populations, putting stress on local services including water supplies and sewage treatment (Peak Park Joint Planning Board, 1989, p. 122).

Stressed in recent studies of tourism is the interdependence which exists between tourist, place and host community, and the need to develop tourist policies that are sustainable and not based simply on exploitation. The approach of Muller differs from most others in emphasizing the part that individual tourists can play as consumers. Rather than conforming to what the market may pressurize them to do, they can exercise a deliberate choice, taking a critical view of their own enjoyment of tourism in the light of its effects on the environment (Muller, 1990, p. 18). Such stances have led to consideration of the role that might be played by 'green' tourism in future policy-making.

In recent years, interest has grown in the notion of 'green tourism'. The term is taken to encompass a number of ideas, as follows (Lane, 1988, p. 61).

- Tourists who are sympathetic to green tourism tend to be value- rather than price-conscious and are socially and environmentally considerate.
- Green tourism initiatives are small-scale and involve slow developments by local interests, strengthening, not replacing farm economies, reusing existing buildings, adopting 'low tech' solutions and car-free concepts.
- Tourists undertake repeat visits and seek experience.
- Heritage is an important ingredient of green tourism.

Central to the concept of green tourism is understanding and explaining the relationship between the tourist and the host. In the past it has been unusual for local communities to be involved directly in the actual planning of tourist facilities and in considering the appropriateness of particular tourism ventures in their localities. Particularly in communities with declining rural industries and services, tourism is often put forward as an alternative way of generating income (Rural Development Commission, 1989). Most communities lack expertise to identify the best ways of attracting visitors, particularly approaches which bring benefits yet do not destroy the character of a rural community. However, the approach adopted in the Rural Tourism Development Project (RTDP) aims to demonstrate how local communities can produce their own tourism packages, emphasizing community involvement and local self-help (Lane, 1988, p. 62).

The RTDP operates through a forum set up in a village to identify tourism strategies, discover strengths and weaknesses and develop the market potential for tourism. A feature of a forum is that it tackles practical projects to improve visitor facilities such as waymarking paths, creating trails, tourist information points. In particular, the approach can assist participants to increase confidence, learning how to make use of grants or sponsorship and how to approach different tiers of government. The RTDP appears to be a welcome approach to enabling local communities to influence the form of tourism in their localities. It must take its place alongside urban-based initiatives such as community architecture and other self-help ventures.

It should be noted that as a result of the growth in use of the term 'green' tourism, acquiring a 'catch-all' nature, the term 'sustainable' tourism is increasingly being used to convey an image of a balance between visitor, place and host community (Lane, 1991, p. 2).

EVOLUTION OF A NATIONAL STRATEGY FOR RURAL TOURISM IN ENGLAND

Until the mid-1980s centrally inspired policies did little to distinguish rural tourism as a separate strand of tourism policy. For example, a 1981 manual on planning for tourism identified opportunities and constraints on tourism development in the countryside, but made little other attempt to identify a specific rural dimension to policy-making (English Tourist Board, 1981).

The first treatment of rural tourism as a significant strand of policy-making occurred with the 1988 strategy *Visitors in the Countryside* (English Tourist Board, 1988b). In keeping with the promotional approach to tourism development in the 1980s, the strategy asserts the role that tourism can play in strengthening the rural economy, as follows.

- The strategy will support measures which encourage more people to visit the countryside, raise the profile of the countryside as a

225

place to go to, in competition with inland towns and other destinations.

- The rural tourism strategy will maintain and enhance the quality of the rural environment, provide more facilities, improve access and information.
- It will encourage visitors to spend more money by providing more overnight accommodation, developing additional facilities, enhance the landscape providing user-friendly access to informal facilities such as footpaths and bridleways.
- The strategy encourages increased awareness of customer needs, use of local products, minimizing the impact of congestion, erosion, litter and other blemishes.
- Access will be of great importance in influencing potential markets available to different rural areas.
- Areas well placed to generate day visits by the development of new attractions and facilities will be close to major conurbations, but such areas may be subject to green belt policies which will inhibit the achievement of the full potential.
- The strategy stresses the need to define tourist areas of sufficient size to have a meaning in marketing terms.
- It emphasizes the value of high-quality strategic developments such as Center Parcs, Langdale timeshare in the Lake District and Alton Towers theme park.
- It recognizes the importance of the financial assistance scheme offered under section 4 of the Development of Tourism Act 1969. Although assisting in widening tourism opportunities, for example, in provision of holiday cottages, grant aid under this measure was subsequently withdrawn.

The strategy can be seen as part of the continuing attempt to expand the tourism industry. It followed on from the strongly development-oriented *Pleasure, Leisure and Jobs* study which sought to encourage dispersal of visitors, increase availability of grants for farm tourism in less favoured areas, and review the economic criteria for evaluating and ranking road improvements in order to give weight to the commercial significance of tourism and leisure uses (Cabinet Office, 1985, p. 1).

A further influence on rural tourism provision stems from a reactivated Development Commission (now Rural Development Commission) with a much stronger remit to promote economic growth in rural areas in

England (Rural Development Commission, 1989). Measures such as the designation of Rural Development Areas and the preparation of programmes of development for such areas has thrown the spotlight on rural tourism. An important theme in development programmes submitted to the Commission by local authorities is concern with ways in which tourism opportunities might be enhanced.

Absent from the ETB strategy is consideration of the needs of the 40 per cent of British adults who do not take a holiday in a given year. Low incomes, together with disability either of an individual or of a relative, can act as major constraints for a significant minority of the population. In an investigation into holiday making and disadvantage, the Baker report noted that, unlike the situation in France, there was no history in Britain of government directly subsidizing holidays (English Tourist Board, 1989a, p. 48). One reason for this was the existence of low-cost holiday opportunities through guest houses, bed and breakfast establishments and caravanning and self-catering. Some charitable trusts can provide support for disadvantaged groups, but the Baker working party argued that the tourism industry itself could do much to assist: for example, by donating unsold holidays at resorts to low-income families. In discussing rural tourism, commentators have asserted that 'The case for subsidized holidays as part of a social welfare programme is overwhelming' (MacEwen and MacEwen, 1987, p. 85). The term 'social tourism' is not widely used in Britain and it currently features little in promotion of rural tourism. However, the concept has a place to play in any discussion about the future form and scope of national policies for rural tourism.

TOURISM DEVELOPMENT ACTION PROGRAMMES

Acknowledging the need to translate broad objectives for rural tourism into practice, increasing emphasis has been placed on the preparation of detailed programmes describing the ways in which proposals for tourism development can be actually executed. Given the close links between tourism planning and management and marketing and finance, it is not surprising to find that tourism plans place considerable emphasis on finding the right mechanisms to promote programmes. A feature of such approaches is the use of coordinated partnerships involving the regional tourist boards, local authorities, and operators from the private sector.

227

One example of a mechanism to adopt a coordinated approach is the tourism development action programme (TDAP), a 'partnership involving both the public and private sectors, intended to develop tourism activity and expenditure through development, marketing and other initiatives over a short period' (English Tourist Board, 1988b, p. 24). As an example, the Kielder Forest TDAP promoted by the English Tourist Board identifies ways of developing the tourist potential of an area surrounding a major reservoir opened in the mid 1970s, containing a small population but including extensive areas of forest, moorland and farmland (English Tourist Board, 1985b, p. 2).

The TDAP outlines the social and economic background to the area and produces an inventory of accommodation, attractions and means of access. Like other tourism investigations it identifies the strengths, weaknesses and opportunities of the area before listing the key issues confronting tourism in the area. Again, like other studies it identifies the different sectors of the tourist market that might be met by the resources of the area (Table 9.6).

In terms of developing the potential of rural tourism the programme stresses the following (English Tourist Board, 1985b, p. 8):

- identifying and developing additional recreational activities to strengthen existing opportunities;
- developing new attractions, which broaden the appeal of Kielder as a destination for visitors and tourists;
- promoting Kielder as a venue for events at national and regional level;
- encouraging provision of more holiday accommodation offering a wide range of facilities, including major all-the-year-round self-catering complexes as well as smaller developments for all-year or extended season;
- providing many more opportunities for spending money for the visitor, places to visit and see, buy best Northumbrian crafts, eat and drink best regional food;
- preparing and implementing a marketing plan, improving standards of existing facilities, information, signing;
- encouraging investment in the area, especially from the private sector;
- ensuring effective coordination and implementation of marketing, management and development initiatives in the area.

Table 9.6 Kielder, Northumberland: product market fit table

Areas of potential	Long holidays		Short break	Overseas	Youth activity	Family	Elderly	Day
	Mass	Up-market						
Attractive landscape	○	●	●	●	–	○	–	○
Activity holidays	○	●	●	○	●	●	–	–
Water sports/countryside activities	○	●	●	●	●	○	–	○
Major events	–	–	●	○	○	○	–	●
Quality self catering	●	●	●	●	–	●	○	–
Camping/caravanning	○	○	○	–	●	○	–	–
Growth sectors	–	–	●	●	●	–	●	●
Strong off-season	–	–	●	●	○	–	●	○

● Major impact   ○ Limited impact   – Little or no impact

Source: based on English Tourist Board (1985b), p. 9

TDAPS represent one way in which coordinated approaches to tourism development might be adopted. With the growth in the number of potential funding sources for tourism development, county councils have taken an important role in acting as catalysts in pooling ideas and information on tourism matters (Lancashire County Council, 1988). They have commissioned a wide range of tourism studies, often following a formula based on the acronym SWOT: strengths, weaknesses, opportunities and threats to tourism in particular localities. Some hundreds of such studies have been produced in Britain in recent years both by local authorities themselves and by consultants. However, most have been produced for small geographical areas, far too small normally to have an identity that is of more than local importance. Few can match the scale of the identity areas described as having a proper meaning in the English Tourist Board's rural tourism development strategy (English Tourist Board, 1988b, p. 10).

A further promotional strand of policy has been the issue of development prospectuses for rural tourism. An example is that for the Settle–Carlisle Railway which runs through the Yorkshire Dales National Park in northern England. The line was threatened with closure for several years, but public objection resulted in the line being saved from closure in 1989. A factor which may have influenced the Ministerial decision to keep the line open was the potential it offered for development of tourism and the support given by several public agencies. A 1990 development prospectus (Biggs, 1990, pp. 12–13) outlined opportunities as follows:

- new tourist attractions, based on a big increase in numbers of users of the railway line in recent years;
- local and thematic attractions: developing and interpreting these including farm visits, nature trails, pony trekking, cycle hire and industrial archaeology;
- inclusive tours based on coach or rail, ring and ride services, taxis;
- accommodation: hotels, bed and breakfast on farms and self-catering;
- retailing and catering: small-scale opportunities including use of railway buildings;
- residential development, exploiting potential for small-scale schemes outside the national park, encouraging higher year-round use of the railway line;

- industrial and commercial development, particularly at the settlement of Hellifield, with opportunities with a local labour market.

Among the mechanisms to assist development, the prospectus suggests the creation of a development company by the Rural Development Commission and the English Tourist Board. Funded primarily from private sources its task would be to identify, promote and assist in the implementation of business projects along the corridor of the Settle–Carlisle railway line. Although the prospectus identifies several small-scale sites on the corridor, the greatest potential is seen to be at a site at Hellifield. The site lies outside the national park and comprises around 60 ha of mainly farmland with potential for development as a golf course with hotel and conference centre, themed pub restaurant at the station buildings, a railway heritage centre, railway exhibition, craft workshops, holiday accommodation and extensive car parking. Pump-priming finance could be available from the local authority and the site would involve using the existing railway station and vacant former railway land as the focus for the development.

The Settle–Carlisle Railway example illustrates ways in which alliances have been created to achieve rural tourism objectives. However, problems of fragmentation of interests are common, and the difficulties are most clearly exhibited in the failure by public and private agencies effectively to market and promote rural tourism. A trend has been for the creation of consortia, groups of providers who jointly market the tourist 'product.' They include groups of farmers who provide accommodation, such as the Peak Moorlands Farm Holiday Group (Frater, 1982, p. 19). In addition, a number of tourism associations have been created in recent years. Often with secretarial and administrative support from local authorities, such associations work to promote tourism in a locality, particularly in respect of promotion and publicity.

Some of the problems associated with the development of tourism in the countryside stem from the complexity of the relationships between different public and private agencies (Figure 9.3) pressing for different environmental and tourism policies (English Tourist Board/Employment Department Group, 1991, p. 17). From earlier discussion, it could be expected that conflict between different agencies would be most apparent in the national parks and other designated areas. Yet here, at least at a national level, there appears to be accord on the adoption of principles for tourism development agreed between two of the main public agen-

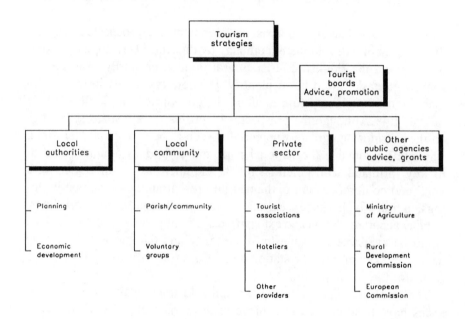

**Figure 9.3   Relationship between different agencies involved in
tourism provision**

cies (Countryside Commission, 1989f). Table 9.7 outlines the principles
which are recommended for tourism policies by the Countryside Commission and the English Tourist Board in national parks. A similar set of
principles has also been drawn up for other areas of countryside in
England and Wales, too.

There is, nevertheless, an underlying tension between those perceiv-
ing tourism as a business and those anxious to restrict tourism development for environmental reasons. Stress has been placed on the need for
positive rather than restrictive objectives if tourism is to play a proper
role in the socio-economic development of rural areas (Tourism and
Recreation Research Unit, 1981, p. 279). Tourism development action
programmes offer a framework for advancing such positive objectives.
However, they are advisory policy mechanisms only, providing a limited
overview. Whether TDAP arrangements work best at a regional and

Table 9.7 Principles for tourism in national parks

Principle	Content
Conservation	Tourist industry should help protect landscapes and wildlife by supporting practical conservation
Enjoyment	Tourism should draw on the special character of the national parks, with emphasis on quiet open-air recreation, culture, history and wildlife
Rural economy	Tourist industry should support the economy of local communities using local employees, products and services and supporting traditional skills and activities
Development	Facilities should respect quality of landscape and environment in national parks, tempered by capacity of site and surrounds and ability to absorb visitors, bringing sympathetic new uses to historic buildings and derelict sites
Design	Development should be in keeping with landscape, seeking to enhance it; major alterations to the landscape are unacceptable
Marketing	Should be designed to deepen enjoyment, appreciation, understanding and concern for national parks

Source: based on Countryside Commission, English Tourist Board (1989)

county level where there are well-established agencies, or at the local level, is a matter for debate (English Tourist Board/Employment Department Group, 1991b, p. 18).

STATUTORY PLANNING AND TOURISM DEVELOPMENT

Local planning authority responses to tourism range from strong constraint policies in areas under pressure for development such as national parks and coastal areas to other locations where, far from tourism being seen as a problem, it is seen as an opportunity to achieve desirable rural change. A number of repeated themes arise in deciding whether, where or when tourist facilities should be provided.

Firstly, authorities express concern about the declining base of serviced accommodation, notably hotels, as recorded in the Bala and Penllyn Local Plan within the Snowdonia National Park (Snowdonia National Park Authority, 1989). In the New Forest, stress is placed on the multiplier value of staying visitors, but concern is expressed about the loss of hotel accommodation because of the changing viability of existing businesses and the conversion of buildings to nursing and rest homes (New Forest District Council, 1991, p. 28). Of interest is the fact that serviced accommodation which has been lost can no longer be replaced under

Plate 9.1   A major problem faced by planning authorities is that of accommodating holiday caravan sites at countryside and coastal locations: Bigbury, Devon, 1991

existing planning policies which confine new hotels and guest houses to built-up areas located outside the New Forest itself. Another issue relates to the need to maintain a good range in the variety of accommodation, including meeting the needs of those seeking cheap and simple bedspaces at hostels, outdoor centres and in huts (Lake District Special Planning Board, 1986, pp. 5–6).

A second theme concerns the problems of accommodating caravans and camping sites in the countryside. From the provider's angle, the situation is one where 'Almost universal opposition by local planning authorities to the granting of consents for new sites on visual amenity grounds ensures that the supply of sites remains fixed, and that new development is restricted to upgrading or extension of existing sites' (Hillary, 1984, p. 99). In part at least, examination of planning policies would appear to underwrite this assertion. In Cornwall, tourism restraint policies are defined on the basis of the environmental capacity of the coast; within these areas, no additional accommodation for visitors will be permitted apart from hotel development, holiday flats and increased densities in touring sites in certain localities (Cornwall County Council, 1985, p. 29). In national parks, policies also tend to be highly restrictive. In the Lake District, for example, landscape areas of special development control are designated where permission will not normally be given to new caravan sites or extension of existing sites. Elsewhere, sites will be judged on such issues as access, the local and wider park environment and effect on local communities (Lake District Special Planning Board, 1986). On the other hand 'positive' provision, particularly for touring caravans, is proposed in some plans within 'preferred' areas. In Lincolnshire, permission will normally be given for transit and touring sites on sites accessible to inland recreational attractions and tourist centres (Lincolnshire County Council, 1982, p. 52). The Structure Plan for Devon produced by the county council provides for search areas for caravan and camping sites. However, this policy is considered to impose constraints on planning policies at the local level since the areas so defined do not 'allow the (South Hams) Council to adopt a more localized approach beneficial to both tourism and the environment' (South Hams District Council, 1984, p. 41). Other problems are associated with 'exempted' organizations which can hold caravan rallies and issue certificates exempting landowners from the need to obtain planning consent for up to five caravans. The situation is one where 'particular organizations are granted special privileges not available to the public at large and

235

which can give rise to situations which are directly counter to national park policy' (Lake District Special Planning Board, 1986, p. 9). Concern has been expressed by the commercial sector which considers that the same arrangement offers an unfair advantage to the 2 000 or so clubs and organizations which hold exemption certificates (Hodge, 1988, p. 13).

A third recurring theme is that of anxiety about the 'swamping' of local communities by staying visitors. In the Peak District, for example, it is recorded that the Edale and Wetton/Alstonefield areas can be overwhelmed with visitors who are caravanning or camping and who place a strain on local services (Peak Park Joint Planning Board, 1989, p. 121). This concern is particularly marked in the Snowdonia National Park where culture and language are seen to be threatened by large numbers of staying visitors. Here encouragement is given to tourism opportunities which are compatible with the natural environment of the area and which help and enhance visitors' appreciation of the cultural and linguistic character of the area (Snowdonia National Park Authority, 1989).

Another theme concerns the problem of devising planning policies which satisfactorily reflect the changing trends in tourism. Because of the changing tastes, planning policies tend to lag behind the realities. By the time that research has been carried out and translated into policies, the latter are likely to be out of date (Hillary, 1984, p. 101). The changing nature of demand is underlined in the case of caravan sites in Devon where the Dartmouth Local Plan records a considerable number of unused pitches in the county as a whole (South Hams District Council, 1985, p. 49). The problems of catering for changing demands of tourism was spelled out by the Edwards Committee review of national parks: 'Planning for tourist accommodation and facilities depends on the accurate anticipation of future leisure preferences. Although such preferences can be given a limited steer through marketing, they often reflect unpredictable changes in public taste and fashion' (National Parks Review Panel, 1991, p. 138). When fashion changes fast, existing facilities may need to be converted to new uses and investment is put at risk... 'we pander to fashion only to create monuments to yesterday's taste...should our parks welcome the latest fashion while insisting that all facilities are of right quality, well designed and adaptable to new uses?'

A final theme which receives attention is that relating to major attractions and strategic tourism projects. These are as likely to be used by visitors as well as by tourists, but the justification for their development is often that they provide 'all weather' alternative attractions of benefit

236

primarily to the tourist. A 1991 investigation into large-scale tourism leisure developments in the countryside called for more positive statements of policy towards such developments and sought to demonstrate to conservation groups that 'knee-jerk opposition to projects in rural areas is not always necessary' (National Economic Development Council, 1991, p. 2).

In national parks, the tendency is to look favourably only on those projects which build on traditional forms of enjoyment, and there is a major presumption against major proposals and tourist projects unrelated to the purposes for which designated landscapes were created. Thus favourable consideration will be given to projects which increase the visitor's appreciation of the national park (Lake District Special Planning Board, 1986, p. 12). However, shared leisure facilities such as swimming pools or leisure centres which might also be expected to be used by local populations may obtain support (Snowdonia National Park Authority, 1989). Such approaches can also be of help in underpinning the costs of providing of local community facilities (Highlands Regional Council, 1990, p. 72).

COMMENT

Tourism development can give rise to fundamental conflicts between amenity interests and economic change and development. Responses to tourism pressure by planning authorities have varied considerably, but increasingly they have recognized that economic benefits can accrue to certain types of tourist project. However, in drawing up policies they have acknowledged the need for a selective approach to tourism development: not all tourism is necessarily bad, not all is good. A trend in recent years has been the growth of pressure for the development of rural tourism not only from the industry itself, but from government agencies which have adopted strong market-oriented briefs towards tourism. A response to this trend has been for planning authorities to join in partnerships for the development of tourism which involve the industry as well as central agencies and can help to exert some control on the market processes. In a highly fragmented industry, such partnerships have also played a role in bringing together different policy-makers and in getting agreement to programmes for tourism development and promotion. Yet the relationship between those programmes and land-use controls remains unclear at times and they cannot be used to disguise quite fundamental conflicts that can arise in land-use planning for tourism.

The conflicts over the development of rural tourism raise important questions about the extent to which it is possible to achieve a 'balanced' approach to rural land-use planning. In areas of designated landscapes, such as national parks, there are normally restraints on tourism development. Yet these are also areas where there are likely to be pressures for strategic tourist developments. Policies based on anything other than restraint are unlikely to be considered but, in adopting such policies, there will also be implications for other policy areas including community development, employment, housing and social provision.

Thought has increasingly been given to finding ways of making tourism more environmentally acceptable. However, 'green tourism' often bears little relationship to accepted good practice in overseas countries. Much needs to be done if green tourism is to take more than the small sector of the market that it occupies at the moment. If it is to increase its stake, then more needs to be done to increase public and private providers' perceptions of the issues involved. In addition, heightened critical awareness amongst consumers can have a part to play in furthering the adoption of green tourism policies by providers.

Chapter 10

Public providers in a period of change

Public provision of recreation can be explained in terms of market failure in the supply of facilities or services. As in the case of services such as education, health, transport and the arts, the public sector is expected to respond to underprovision in recreation by itself supplying facilities and services or by subsidizing supply by other providers (Gratton and Taylor, 1985, p. 121). In addition, governments have regarded recreation as one of the community's everyday needs and provision of it can be seen as part of wider policies for the social services (Department of the Environment, 1975, p. 1).

Local government has traditionally been a direct provider of rural recreation sites and services. By contrast, central government agencies responsible for waterways, water catchment or forestry have tended to see recreation as a secondary activity, which is incidental to their main functions. However, these broad patterns which have developed over the last 50 years have been subject to considerable pressures for change, principally as a result of centrally inspired measures to achieve a different balance between public and private interests. In particular, this has been reflected in the surge of support for neo-liberal economics during the 1980s and concerted efforts to reduce the influence of the state. The impact of the new orthodoxy on the rural environment is complex and is only gradually evolving but it is likely to result in a major change in the context of rural policy-making (Bell and Cloke, 1989, p. 11).

The performance of the public sector in this period of major realignment of state responsibilities is examined in relation to four major providers of rural recreation in Great Britain: local authorities, the Forestry Commission, the privatized regional water authorities, and the British Waterways Board.

LOCAL AUTHORITIES AS PROVIDERS

There is no statutory requirement for local authorities actually to provide leisure services, including countryside recreation. Although this can be seen as a constraint, some providers see advantages in leisure not being a mandatory service. When interviewed as part of one investigation, local authority leisure services officers considered mandatory status could result in loss of flexibility and autonomy in policy-making (Coalter *et al.*, 1988, p. 153). Despite the discretionary status of leisure provision, local authorities have drawn up quite major programmes for the development of rural recreation.

In the years following the passing of the Countryside Act 1968, county councils took the lead in developing rural recreation sites. Early country park designations in the late 1960s and early 1970s show few non-county council schemes. More recently, district councils have taken an increasingly important role in developing rural recreation, particularly following local government reform in 1974. By 1990, just under half of expenditure on country parks and other related amenities was by county

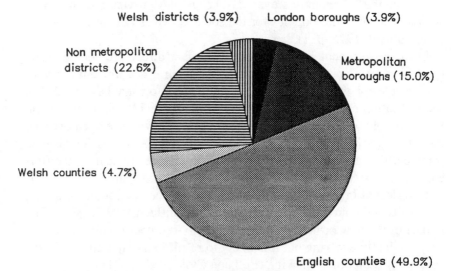

Welsh districts (3.9%) London boroughs (3.9%)

Non metropolitan districts (22.6%)

Metropolitan boroughs (15.0%)

Welsh counties (4.7%)

English counties (49.9%)

Figure 10.1 England and Wales: expenditure on country parks, amenity sites, picnic sites and nature reserves by local authorities, 1990–1991

Source: based on Chartered Institute of Public Finance and Accountancy (1990), p. 3

councils. Expenditure by local authorities in a sample of 323 out of 450 local authorities was estimated to be £40 630 000 (Figure 10.1; Chartered Institute of Public Finance and Accountancy, 1990, p. 3).

Although traditionally seen as a 'social service', leisure and recreation provision can offer a financial return on some investments (Figure 10.2). Thus, for golf courses most local authorities are able to cover gross expenditure costs. In the case of swimming pools then returns barely equal half of expenditure. The level of income for countryside sites varies between about 12 and 20 per cent of gross expenditure. That even these sums were recovered is perhaps surprising, given the problems of extracting payments from visitors at open spaces which often have many access points.

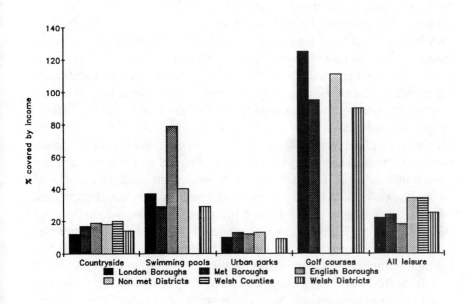

Figure 10.2 England and Wales: income as a percentage of gross expenditure on leisure and recreation, estimates 1990–1991

Source: based on Chartered Institute of Public Finance and Accountancy (1990), p. 5

The organization of rural recreation provision

In the late 1960s and early 1970s, planning departments of county councils frequently took on responsibilities for policy development, site identification, design, development and management. Specialist skills or services not available within a planning department would be obtained as part of 'internal trading' arrangements with other departments. Thus, a planning department might be responsible for policy formulation and site development, but management would be undertaken by another department: for example, a county estates department. Special committees were sometimes created to deal primarily with recreation and countryside matters (Miles and Seabrooke, 1977, p. 38).

Rural recreation activities became a central focus of specially created leisure services departments. The result was an increasing separation of the county statutory and informal plan-making from site design, implementation and management. This separation has not been without its problems and gave rise to conflict (Miles and Seabrooke, 1977, p. 42).

A further trend has been for rural recreation to be provided by district councils following local government reorganization in 1974. Even metropolitan district councils found that significant stretches of countryside were within their areas. In all types of district authorities, unified leisure services departments were created which bridged a wide range of facilities, urban and rural, indoor and outdoor. At first, district interests were primarily involved in managing parks and open spaces in urban areas. However, this was not always the case and districts now undertake major programmes of urban fringe recreation developments (Salford City Council, 1989, pp. 8–9). In the expansion of recreational services departments or sections, the role of the leisure profession was seen to be crucial (Kirby, 1985, p. 72). However, fragmented professional structure has caused problems in finding an appropriate identity for those working in the field (Countryside Commission, 1990e, p. 11).

A trend has been for authorities to provide leisure facilities in conjunction with other agencies. Such cooperative approaches have included all stages of the recreation site development process, including shared finance and management (Figure 10.3).

Joint management schemes have been widely used and can involve a wide range of interests from different agencies. For example, officer working parties can provide a basis for cooperation between several participating agencies who control their recreation schemes either sepa-

242

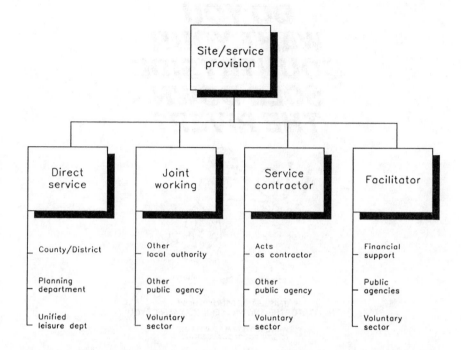

Figure 10.3 **Arrangements for site identification, design, development and management of rural recreational sites by local authorities**

rately or jointly with others. Joint working arrangements in Greater Manchester instituted by the former County Council provided financial support for recreational and environmental projects for schemes undertaken as part of an agreement made jointly with district councils (Maund, 1982, pp. 83–85; Elson, 1986, p. 210). Policy frameworks were set by joint members' committees who were committed to agreed programmes of work extending outside individual members' own districts. Prior to the demise of the former county council in 1986, there was concern about the possible demise of joint working arrangements. In 1989, local concern was expressed in the case of the Mersey Valley area when it appeared that Trafford Borough was intending to withdraw from the shared joint working arrangements with Manchester and Stockport which operated in that area. Such a withdrawal would enable firmer internal

243

**DO YOU
WANT YOUR
COUNTRYSIDE
SOLD DOWN
THE RIVER?**

*THIS LEAFLET SHOWS HOW
THE LOSS OF THE GMC WILL SERIOUSLY AFFECT YOU*

*WRITE TO YOUR M.P. AND FIGHT
TO SAVE YOUR LOCAL SERVICES*

Figure 10.4   Abolition of the metropolitan counties in 1986
Source: Greater Manchester Countryside Unit

control to be maintained by the local authority but it was feared that a valley-wide, unified approach to management would be lost (Figure 10.4).

A further variation on this theme has been for joint management schemes devised with managers of other resources such as forests and woodland. Here, the partner could be a private or voluntary organization but the precise nature of the link-up would depend on the nature of the mutual benefit obtained by each participant. The considerable interest in such arrangements reflects the legal and financial constraints which now face local government. In particular, the impact of the Community Charge, introduced in 1990, focused attention on its possible effects on revenue budgets and capital programmes and has doubtless encouraged search for partners to share the burden of provision.

244

Local authorities are unlikely to be the major providers of rural recreation facilities as they were during earlier periods of major public funding (Smart, 1990, p. 186). Increasingly, the local authority might be only one of several 'partners' who might be used to implement schemes. For example, the broad and flexible approach of groundwork trusts may make them attractive partners for local authorities in tackling specific problems in urban fringe areas (Jones, 1990, p. 64). Partnerships might include trading arrangements whereby a county council provides a countryside management service for a district council and avoids the latter authority having to replicate an up-and-running service.

The change in the climate of public spending in Britain has resulted in greater concern to see that the public obtains value for the money spent on its behalf. In Britain the Audit Commission has scrutinized several aspects of local authority expenditure in leisure and recreation provision (Audit Commission, 1988, 1989, 1990). Under the provisions of the Citizens' Charter performance criteria for some at least of the 200 or so suggested indicators of local authority service delivery are likely to include recreation services (Audit Commission, 1991, p. 4). In respect of rural recreation provision, cost-consciousness has been on management agendas for several years. Witness to this has been a number of marketing studies which have investigated ways of efficiently delivering services to visitors. An additional influence on policy has been a growing awareness of the limited constituency of users of countryside recreation facilities. That it is the better-off sections of society who benefit from rural recreation has led some to question how far public recreation facilities should be subsidized or whether fee income levels should be increased (Reiling et al., 1983, pp. 203–205).

In reviewing the effectiveness of service delivery, the Audit Commission emphasizes the need to set targets; to get to the right customers in the right way with the right services; and to keep to stated policies. Applying these principles of review directly to countryside recreation is not quite so straightforward as it might be with some other local government services, such as education. 'Hidden' benefits or costs may be borne by other departments or voluntary groups and can be difficult to quantify. However, an indication of how performance criteria might be applied to rural recreation is given in Table 10.1.

Difficulties can arise in clarifying the relationship between economic efficiency and performance and the pursuit of environmental or social goals. The national parks efficiency study cited examples of projects

245

Table 10.1   Measurement of effectiveness
of delivery of countryside recreation service

Issue	Example of assessment
Resources used	Cost or number of staff, vehicles, matching staff to demand, running costs per unit of use
Users	How many people use facilities/service in comparison with 'need' or targets set? e.g. elderly, people with disabilities Reaching more or different customers, marketing
Service provided	Centralized/decentralized structure Number of facilities, hours of opening
Quality of service	Standards for key features of service, number of complaints; visitor surveys, staff training and motivation
Ultimate results	The outcomes or contribution to quality of life: overall estimate of outcomes, e.g. trends in use of facilities

Source: based on Audit Commission (1990), pp. 3 and 64–66

where liabilities had been acquired without full justification in terms of need, appropriateness or consequences of continuing maintenance (Arthur Young, McClelland, Moores and Co., 1984, pp. 27–28). Expenditure on car parking, toilets and an information point did not 'appear to be based on a clear identification of need'. Or, 'opportunities to generate income to offset the costs of facilities provided were not always rigorously pursued.' These examples suggested there was scope for reducing the net costs of running car park sites and hostels; and for increasing income from car park charges in urban centres, villages and heavily used locations.

Such approaches as these raise important questions about the objectives and functions of recreational planning and management and the value which is placed on the less tangible social and environmental considerations. As a minimum, providers are expected to say whether broad social benefits justify the resources involved. Comparison of the 'value for money' of different facilities and services could follow from such financial appraisals, including, for example, examination of resource costs per admission to sites (Coopers and Lybrand, 1979, p. 3).

Despite the difficulties of assessing the 'return' on rural recreation, some have long argued for a more rigorous and questioning approach to provision. Review techniques have their drawbacks, but it is now generally accepted that they perform an important part of the process of planning and management. A reviewer in 1990 noted that within the changed climate new working relationships with other services had evolved; new budgetary regimes had been introduced with a constant need for review of objectives and performance; increasingly, there were moves towards income generation from alternative sources of finance, preparation of full business plans and, possibly, full privatization of countryside services (Flanagan, 1990, p. 3).

The introduction of competition into provision of local authority services

Deregulation of public transport, opting out of schools and the privatization of water authorities are only a few instances of attempts to create public services that are intended to be more efficiently run and that result in cost savings. For providers of recreation services the spur for change has come from a variety of sources, but of particular importance has been the Local Government Act 1988. An important component of the Act was a requirement for local authorities gradually to put much of their work out to competition in the period 1990–1994. Compulsory competitive tendering is considered to result in improvements in the effectiveness of services, as client departments detach themselves from the day-to-day problems of running services and increasingly question how far provision matches the varied demands of the community (Audit Commission, 1988, p. 2).

In Britain, competition for tendering to undertake work done on parks and open spaces was introduced in several phases. Under the Local Government Act 1988, local authorities were required to divide their recreation services into 'contractor' and 'client' divisions, with the former having to compete with other tenderers for contract work. The provisions apply primarily to urban recreation, particularly maintenance of

247

parks and open spaces. A section of the Act specifies that maintenance work involving research or specific conservation activities may be excluded from the tendering process. Of course, this may not always remain the case. In countryside recreation, where continuity of management style and joint working can be vitally important in achieving stated goals, it remains to be seen whether the market will be able successfully to take account of such activities (Flanagan, 1990, p. 3).

Different strands of argument, seemingly at the opposite ends of the political spectrum, appear to be converging towards agreement on the need accurately to measure the full costs and benefits of public policy-making. In the case of 'recreation as welfare' policies: 'The need to target public expenditure as carefully as possible across the whole range of community and public services is a reminder that recreation investors need to identify the main beneficiaries of their resources' (Countryside Commission, 1989a, p. 6). This stress on careful scrutiny of policy delivery is not all that different from some of the assertions made by the Audit Commission, which has articulated the need for a strong market dimension to local authority operations.

Representation, influence and interest

Although local authorities widely assist others to promote recreation policies rather than taking a lead role themselves, restrictions have gradually been introduced to limit that involvement. In a measure aimed amongst other things at curtailing local authorities' control and financial interests in 'arms-length' companies and 'companies subject to local authority influence', government passed the Local Government and Housing Act 1989. The Act enables the Secretary of State to make restrictions on the involvement that local authorities can have in trusts which may be subject to their influence. A trust seeking local authority assistance in developing a country park would now note that section 72 of the Act places restrictions on the extent to which the authority can participate in such a venture. A trust is considered to be 'subject to local authority influence' if 20 per cent of voting rights are held by persons associated with the authority or if over a third of the trust's income is made up of contributions from local authorities. Desirable as public authority involvement might be, this section is likely to limit the support that 'alternative' agencies can make to recreation policy-making. A related restriction enables the Secretary of State to attribute to the local authority's cash limits the whole of the expenditure of the trust concerned. The implications of this element of the legislation could be to restrict significantly the ability of a local authority to act as a facilitator, even in a modest way.

Despite the problems described above, in developing strategies for leisure and recreation, the local authority will remain the only body with an electoral mandate to act on behalf of the whole community (Benington and White, 1988, pp. 251–252). It is argued that local authorities can provide inspired leadership to 'harness the energies of many different agencies (public, voluntary and private) behind a common vision and sense of direction for the leisure services for the whole community.'

THE FORESTRY COMMISSION

The second public provider considered is one for whom recreation has generally been incidental to the planting, management and harvesting of timber. The Forestry Commission was created in 1919 at a period when the need for increased home timber production was being expressed. Sheail records that a first 'forest park' was opened to visitors in Argyllshire in Scotland in 1936 with the number of people staying overnight increasing from 20 419 in 1937 to 30 870 in 1938. Further national forest parks were opened in the Forest of Dean in 1939 and in Snowdonia in 1940. In spite of a number of practical difficulties, '...the Forestry Commission became the most important statutory body for the provision of facilities for outdoor recreation' (Sheail, 1981, p. 190). During the immediate post-war years, the Commission continued what must with hindsight seem a considerable expansion of its recreational activities by the creation of forest parks in Glenmore (1948), Queen Elizabeth Forest (1953) and Border Forest (1955).

Commission interest in forest recreation continued, with major studies being undertaken of visitor behaviour in selected forests (Mutch, 1967; Colenutt and Sidaway, 1973). Firm encouragement was given to increased recreation provision in the forests under the Countryside Act 1968 for England and Wales and the Countryside (Scotland) Act 1967. Hall records that between 1970 and 1972, the number of picnic sites increased from 133 to 195, car parks from 122 to 150 and forest rails and walks from 124 to 262. However, he also noted that Commission forests were still poorly advertised, relatively unknown and badly signposted (Hall, 1974, pp. 149–151). The value of forests was nevertheless considerable:

- The recreation potential of the forests was greatly enhanced by there being a unified national ownership.
- The forests had the ability readily to absorb cars and their occupants.
- Limitations were present in the form of constraining legal agreements, problems of peak loading and reluctance on the part of forest workers to have to enter into activities very different from what they had been trained for (Hall, 1974, p. 161).

An important influence, too, was the status of the Commission as a government agency, subject to external financial control from the Treasury. In this situation, 'more heady enthusiasm rapidly wilts in more difficult economic circumstances, and recreation, marginal to other operations, is an early candidate for cuts' (Patmore, 1983, p. 197).

Present-day organization

Today, Commission woodland amounts to just under half of the 2.1 million ha of forest in Great Britain. The resource is widely distributed but since much of it is residual land and a by-product of the agricultural industry, occupying poorer-quality land, it is not always in the right place for recreational use (Scott, 1989, p. 15). Management in Britain is undertaken through seven regional conservancies, but policy is largely determined by 65 managers at local district level. In theory, visitors are welcome in all forests on foot, although adherence to this principle will vary greatly depending on management and protection of the forest and legal agreements which may be in operation (Table 10.2).

The two functions of the Commission are reflected in the activities of the Forestry Authority which seeks to encourage forestry planting, notably through the operation of a Woodland Grant Scheme; and secondly, through the Forestry Enterprise which directly undertakes forestry planting and management programmes itself. In the 1980s much investment took place in private forestry because planting qualified for tax benefits. However, from March 1988 fiscal policy changes reduced the taxation advantages. In order to ensure that afforestation remained an attractive

Table 10.2
Great Britain: Forestry Commission recreational facilities, 1989

Camping/caravan sites	32
Picnic places	185
Forest walks/trails	246
Visitor centres	8
Arboreta	4
Cabins/holiday homes	71
Forest drives	11

Source: Forestry Commission (1991), p. xxvi

proposition, a substantial increase was made in grants paid for planting schemes. Investors received around £250 per hectare for planting. However, the actual take-up of the opportunities seemed small compared with the previous arrangements and the Government's target of increasing the total area of forest seems unlikely to be achieved (Tompkins, 1990, p. 70).

A problem which will persist into the future concerns the effects of 'privatization' of Forestry Commission land. It can both acquire and dispose of land under the Forestry Act 1967. The Commission can dispose of land for any purpose but the land should be surplus to requirements or should form part of a programme of land disposal required by government. The latter requires the Commission to dispose of some 100 000 ha of land between 1989 and the end of the century, with no less than half that area being disposed of within the first half of the period (Hansard, 1989).

The total area of land in Commission ownership and which is managed as part of the Forestry Enterprise was some 1.39 million ha in 1990. As part of the disposals policy, 1989–90 saw the sale of almost 8 000 ha of land of various categories with income from disposed land, buildings and plantations amounting to £12 955 million (Table 10.3).

Today, recreation is an important component of Commission activity, with a significant increase in the numbers of recreational facilities in 11 forest parks and other woodlands. Many facilities are targeted at the day visitor, and include paths and forest roads for walking, and in some instances pedal cycling; car parks, picnic places, viewpoints, forest walks,

251

Table 10.3   Great Britain:
disposal and acquisition of Forestry Commission land, 1989–1990

	Disposed *(ha)*	*Acquired* *(ha)*
Plantations	4 509	1
Planting land	476	444
Other land	2 866	60
Total	7 851	505

Source: Forestry Commission (1991), p. xxiii

overnight accommodation, such as caravan and camping sites and self-serviced accommodation. A 1989 survey showed, too, that forests offered a wide range of specialist pursuits and emphasized the scale of the resource as a whole (Travis, 1989, pp. 30–31).

The General Household Survey of 1987 included questions on visits to forests (Office of Population Censuses and Surveys, 1989b, p. 65). The results suggest that visitors seek a surprising degree of 'organization' at sites, wishing to see more than just access to woodland and generally expecting provision to extend to toilets, nature trails, car parks, picnic areas, visitor information centres and much of the other 'equipment' found at rural recreational sites.

National forestry policy

The 1980s have been described as a decade of transition for forestry policy as the industry moves from an 'industrial' to 'post-industrial' era (Mather, 1991, p. 247). Changes which have taken place in recent years include moves to remove Forestry Commission activities from Treasury control, the sale of Commission land to the private sector, the setting of targets for planting at around 33 000 ha per annum, and a general move to increase the efficiency and commercial effectiveness of the Commission. Afforestation in Britain is highly dependent on financial incentives and despite moves in the 1980s to reduce dependence on public subsidy, in 1989–90 some £61 million of grant in aid was received from government (Forestry Commission, 1991, p. 10).

In disposing of land, the Commission is required to work to guidelines set by government. The Commission is keen to 'consolidate and rationalize the Commission's forestry estate in an orderly manner, taking account of wood supply commitments and the use of its forests for public access and recreation' (Forestry Commission, 1991, p. 15).

The disposal programme has been the subject of considerable criticism. The Ramblers' Association cites the example of Pen Wood in Somerset, where car parks and picnic areas shown on the Ordnance Survey map have been removed by the new private owners. It points out that 'landowners get important recreational benefits from their own woodlands and that there is a certain reluctance to want to share that with other people' (House of Commons Agriculture Committee, 1990, p. 217). Loss of permissive access is of particular concern. Access to forest areas may not be lost altogether but it is very much more restricted. In one case, 'general access before sale was replaced by access confined to a short permissive footpath' (House of Commons Agriculture Committee, 1990, p. 217).

In response to such criticisms various policy responses have emerged including an announcement from government that the Forestry Commission should give advance notice to local authorities of intended disposals of woodland under its management (Hansard, 1990). The Commission could then enter into legal agreement with local authorities ensuring continued public access after sale. Whether the local authorities would have the resources or interest to enter into such agreements is unknown. In addition, these arrangements would not appear to apply to woodland which at present is not used for recreation but which might be used for that purpose in the future.

However, any curtailment of the ability of the Commission to sell land to anyone it feels appropriate will limit its ability to meet its requirement to dispose of plantations, and affect its economic efficiency. The latter is a central plank in the policy of reducing dependence on the Exchequer for subsidy.

Policy development in the future

A more strongly commercial approach has also been adopted by the Commission towards recreation policies. Thus, between 1986 and 1990, the yield on commercial recreation activities doubled from 5.7 to 10.7 per cent. Despite this, subsidy continues to be paid to the Commission for the conservation, amenity and recreation value of Britain's forests. Over the three-year period 1987–90 some £27 million was received in Exchequer subsidy under this heading (Forestry Commission, 1991, p. 40).

There is every incentive for the Commission to continue to increase the commercial return from recreation, including, for example, provision of camping, caravan and chalet sites. In some locations there may be scope for more strongly focused commercial tourism development. Currently, the Commission's forests are visited by some 50 million people a year, although demand is uneven with a levelling-off of visits among some categories of visitor. A proportion of visits can be directly measured in terms of commercial returns to the Commission in the form of payment for fees. Attempts are also being made to quantify the value of the non-commercial benefits of forests (Forestry Commission, 1991, p. 11).

Some degree of public financial support for forest recreation seems inevitable. Continued availability of that help could depend on the Commission's obtaining as wide a constituency of support as possible by increasing public awareness of and sympathy for the forest environment. An indication of efforts to widen this constituency was seen in 1989, when the Commission launched a campaign to promote forestry under the maxim *Great Britain: Great Forest* (Forestry Commission, 1989). This campaign, with its emphasis on the amenity value of forests and as resources in whose management the community can share, is a further indication that recreation is now a central plank of Commission policy.

Community forests and the new national forest in the English Midlands

A 1987 Countryside Commission policy statement advocated the creation of forests in urban fringe areas (Countryside Commission, 1987b, p. 23). Twelve areas were subsequently identified as possible locations for 'community forests' with the Forestry Commission as a central partner in the initiative. The idea of such forests is that people are able to visit them easily and that within them it is possible to undertake a wide range of recreational activities. The area of such forests could be quite large, ranging from say 12 000 to 17 000 ha. They may be continuous but they could comprise networks of interconnected woodland areas with roads, bridleways and footpaths linking them.

Project teams have been created in order to implement the community forest initiative with the most advanced work being in south Tyne and Wear, in south Staffordshire and east London. An important feature of the initiative will be forestry expansion in areas which are relatively well endowed agriculturally when compared with the traditional upland af-forested areas. Although there will be considerable reliance on private owners participating in the scheme, much will depend on there being sufficient benefits to make it worthwhile for them (Countryside Commission, 1990a, p. 18). Bishop (1991, pp. 8–10) reminds us of the constraints within which community forests will operate.

- Limited funds mean that scope for public-sector land acquisition will be minimal; the Forestry Commission is in a good position to purchase land, but urban fringe land prices may make this prohibitive.
- Investigations with landowners suggest that even with enhanced fiscal incentives, owners are unlikely to be interested in planting schemes if unlimited public access is required as part of a grant offer.
- 'Positive planning' would seem to offer opportunities with the use of planning agreements and conditions securing the development of woodlands as after uses. However, this could be in conflict with landscape protection policies: for example, in green belts.
- Community forest concepts need to be accompanied by strategic-level planning in order to implement major landscape and land-use restructuring in urban fringe areas.

Inevitably there is likely to be a close relationship between community forest initiatives and the statutory planning system. An indication of such a relationship is to be seen in the draft Thames Chase community forest plan (Thames Chase Team, 1992). Here, initiatives for the South Hornchurch community forest zone are expressed in the form of illustrative 'visions' which outline a number of possibilities including a car park, visitor centre, recreational activities, landscape improvement measures and mineral extraction resulting in the creation of a new lake (Figure 10.5).

Any proposals would be, nevertheless, strongly influenced by established planning policies, for example, in respect of mineral extraction, tipping and earth-moving as well as the interests of local residents. The

255

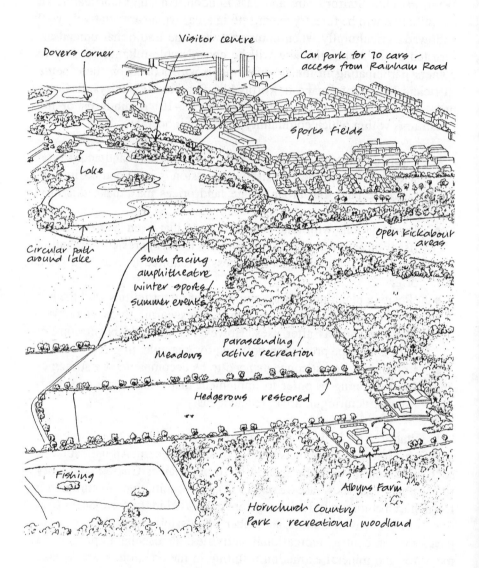

Figure 10.5   Thames Chase community forest. 'Vision' for part of
South Hornchurch community forest zone
Source: Thames Chase Team (1992), p. 68a

vision notes that 'The London Borough of Havering does not necessarily share this vision.' As local planning authority, it would need to be convinced that the benefits outlined would outweigh the impact of developments (Thames Chase Team, 1992, p. 68a).

The cautious approach to introducing exceptions to existing planning strategies is underlined, too, in the Thames Chase treatment of 'positive' forest planning policies. Interpreted as possibly opening the doors to development in the green belt, it is made clear that local authorities are determined that only previously acceptable developments will be considered favourably. Therefore, the prospects in this particular example of using exceptions policies to trade-off community forest gain against normally unacceptable developments, will be slight.

It is not surprising to find that achievement of planting targets will depend to a considerable degree on a package of central financial supports. The draft plan indicates expansion of the total woodland area from about 960 ha in 1992 to almost 3 000 ha by the year 2042, an increase in the woodland component of the community forest area from approximately 10 per cent to about a third (Thames Chase Team, 1992, p. 91). Core finance is expected to come from the Forestry Commission's Woodland Grant Scheme (45 per cent), community woodland supplement (28 per cent), better quality agricultural land supplement (7 per cent) and the Ministry of Agriculture's Farm Woodland Premium Scheme (20 per cent). Once established, woodland management grants will also be available to owners. About 28 per cent of the forest area is in public ownership, primarily five local authorities. Assuming that this land remains in the hands of those bodies, then they could be expected to make a major contribution to planting and access programmes for the community forest.

Implementation issues are likely to feature prominently in the case of the much larger-scale new national forest in the English Midlands. Extending up to 400 km^2, the scheme is designed to provide a major new forest resource (Countryside Commission, 1990c). The project is to depend on voluntary agreements to plant, supported for example by business sponsorship, private donations, central government grant for derelict land reclamation and the use of planning agreements (Bell, 1991, p. 22). The vast majority of the land is in private ownership and, as in the case of the community forests, performance will need to be based on a 20- or 30-year time span.

257

In that time it will become clear as to who will manage the forests, what might be the most appropriate forms of planting and, most importantly, what might be the roles of the Forestry Commission, local authorities and other non-profit organizations such as environmental trusts.

WATER RECREATION IN AN ERA OF PRIVATIZATION

The history of provision of water supplies has been dominated by the existence of many small public and private providers and a number of attempts by government to rationalize patterns of provision. Municipal authorities in the north of England sought to meet the local demands for water supply including the burgeoning needs of manufacturing industry in the nineteenth century. In expanding water supplies, private and public providers also acquired not just land for reservoirs themselves, but for the surrounding catchments, control of which was felt necessary in order to protect the quality of water. At one time, therefore, local authorities were able to count among their assets reservoirs and many hectares of managed rural estate. The estate was mainly upland moorland, some of which was set aside for timber-growing. A distinctive upland landscape became associated with the water supplier's rural land inventory: stern architecture, woodland, dams and notices restricting public access.

Various attempts were made to bring an element of national or regional planning into water supply, pollution control and drainage (Parker and Sewell, 1988, pp. 760–761). Rationalization of water supply under the Water Resources Act of 1963 resulted in the creation of the Water Resources Board with a remit to advise government on planning and provision of water. Further and more significant reform continued with the Water Act of 1973. Under the Act the local authority providers were amalgamated into nine regional water authorities for England and one for Wales. The new authorities inherited all the assets (and liabilities) of the previous owners. Their responsibilities were comprehensive: water supply, sewerage, flood protection, navigation, recreation and conservation. Private water-supply companies, responsible for about a quarter of all water supplied, fell outside the administration of the new regional water authorities.

Some limited encouragement to recreation provision was given under the Water Resources Act of 1963 which permitted river authorities to

258

provide for public use of water spaces for recreation. Under section 22 of the Countryside Act 1968, a requirement was placed on water suppliers to take into account questions of recreation and conservation. In addition, section 20 of the Water Act 1973, indicated that 'every water authority and all other statutory water undertakers may secure the use of water and land associated with water for the purpose of recreation.' Further emphasis was placed on the recreational role of the new water industry by the creation of a short-lived Water Space Amenity Commission, which could offer advice on how the water authorities might undertake their recreational functions.

The record of the water authorities in providing for rural recreation

Other than providing facilities for anglers, water suppliers have only in recent years begun to take a significant interest in catering for informal recreation on a major scale. The reasons for this late concern have been recorded by Parker and Penning-Rowsell (1980, pp. 157–169).

- Recreation can lead to pollution of reservoir water and recreation has been seen as incompatible with safeguarding drinking water supplies.
- As a newcomer amongst water industry responsibilities, recreation was viewed with antipathy by water engineers and scientists.
- Access to water space for recreation was seen as important but not if it jeopardized the quality of water supplies and was not at least partly self-financing.
- The professional standing of water recreation and amenity planning within the water industry was weak.
- The techniques for resource appraisal, including social benefits, carrying capacity and environmental impact of recreation were often distrusted by water engineers because of imprecision.

Despite a traditional reluctance to undertake recreation provision, the ten authorities created under the Water Act 1973 expanded the range of facilities available to the visitor, appointing specialist officers to deal with recreation and conservation responsibilities.

A wide range of water-based activities is provided at reservoirs. Besides angling, sailing and water-skiing, provision is also made for other

259

pursuits such as horse-riding and birdwatching (Water Authorities Association, 1988, p. 52). Control of most activities is vested in clubs with membership being a requirement before undertaking pursuits. In the case of more informal activities such as birdwatching relatively unrestricted access appears to be permitted.

A further indication of the scale of the water authority recreation resource is provided by looking at the range of facilities provided for the casual visitor. From a very limited provision in 1973, the range as recorded in 1987 was quite extensive (Figure 10.6).

An indication of the approach to recreation provision is provided in a study of the water industry in the countryside (Eachus Huckson Partnership, 1988). The study revealed that a wide range of planning and management practices had been adopted by water authorities as part of their

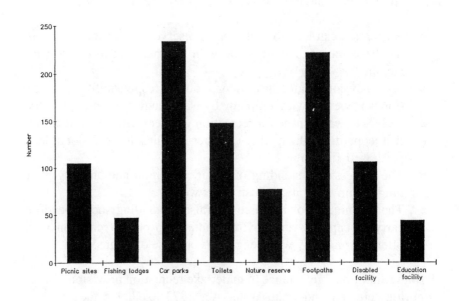

Figure 10.6   England and Wales: amenity and recreation facilities on water authority land, 1988

Source: Water Authorities Association (1988), p. 52

remit towards recreation and amenity. For example, the designs of reservoirs paid considerable attention to the way in which recreation provision could be made; planting and management schemes sought to create an attractive setting for visitors; river engineering schemes deliberately sought to widen opportunities for public enjoyment. Of particular importance have been water authority efforts to create permissive (concessionary) access around reservoirs (Figure 10.7).

Water authorities have thus became major providers of rural recreation, with large numbers of visitors making use of reservoirs and other sites. The South West Water Authority, with the smallest land holdings of all authorities, was able to attract some 25 million visitors to its properties in 1988–89 (South West Water Authority, 1989, p. 19).

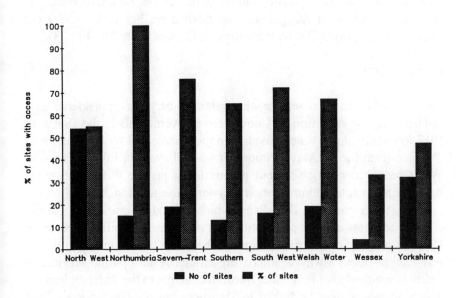

Figure 10.7   England and Wales: permissive access on water authority land holdings
Source: Countryside Commission (1989i), p. 9

As major landowners, water authorities have been able to play important roles as partners in the planning and management of rural land uses. They have been members of joint planning, programming, funding and management arrangements with local authorities and other bodies. In 1986, the North West Water Authority recorded its involvement in 32 formal joint working arrangements with its partners (North West Water Authority, 1986, pp. 15–16). In looking at regional water authority achievements, the record has generally been one of developing reservoirs and their catchments for quiet, informal recreation. However, this has at times been thrown into doubt, witnessed by proposals to provide mechanized water-skiing facilities at Bottoms Reservoir in Longdendale, east of Manchester (Peak Park Joint Planning Board, 1991a, p. 6). Located in the Peak District National Park, the proposal conflicted with that authority's policies for the area and was refused planning permission.

In 1988, total land ownership of the water authorities was estimated as being just under 200 000 ha. About a quarter of this total was in the hands of the North West Regional Water Authority, reflecting the extensive catchment areas in the hill country of the region. Southern Water, on the other hand, with far greater dependence on boreholes and river extraction had only 3 700 ha (Countryside Commission, 1989i, p. 3).

Privatization

As a publicly provided service, the water industry was considered as a candidate for privatization by Conservative governments in the 1980s. In 1987, commitment to water privatization was indicated by the Conservative manifesto for the May elections. It was followed in July of that year by a Green Paper which set out proposals for private water authorities who would operate within a national system of regulation. The following year saw the release of a Blue Paper which refined several aspects of the original concepts and the publication of a parliamentary bill in December 1988. As with the other privatizations of the 1980s in Britain, the initiative was seen as being a way of improving efficiency in a public service. In addition, it would give far greater freedom of action to the water authorities who would no longer be linked to Treasury control. The leaders of the industry such as the Chairman of Thames Water, Roy Watts, were some of the most foremost advocates of privatization.

The passage of the Bill through Parliament in early 1989 saw a great deal of opposition levelled against the legislation as proposed. A study undertaken for the Council for the Protection of Rural England high-lighted two issues in particular. Firstly, there was concern about asset development which might be undertaken by subsidiaries of the privatized water companies (Bowers *et al.*, 1988, p. 25). While some developments would be subject to planning control, others would fall outside the control mechanism. An example of the potential effects of privatization was seen in the case of Rutland Water, where the 1980s had seen a gradual encroachment of commercial interests. This was reflected in the intensification and privatization of fishing in 1987 when the fishing rights were sold on a 9-year lease to a private management company. Subsequently, the permissible fishing period was extended into the winter months, the most disruptive to wildlife, without seeking the consent of the Nature Conservancy Council (NCC). 'When the NCC challenged this decision, Anglian water threatened the NCC with legal action on commercial grounds for seeking to "undermine the viability of the fishing and sale of rights"' (Bowers *et al.*, 1988, p. 27).

Such a move was considered to mark the end of a tradition of voluntary cooperation between local nature conservation interests and the diffusion of management responsibility to private agencies who did not share the same statutory obligations towards the protection of the environment as the water authorities.

Secondly, opposition focused on the loss of access to areas where the public had been traditionally free to wander. Extensive areas of land opened up by water authorities were often based on permissive access rather than on statutory rights of way or on formally defined access agreements with planning authorities. The potential loss of access to such land was identified as a major concern (Countryside Commission, 1989i, p. 9).

The Water Act 1989

In practice, modifications made to the Water Bill resulted in its opponents achieving some modest success. Thus, environmental duties are placed on the water companies themselves. Section 8(2) of the Act requires companies to have regard to the 'desirability of preserving for the public freedom of access to places of natural beauty, and to buildings, sites and other objects of archeological, architectural or historic interest'. However, this provision does not apply to commercial subsidiaries. Under section 10, a code of practice for water companies seeks to

263

ensure that conflict is minimized when land is offered for sale in designated areas such as national parks and that management plans are drawn up by the companies. However, some of the key elements which were criticized by the opponents to the Bill remained in the Act. Retained, for example, is the clause indicating that nothing in the provisions of the Act 'shall require recreational facilities made available by a relevant body to be made available free of charge'. In addition, the scope for representation by recreation and conservation interests on advisory bodies was significantly reduced compared with what was sought by voluntary groups (Mersey Basin Campaign, 1989, p. 15).

An indication of policies in the post-privatization era is provided by one of the new companies in the North of England (North West Water Group plc). The Group has six subsidiaries including North West Water Limited (water supply and sewerage services), NWW Properties Limited (property development and management), and other companies providing specialized engineering and consulting services (North West Water Group, 1990, p. 42).

Aware of the importance of access issues in its extensive land holdings, North West Water Limited formed a conservation, access and recreation advisory committee, the first such body to be created by the new water companies. This is a forum for considering the use of company land holdings from the amenity aspect. The company published a commitment 'to promote freedom of access, in a manner compatible with reasonable operational, land and conservation requirements' (North West Water Ltd, 1990, p. 1). In addition, there has been a continued programme of recreation and interpretation schemes including £1.5 million funding for converting a disused railway for walking, cycling and riding (Payne, 1991, p. 8).

The activities of one of the subsidiary companies within the North West Water Group have been the cause of concern. In 1990, NWW Properties Limited sought to develop a 100 ha site at Kingswater Park, at Audenshaw east of Manchester. The scheme involved provision of a golf course, hotel, housing and offices with access to the Greater Manchester outer ring road (Building Design Partnership, 1990). The existing uses of the land include water areas and two golf courses. After-uses to ameliorate the effects of the development included the creation of a new golf course, the relocation of the two courses there at present, extensive landscaping and improved access to informal recreation. The local planning authority, Tameside Metropolitan Borough Council, was aware of the opportunities for employment generation at the site which were estimated at some 6 000 jobs. It was mindful to approve the application but there was considerable opposition to the proposal, reflected in a 22 000 signature petition. Manchester City Council, whose boundary extended up to the site, expressed its opposition to the scheme. The controversy associated with the application was such that it was called in by the Secretary of State for the Environment for his consideration.

Another indication of the way in which water company policy has evolved is provided by Welsh Water plc. The company has placed around 17 000 ha of land in the Elan Valley in the hands of the Welsh Water Elan Trust (Welsh Water plc, 1989, p. 1). The Trust was granted a 999-year peppercorn lease on the land together with a £100 000 endowment. For the first three years of the Trust, a further £30 000 was made available to help with running expenses. The lease controls some of the activities which can be undertaken by the Trust and, for example, it prevents commercial development by the trustees of the foundation. Welsh Water itself holds on to around 800 ha, mainly fenced land around the reservoirs in the Elan Valley. However, the creation of the Trust has not been without criticism. Concern has been expressed about the limited scale of the endowment, which seems far too small for dealing with the problems likely to be faced in an area facing agricultural decline (Anon, 1989).

Separate from the water companies is the National Rivers Authority (NRA) which has a central role in managing water resources, pollution control, flood protection, land drainage and freshwater fisheries. It has a major recreational portfolio, including rivers, associated recreational land and public rights of way. It has duties to 'develop the amenity and recreation potential of waters and lands under NRA control' (National Rivers Authority, 1990, p. 49). This involves:

- producing corporate strategies for recreation and amenity;
- adopting the Code of Practice on Conservation, Access and Recreation required under section 10 of the Water Act, 1989;
- promoting water recreation generally but in particular the use of the NRA's own recreational facilities;
- recovering as far as practical from users the costs of providing NRA recreational facilities;
- ensuring proper consideration of recreational issues by regional recreational and amenity committees.

In practice, the tasks involved include those of identifying the wide range of NRA assets where recreation facilities exist or could be provided; producing management plans for all sites owned or leased by the NRA; assessing the potential for increasing visitor usage and income potential of each site; seeking the involvement of recreation bodies; and undertaking collaborative projects (National Rivers Authority, 1990, p. 49).

It was unlikely that the architects of the privatization process expected countryside recreation to be a central issue in their designs for the water industry. However, the process of privatization succeeded in introducing an unexpected degree of debate about the provision of, payment for, and use of recreation facilities in the countryside.

THE BRITISH WATERWAYS BOARD

A fourth public provider considered is the British Waterways Board. It was created in 1948 when the inland waterways of Britain were nationalized. The extent of the resource includes a 3 500 km network of inland waterways, 90 reservoirs as well as extensive areas of other land. The Board's estate includes natural rivers and constructed waterways, the majority of which date from the late eighteenth and early nineteenth centuries. Following nationalization, the waterways system was the subject of several initiatives designed to inject new life into a run-down resource. In 1962 the waterways were transferred from the British Transport Commission to a separate British Waterways Board. Given the long-term problems facing the waterways systems, with major maintenance backlogs and many near-derelict canals, a development strategy was introduced under the provisions of the Transport Act 1968. The strategy sought to rationalize the existing system, classifying waterways into three categories as:

- commercial waterways, principally used for freight transport;
- cruising waterways, used principally for recreation;
- 'remainder' waterways, amounting to about a quarter of the waterway mileage and whose future was uncertain.

In respect of the 'remainder' waterways, government had asserted that for three years from the passing of the Act, 'no action would be taken by the Board, without the consent of the Minister of Transport, which would present their ultimate restoration' (British Waterways Board, 1969, p. 1). Although these waterways might be improved and used for recreation depending on local circumstances they might also be filled in or used for development. The strategy was the subject of great controversy, for it was launched at a time when the inland waterways restoration lobby was pressing for the retention and restoration of the waterways network in Britain (Bolton, 1991, pp. 231–232). In particular, the proposals for 'remainder' status waterway proved an effective target for the lobby. The 1960s and 1970s saw major and admirable achievements by waterway activists in restoring canals to navigation in the face of indifference on the part of their owner.

Inland waterways are now very different from their state on vesting day in 1948. Few canals are now used for the carrying purposes for which they were originally designed and significant income is derived from recreational activities and from supply of industrial water. However, with the decline of much manufacturing industry in Britain in recent years, the returns in the latter sector have decreased noticeably.

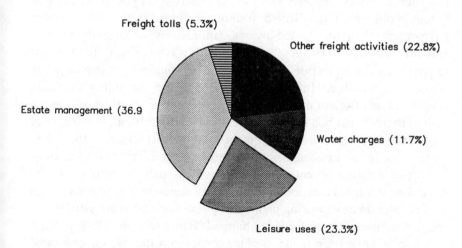

Figure 10.8 External revenue sources of the British Waterways Board, 1987–1988 (total external expenditure was £20.6 million)
Source: British Waterways Board (1989), p. 3

Despite these different sources of income, the Board receives a significant grant from central government, amounting to some £43 million in 1987/88 (Figure 10.8).

Since the early 1980s, Board activities have reflected a new commercial imperative. Objectives set by the Department of the Environment in 1984 expected the Board to expand profitable activities in conjunction with the private sector where possible. There is a central aim of maximizing revenue with priority being given to increase in value of the waterways for the nation (British Waterways Board, 1989, p. 3). There is also a recognition that much of the land associated with the waterways system has considerable commercial value. The value of this land is realized through sales, which amounted to over £5.5 million in 1987/88. In addition, income has been enhanced by joint ventures in conjunction with third parties in marina, hotel, housing and office development.

The recreational value of the waterways has been recognized for a considerable time and a number of investigations have been made of their use for recreation and tourism (British Waterways Board, 1986). In a study of the income and operations of the waterways system, the cost to the community of maintaining the waterways system was shown to be considerably less than for other comparable and frequently used facilities such as parks and swimming pools (Harrison, 1978, p. 20). A persistent problem for the British Waterways Board is that of obtaining payment for benefits gained by recreationists who currently use the network of canals in Britain. For the Board, it is important that the cost of providing the recreational resource is levied amongst as large a group of users as possible. However, much depends on the ability to obtain revenue in an efficient manner. This can be done relatively easily in the case of recreational boaters and anglers. It is more difficult in the case of walkers and cyclists whose movements may be much more diffuse than other users. In its attitudes to access, therefore, the Board will be anxious to protect existing revenue-earning activities such as angling. At the same time it might be expected to permit revenue-earning activities such as cycle hire on canal towing paths, if physical conditions are satisfactory and if other users' interests are not harmed (Banister, *et al.*, 1992, p. 158).

Attempts have been made to place a value on the overall economic benefits of the waterway system. A 1989 study suggested that the full value of informal recreation was around £63 million, and that land drainage charges, if the Board was able to charge for them, would be £20 million (British Waterways Board, 1990, p. 4). This estimate is of interest but it illustrates the problems of realizing the full financial value of a linear recreational facility such as a canal. Although receipts from boating, angling and other priced activities generated some 25 million visits to the inland waterways, it is estimated that there were over 130 million 'informal' visits by towpath walkers and others who have free access to the network.

Income will continue to come from established uses as well as the new more commercial activities, including income from providers of recreational facilities on the towing path. In addition, the Board could continue to expect financial support from bodies such as the Countryside Commission or the Sports Council who, operating to national objectives, may be anxious to achieve wider access to water or to the countryside. The principle of partnership operations is well established through a number of experimental schemes including projects to widen access to waterway towing paths for cyclists (British Waterways Board, 1989).

In 1990, the Board sought to increase its flexibility in the management of its resources through the British Waterways Bill. The initiative removed many legal obstacles faced by commercial subsidiaries of the Board. However, the Bill drew opposition, particularly from those who by custom had access to waterway facilities and now found their traditional enjoyment threatened. Humble Petitions lodged by both the Ramblers' Association and the Cyclists' Touring Club stressed that the Bill offered no protection for the possible loss of continuity of permissive access routes on towing paths (Cyclists' Touring Club, 1991). Sale of land by subsidiaries could result in the new owners' denying public access to towing paths or land to which there had previously been unrestricted use. In response to the Petitions the Board amended the clauses of the Act so as to preclude the clause from being used to authorize the disposal of the waterway channel or towing path. In addition, it issued a policy statement reaffirming its commitment to the retention of the continuity of the waterways themselves and associated towing paths (British Waterways Board, 1991).

The sale of waterway property has been the cause of some controversy in other respects. 'Hundreds of canalside homes, offices and public amenities are auctioned or sold privately in the biggest disposal of assets by British Waterways' (Hencke, 1991). Among the property sold, it was reported, were woods and open spaces of a stretch alongside the Grand Union Canal at New Bradwell near Milton Keynes.

While enhanced commercial returns could help clear the backlog of waterway repairs, the cost could be the loss of character and quiet enjoyment traditionally associated with the waterway system. '...it is vital that future developments should retain their (canals') historic character and atmosphere and make a contribution towards their authentic purpose as navigations' (Bolton, 1991, p. xviii).

COMMENT

In Britain the Thatcher years have had a major impact on the delivery of recreation facilities by public agencies. The latter have been faced with total privatization or have been made to adopt a much stronger commercial dimension to their activities. A result of this has been that, rather than presenting a broadly unified approach to policy-making, the evolving organizations now present contrasting and sometimes contradictory policies towards recreation. One branch of a public agency or privatized public agency will be able to demonstrate that it is doing much to promote recreation for a broad public, but another branch, most probably a commercial subsidiary, may well be demonstrating the opposite.

An important theme which has emerged has been the threat of loss of land to which there has traditionally been free access. Where previously access has been allowed on a permissive basis without formal agreements, there is a danger that recreational resources available to the public will decrease. The insertion of clauses into legislation and the drawing-up of codes of practice have aimed to offset the adverse effects of the loss of access land. However, the commercial dimension of public providers can no longer permit the same degree of unrestricted, and generally unpaid, access which existed hitherto.

For local authorities, changes during the 1980s have meant that their roles as direct providers of recreational facilities have been increasingly constrained. Their future contribution will revolve around initiatives shared with other agencies: for example, in the creation of community forests or in contributing to the activities of environmental trusts. Uncertainty remains over their relationships with their traditional 'partners' in joint recreational planning and management programmes. To what extent the consensus that marked earlier working relationships will persist is unclear.

Finally, a question remains over the long-term commercial objectives of the market-oriented providers' ambitions. Development strategies drawn up during a period of relative prosperity in the late 1980s reflected a general buoyancy of outlook. The ensuing recession reminded us of the dangers of over-reliance on speculative commercial ventures, and targets have had to be moved downwards. Where recreation provision has been dependent on finance from such ventures, there is a danger of activities such as maintenance suffering because of the withdrawal of funding support.

Chapter 11

The voluntary sector in rural recreation planning and management

Despite the important role of government in supplying goods and services not provided by the market, gaps in provision persist which have to be filled by the voluntary sector. In democratic societies governments tend to be responsive to majority wants, and as a consequence there emerges a need for other bodies to respond to the demands of persons who feel intensely about particular activities, such as the preservation of historic buildings or landmarks (Weisbrod, 1988, pp. 6–7).

In Britain, governments have often been slow to face up to a number of problems associated with countryside recreation. For example, at a local level, it has often been difficult to get local authorities to attend to their legal responsibilities in respect of public rights of way. The response in such situations has been for voluntary-sector organizations to fill the gap.

A key feature of voluntary organizations is that their activities are not undertaken for financial profit, and the term 'non-profit' has increasingly come into use to describe all voluntary organizations. However, such bodies vary enormously in scale and modes of operation. Weisbrod reminds us that non-profit groups can be big businesses which have to respond to changes in prices or in demand. Like users of 'with profit' services, consumers of non-profit services are sensitive to price changes. In addition, prospective donors are influenced in deciding the size of their contributions by the prospect of tax deductibility. However, of great importance to non-profits is the giving of time and non-monetary contributions in the form of voluntary labour (Weisbrod, 1988, p. 4).

Murphy draws attention to the great variety of voluntary bodies, which include mutual aid organizations, self-help groups, volunteer organiza-

272

tions, voluntary organizations, and private non-profit social service organizations (Murphy, 1983, p. 5). They include bodies which are almost wholly sponsored by government, staffed by professionals but directed by an independent board and regarded as 'quasi voluntary' organizations. In identifying the characteristics of voluntary organizations he suggests (p. 6) that:

- the contribution of resources including money, time and materials from independent sources, exceeds in value the contributions from statutory sources;
- the organization has a constitution that guarantees its independence and autonomy;
- the membership of the ruling body is composed of a majority of independent members of the organization;
- the activities of the organization are so arranged as to maximize voluntary participation and to minimize the distinction between those who give services and those who receive them.

In addition, it is worthy of note that, in achieving their goals and avoiding tax liabilities, many voluntary organizations find it valuable to operate as companies limited by guarantee with charitable status.

Table 11.1   Characteristics of voluntary organizations

Receive money from donations and gifts

Obtain some degree of taxation relief in carrying out their operations and often have trust status

Are often qualified to receive grants or subsidies from government or sponsorship from 'for profit' organizations

Often have close links with government

People volunteer their labour to them, but they may employ full-time administrators or professional staff

Those who benefit from use of not-for-profit services normally have to pay for that service, although in practice this may be difficult to achieve

---

As a broad categorization, voluntary-sector organizations may fall into 'interest' groups, pursuing common interests of the membership; or they may be 'principle' groups who stand for and champion particular sets of values (Lowe and Goyder, 1983, p. 33). Interest groups will tend to be locally based, perhaps concerned with one particular site. Principle groups are more likely to be nationally based but they may have local branches. The Council for the Protection of Rural England and the Ramblers' Association provide examples of the latter.

THE VOLUNTARY SECTOR AND RURAL RECREATION

Voluntary organizations concerned with rural recreation share a number of characteristics with the bodies described so far in this chapter. They are extremely diverse in character and can include a body such as the National Trust, perceived by many as a national 'quasi voluntary' organization performing tasks little different from those of government agencies.

Recreational voluntary groups have long sought to influence policy-making. In inter-war Britain, they were active in promoting the idea of national parks and in advocating the need for a new planning system for post-war Britain. Growth of leisure in the 1930s fostered an increase in voluntary-sector activity. 'The outdoor amenity bodies had a new found importance at a time when there was popular interest in physical recreation and outdoor activities such as cycling, hostelling, camping and rambling' (Cherry, 1975, p. 154).

Sheail records that in this same period voluntary organizations also became regulators of the use of the countryside for recreation. Following attempts to control random and indiscriminate camping, the Camping Club of Great Britain was deemed responsible enough to be able to manage its own sites in an efficient way and was exempted from planning controls (Sheail, 1981, p. 202).

Distinct from the work of voluntary organizations as regulators or as interest groups pressing for particular policies or acting as providers, are the many who join recreational organizations in order simply to share their enjoyment of the countryside with others. Their origins extend back a considerable period: the Cyclists' Touring Club, for example, dates from 1878; the Ramblers' Association, an amalgamation of a number of rambling organizations, was founded in 1932; and the Youth Hostels Association was founded in 1930.

Many local organizations are likely to be affiliated to regionally or nationally based organizations, some of which will have governing status, determining regulations and codes under which the activities are undertaken. This applies primarily to sports which take place in the countryside, but recreation bodies are equally likely to provide members with codes of behaviour. Participation in the voluntary sector in rural recreation demonstrates a number of features, as follows:

- *Recreation: enjoyment.* People join together in clubs for enjoyment of rural pursuits, with a need for varying degrees of organization; normally organized on a voluntary basis by members.
- *Recreation: campaigning.* Members join together to achieve certain targets: for example, access to the countryside, countryside policies which favour members' interests.
- *Recreation: governing bodies.* Some countryside sports and recreational activities have governing bodies to ensure that the activity is undertaken in a proper manner. Often these have paid professional staff, but will still rely on substantial voluntary support, particularly at a local level.
- *Recreation: conservation.* Much countryside volunteering is concerned with conservation of rural resources, some of which might have a recreational function.

Although sharing a common interest in the countryside, it cannot be assumed that recreational voluntary organizations automatically have strong links with the wider environmental movement. As the 1986 investigation into *Access to the Countryside for Recreation and Sport* demonstrated, the dynamics of voluntary groups in the countryside are fluid and not free from conflict. Groups can act in a very committed way, pursuing their members' interests, perhaps against the interests of other voluntary organizations (Centre for Leisure Research, 1986b, p. 13).

In reviewing the role of recreational voluntary groups, an issue which arises concerns the seeming contradiction which arises in the use of the term 'voluntary sector'.

If one considers a number of strictly recreational countryside activities – rowing, birdwatching, angling, etc. – it is difficult to see how

275

these activities (whilst undoubtedly performed voluntarily) bear any relationship with volunteering; most anglers would be puzzled if asked to recollect when it was that they first volunteered to go angling (Hoggett and Bishop, 1983, p. 38).

The authors contrast the activities of most participants in voluntary organized recreation in the countryside with those who seek to promote voluntarily organized conservation work in the countryside. They remind us of the distinction between recreation, which is most commonly concerned with resource consumption, and conservation, which is concerned primarily with resource management.

VOLUNTARY LABOUR

In reviewing the role of the voluntary sector, the Edwards Panel acknowledged its value in practical voluntary labour, countryside management, outdoor activities and in providing information services (National Parks Review Panel, 1991, p. 115). However, it also highlighted the other contributions made by volunteers:

- national park societies which offer support, encouragement, practical assistance and constructive criticism;
- voluntary ranger services which assist in visitor management;
- trusts and charitable organizations which raise money and conduct business independently and can work successfully with the park authorities.

Of interest is the Panel's view that, although authorities consult voluntary groups during the preparation of major policy documents, 'otherwise voluntary sector expertise is often neglected' (National Parks Review Panel, 1991, p. 117). In addition, the Panel stressed the need to provide sufficient resources for voluntary sector activity to thrive, to set up park-based volunteer services to cover activities from the scholarly to the manual, and to establish direct contact with local groups. On a cautionary note, however, it felt that the voluntary sector needs support but not at the expense of its independence.

It is important to distinguish between the beneficiaries of voluntary effort, be they members of a voluntary group or other recipients of support, and the role of volunteers themselves. Volunteers have played a major role in implementing countryside policies, including those for recreation. The scale of that involvement has been recorded in a survey of 146 local authorities, national park and water authorities, which indicated the range of volunteering effort directed to countryside recreation and conservation (Simpson, 1983, p. 93). The survey findings show that several types of volunteer are engaged in this type of work: British Trust for Conservation Volunteers, schools and local conservation corps; local societies including local branches of the Ramblers' Association, British Horse Society and anglers; individuals who are recruited directly by public sector providers; and, lastly, other volunteers including scout groups and military groups. Most work undertaken is best described as 'countryside conservation'. Almost all of the sample of respondents had worked with volunteers on conservation tasks (tree planting, scrub clearance); countryside management (fencing, path construction); ranger and patrolling services (some manual work but also providing information services). Often, voluntary wardens have been able to do work which might be difficult for full-time staff to undertake: for example, at weekends. The investigation is useful in indicating some of the limitations of the use of voluntary labour by resource agencies.

- Arrangements for organizing the volunteer effort seem to vary greatly, often with organization being only a very minor part of a professional's responsibilities.
- Costs of employing volunteers can sometimes be considerable if all servicing costs are taken into account, including administration and training.
- Some agencies found that volunteers, by the nature of their work, were doing it as a hobby or interest and clearly did not look on voluntary work with exactly the same commitment as might be expected from contract labour.
- The complications of using voluntary labour mean that, in some circumstances, it might be more efficient to use full-time contract staff.

Simpson concludes that the volunteer resource is capable of further involvement in conservation and recreation effort, but that clients and volunteers need to follow clear principles of operation so that the labour needs meet the nature of the work which is required to be undertaken.

The need to involve other groups than the traditional activist has been stressed by other observers. '...if labour-intensive conservation and access tasks are the traditional way of using volunteers in national parks, I believe that a long-term strategy on volunteering needs to concentrate on the involvement of local communities and local residents' (Archer, 1988, p. 39). In another review, it was found that most volunteers in national parks were resident outside the parks themselves. In addition, residents of national parks tended to undertake wardening activities while 'outsiders' were more involved in landscape conservation and maintenance (Darling and Buchanan, 1985, p. 13).

It is clear that, although volunteers can be seen as a valuable resource, there is a need to consider very carefully what tasks might be undertaken by them. In national parks, it is suggested that the volunteer effort must be seen in relation to the wider involvement of different groups in the community and as part of an attempt to develop broad local support for the park authorities' work (Darling and Buchanan, 1985, p. 37).

THE VOLUNTARY SECTOR: ENVIRONMENTAL TRUSTS

A number of voluntary-sector organizations have found it advantageous to obtain trust status as a way of providing stability and enhancing recognition by possible sponsors. The names of the trusts involved in rural recreation provision, incorporating terms such as 'environmental', 'land' or 'development', provide clues to the particular emphasis of their operations.

The trust mechanism can have a wide appeal. A major review of development trusts concluded that: 'Trusts can appear to be all things to all people, appealing to a wide range of political viewpoints: entrepreneurial yet responsive to community interests; independent of the public sector yet working with councils and quangos; concerned with the well-being of a particular locality – not a particular group or interest' (Warburton et al., 1989, p. 3). The review also stresses how trusts can encourage substantial community involvement; cross-subsidize from commercially viable activities to non-profit making schemes; and 'package resources, including grants, loans, effort, enthusiasm, skills and energy from organizations and individuals'.

The value of the trust mechanism has been recorded in a review of countryside change in Britain and the impact that this may have in encouraging the growth of conservation, amenity and recreation trusts (CARTs) as managers of rural land (Hodge, 1988, p. 372). A review specifically of land trusts (Lapping and Hoagland, 1985, p. 172) records that, although such bodies may follow different strategies and operate at different geographic scales, they have a number of distinct characteristics.

- They are able to be flexible and dynamic in acquiring open spaces, in meeting landowner needs and providing stewardship over valuable resources.
- They are able to draw out private resources and inspire individual initiative.
- They benefit from non-profit tax-exempt status.
- They are free from the bureaucratic agendas of government.

An interesting aspect of trust revenue-earning activities concerns the 'partial development' of land in a trust's ownership as possibly the only way of ensuring continued funding for a trust. Partial development involves a trust purchasing property with landscape or recreational value, then paying back its investment from receipts obtained by selling part of the property for development. This is extensively undertaken by land trusts in North America and its application in Britain is seen in a number of examples, including Sustrans Ltd (below) and in the activities of the Scottish Green Belt Company (Groome, 1990, p. 59).

Consideration is now given to the operation of three voluntary organizations who assist in the provision of rural recreation facilities. Each is a trust, but they have adopted different approaches to developing and managing recreational resources.

Groundwork trusts

An example of a 'top-down' initiative started by a central government agency is the Groundwork trust of which there exist over 28 in England and Wales. The Groundwork trust concept stemmed from several years of experiment by the Countryside Commission in running countryside management experiments in areas such as the English Lake District, Snowdonia and urban fringe areas. The original Groundwork scheme was first seen as part of public-sector initiative to link smaller-scale environmental improvements with derelict land programmes in urban

279

fringe areas. However, under the instigation of the Secretary of State for the Environment, Michael Heseltine, the model changed from being a public authority initiative to that of a trust mechanism and reflected the Secretary's admiration of the enterprise trust movement (Warburton *et al.*, 1989, p. 50). Encouraged by the early success of the Groundwork trust at St Helens, established in 1982, government invited local authorities in northwest England to submit bids for a further five environmental trusts. An incentive for the local authorities to make bids was that Groundwork areas would have access to an allocation of derelict land grant of £3 million together with a special allocation of Countryside Commission funding. The Groundwork North West initiative had several aims, including the following (Countryside Commission, 1983, p. 3).

- Clear dereliction, carry out environmental improvements and find productive uses for wasted assets.
- Improve access to rural recreation, provide small-scale recreation facilities and improve the management of rights of way.
- Improve understanding between town and countryside.
- Conserve and enhance good environments for wildlife, agriculture, leisure and recreation.
- Assist farmers in realizing the full potential of their land, bringing neglected land back into production.

The trusts created at this time were in Salford/Trafford, Rossendale, Wigan, Oldham/Rochdale and Macclesfield. All the areas contained extensive urban fringe areas, although Macclesfield differed from the others in suffering from much less dereliction and decay. The main features of the trusts are illustrated in Table 11.2. Since the first trusts were created in the early 1980s, others have been created outside the northwest of England in locations ranging from Merthyr Tydfil in Wales to East Durham in northeast England. Approaches vary from one trust to another, but the features indicated in Table 11.2 are to be found in most. The Groundwork Foundation is the national charity which provides support and guidance to the local trusts and has been centrally involved in extending the Groundwork approach from its origins in northwest England.

An illustration of the role of a trust in providing for rural recreation is provided by that of the Macclesfield and Vale Royal Groundwork Trust. Unlike the terrain found in some trusts, the trust's area includes extensive attractive countryside within its 500 km^2, is popular for outdoor

280

Table 11.2 Key characteristics of Groundwork trusts

Initial core funding from central government, tapering off so that trusts would eventually be substantially self-supporting

Support from local authority partners

Charitable status, companies limited by guarantee

Possibilities for fee-earning activities

Sponsorship and secondment from the private sector

Working together with the voluntary sector through groups or individuals

Boards of trustees, from the public, private and voluntary sectors

Developing programmes of action in partnerships

---

recreation and has long acted as a 'green lung' for Manchester. However, expansion of the trust's area in 1988 to include the neighbouring district of Vale Royal increased the proportion of derelict land.

Like the other trusts, it receives partial core funding from government via the Countryside Commission. This is tapered over a 5-year period with the aim of obtaining what other financial support is available nationally and locally to achieve its objectives. Significant sums come from grants, including those from local authorities and sponsorship, but considerable amounts are also associated with handling projects and in running a consultancy, Adelphi Environmental Consultants Limited, which is a commercial company making an annual covenant from profits to the parent trust (Macclesfield and Vale Royal Groundwork Trust, 1990, pp. 9–10). In 1990, there were 12 members on a board of directors including six district and county councillors and six other members including representatives of the local business and industrial community.

Work has been undertaken under several themes: improving the environment including working with business and industry, with industrial estates and environs of former cotton mills; undertaking environmental improvements with local communities; on the basis of core funding, extracting money from other sources including, sponsorship, gifts in kind, financial packaging and 'grantsmanship'.

Table 11.3   Macclesfield and Vale Royal Groundwork Trust: recreational initiatives

Theme	Example
Access routes	Improvement of Macclesfield Canal and Trent and Mersey Canal towing paths.
Increasing participation	Cycle-hire schemes at Bollington, Tatton Park and Delamere Forest. Canoe hire. Events, walks.
Interpretive guides and centres	Walking, cycling, disabled and public transport guides; theme walks on industrial archeology, local history; Peaks and Plains and Marston Discovery Centres.
Volunteers	'Groundworkers' practical conservation and access projects staffing of Discovery centres; write publications; account for 20 per cent of Trust's total staffing resources.

Source: Macclesfield and Vale Royal Groundwork Trust (1984–1989)

A major component of the trust's activities have concerned widening access to leisure in the countryside of east and mid-Cheshire. Table 11.3 shows the wide range of schemes. In undertaking these different initiatives, much use has been made of funding support from public and private sources. Although the trust did not get as involved as some others in temporary employment programmes in the mid-1980s, some assistance was received from that quarter. In more recent years the trust's efforts have become more focused on urban and environmental improvement in conjunction with the private sector: for example, as part of the 'Brightsite' campaign in which Groundwork trusts have participated.

Groundwork trusts have succeeded in introducing a new diversity to rural recreation provision. In addition, they have managed to adapt a nationally-instituted initiative to local conditions and resources (Trépanier and Ouellet, 1986, p. 156). However, despite the success of projects and increasing revenue-earning capacity, the trusts are unlikely to fulfil their roles without public-sector funding support (Warburton *et al.*, 1987, p. 54).

In his investigation of Groundwork trusts, Collis also notes their impressive track record in getting practical projects on the ground. Even so, trusts were not found to be immune from the normal constraints that confront agencies attempting to implement environmental policies. 'Groundwork's success lies not, therefore, in the absence of red tape but in the quality of its staff. It takes capable people to be able to meet a host of financial and other performance measures, to work simultaneously with public, private and voluntary sectors and still get things done quickly and effectively' (Collis, 1990, p. 36). In addition, he argues that the 'top-down' nature of Groundwork trusts means that they must be seen as a political initiative, reflecting central government's belief that local government cannot work in an innovative and entrepreneurial way.

Sustrans Ltd, the railway path and cycle route construction company

Sustrans follows in the tradition of self-help in the provision of recreational facilities. It is both a 'principle' group arguing for a better-balanced transport policy in Britain and an 'interest' group which actively promotes opportunities for cyclists and walkers. Its most outstanding contribution has been its association with the provision of over 300 km of recreational routeways in Britain.

Sustrans was founded in 1985. It originated through the Bristol-based cycle campaign Cyclebag which was founded in 1978. Cyclebag was intent on improving facilities in town and countryside for cyclists of all kinds. However, the group became very closely associated with the conversion of disused railways to 'railway paths' for use by cyclists, walkers and the disabled. Using voluntary labour and making use of various government job-creation schemes, the group constructed a 15 km section of recreational pathway on the disused Bath to Bitton railway line in Avon in the West of England. From this first exercise emerged the

Railway Path Project which expanded its operations from Bristol to the rest of Britain. The organization undertook feasibility studies for local authorities and other public providers who were considering developing railway paths. In addition, the Project, renamed Sustrans Ltd in 1985, undertook railway path construction work itself, acting as a managing agency and using staff recruited under job-training schemes.

The principal objective of the organization is to improve conditions for walkers, cyclists and the disabled through the creation of networks of safe and attractive routeways. The company is limited by guarantee and is registered as a charity. It directly employs its own staff including a company engineer, accountant, bridge engineer and a senior ranger. The company has a board of directors and the public are able to become members of Sustrans (with voting rights) or supporters who make financial subscriptions to the company.

Most of Sustrans' routes comprise disused railways but lengths of path have been constructed on canal towing paths and on other locations too. An important feature of Sustrans' paths is the attention to detailed design matters, in particular the quality of surfaces, path camber, drainage and barriers. Attention is paid to the needs of specific classes of user such as cyclists and the disabled whose requirements are often poorly understood and have been given too little thought by designers. Around 45 schemes have been undertaken so far. Initially, schemes tended to be identified by Sustrans but, as the company has become better-known, most projects originate through invitations from landowners to Sustrans (Figure 11.1).

In carrying out projects Sustrans employs a number of approaches:

- direct purchase of a site by the company with liabilities such as viaducts and bridges as well as assets such as the track itself and ballast (local authorities may act as guarantors);
- lease of a site to Sustrans, normally from local authorities, with a scheme undertaken to Sustrans' plan and with the company receiving payment as the management agency;
- design and construction of sites on behalf of a client, with sites then being managed by their owners or in partnership with Sustrans;
- design consultancy service, with Sustrans advising only on the feasibility of projects at locations such as forests or on disused railways and canal towing paths.

284

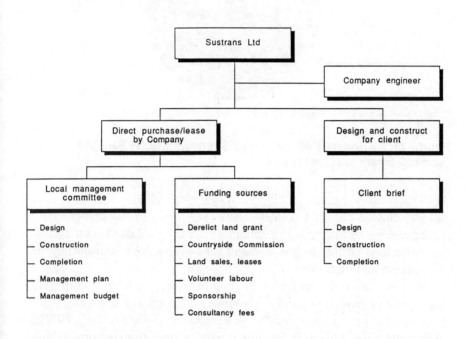

Figure 11.1   Sustrans Ltd: development of linear routeways
Source: correspondence with Sustrans Ltd, 1991

The company receives no core funding and is highly dependent on obtaining contracted work, mainly from local authorities. A small amount of sponsorship is obtained but the company's continued existence is also bound up with obtaining income from partial development of land in its ownership. This has been accomplished by direct land sales including sections of track alongside residential property, the granting of wayleaves and receipt of income from leases (Figure 11.2). For each route, it is intended that income from sales and other sources will pay for the costs

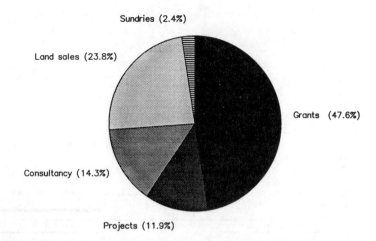

Sundries (2.4%)

Land sales (23.8%)

Grants (47.6%)

Consultancy (14.3%)

Projects (11.9%)

Figure 11.2   Sources of income of Sustrans Ltd, 1990–1991
Source: Sustrans Ltd (1991a), p. 4

of maintenance and management. However, in 1990 the company recorded delays in setting up maintenance funds associated with certain
routes because of the drop in demand for development land during the
recession at that time.

The financial problems facing the company are probably no different
from those of many land and environmental trusts. The company finds
itself caught in a vicious circle. A newsletter (Sustrans Ltd, 1991b)
asserts that the company is the only organization seriously approaching
the problems of safe route provision for the non-motorized traveller. Yet:

> ... lack of official and public awareness impedes our dealings with
> national and local government and restricts our ability to raise fund-
> ing through business sponsorship. The simplest way to the publicity
> we need is through a stream of new (route) openings and an ever-
> growing route network carrying an ever-growing load of satisfied
> customers. Slow progress with officialdom and fundraising handicaps
> our route construction programme; the circle is complete.

The company questions the role it has in providing public recreational
facilities, work that local authorities themselves should rightly be doing.
The company has considered charging users for visiting its properties

but, besides the practical problems of implementing a payment scheme, has found resistance amongst the public and faces a moral dilemma since much of the finance for developing (but not maintaining) schemes has come from public sources.

The National Trust

The third voluntary organization considered is the National Trust. Founded in 1895, its prime objective is to work for the preservation of places of historic interest or natural beauty in England, Wales and Northern Ireland. Its importance, though, as the provider of major recreational resources and as an effective determinant of rural recreational policy makes it worthy of some detailed consideration in this chapter. The Trust is able to acquire property by means of gifts or bequests, direct purchases or is able to receive property in lieu of inheritance tax. Through an Act of 1907, the Trust is constituted as a statutory body which is able to make its properties inalienable and to create its own bylaws. It is therefore quite different from any of the other voluntary-sector organizations considered elsewhere in this chapter.

National Trust properties are widespread in England, Wales and Northern Ireland, although there are local concentrations. For example, the early years of the Trust showed a clear bias in favour of acquisitions in the south of England and in Cumbria (Tunbridge, 1981, p. 105). In the 1930s, ownership had extended into substantial areas outside southeast England: for example, in Wales and in Derbyshire. In the post-war period, many stately homes were acquired as a result of government legislation which bestowed donations to the Trust in lieu of death duties. An acquisition programme of particular note was Enterprise Neptune from 1965 onwards which resulted in the Trust's gaining some 820 km of coastline (Raikes, 1990, p. 19). In 1990, the Trust owned some 228 713 ha of land and had covenants over a further 31 402 hectares. This results in the Trust owning a little over 1 per cent of the total land area of Britain, including many areas of outstanding scenery.

The importance of the Trust as a provider of recreational land is clearly apparent. Several different types of Trust land and property offer a wide range of recreational activities: open land, downland, moorland, country parks, woodlands, farm and nature trails, all of which can be perceived as part of the total stock of recreational resources. A review of Trust properties in southeast England reminds us that in that region the

Trust is one of the major recreation providers and managers (Tunbridge, 1981, p. 112). This means that it is able to exert a significant influence on channelling recreational demands in particular directions. As a major landowner, too, the Trust has been able to influence such initiatives as the creation of long-distance footpaths. The South West Coast Path links over a hundred Trust properties and 'given the variety of pressures on coastal land in this attractive part of the country, the path would be a doubtful proposition without the Trust' (Tunbridge, 1981, p. 112).

The success of the Trust has been recorded on a number of occasions and it is clear that it is carrying out activities that might otherwise have been left in the hands of public agencies (Lowe and Goyder, 1983, p. 139). It is a voluntary organization with tax-free status as a charity but is also a major recipient of central government grants through bodies such as the Nature Conservancy Council, the Countryside Commission and the Forestry Commission.

Over the years, there has been criticism from outside and from within of the Trust's policies. With the growth in rural recreation, Trust properties have been put under increased pressures from visitors. Yet it appears that the Trust has been slow to respond to the challenge of mass leisure (Lowe and Goyder, 1983, p. 148). It is argued that the Trust faces a dilemma, in having to cope with large-scale leisure demands while seeking to achieve the primary objective of protecting buildings and sites. In addition, preservationist attitudes have inhibited acceptance of modern techniques of recreational land management which might be advocated by a body such as the Countryside Commission (Lowe and Goyder, 1983, p. 149). Thus only a very small proportion of the total of 220 country parks in England and Wales are on Trust land.

Since those observations were made, however, there is clear evidence of a wide range of initiatives to deal with recreation issues. These have included 'Countryside comes to town' events in south London and Salford; major involvement in improvements to rights of way on Trust property; meeting the requirements of people with special needs; and adopting a keener and popular approach to sponsorship and promotion of Trust properties and activities. All these have been undertaken at a time when the Trust has been conscious of criticism of its closed nature and the frustration of some, anxious to have an influence on its policy-making.

Besides being a champion of the protection of landscapes and buildings, the campaigning role of the Trust is also of interest. Over the years it has played a major role in preventing undesirable development from taking place in the countryside. However, to retain its independent status, 'the Trust uses its influence judiciously and it assiduously avoids the image of a pressure group' (Lowe and Goyder, 1983, p. 144). In practice, this has meant that it has concentrated its efforts on safeguarding its own property although it has used its own channels of access to government to give support to environmental pressure groups. It is noticeable in recent years that the Trust has campaigned quite openly on a number of environmental issues. These include water privatization, where the Trust helped strengthen safeguards for conservation and public access on land retained by the newly privatized companies; and the need to ensure the survival of a strong planning system which is not watered down by weak strategic planning policies or too lenient in interpretation of policies through the system of planning appeals (National Trust, 1990, p. 6).

Unlike most other agencies discussed in this chapter, the National Trust is able to recruit large numbers of members whose fees make a

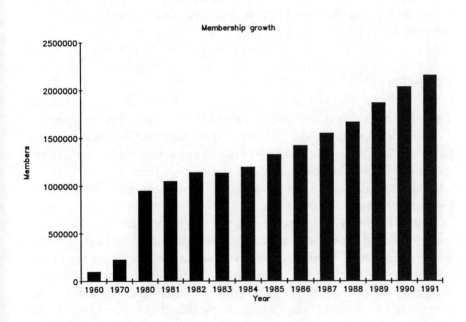

Figure 11.3   Membership of the National Trust
Source: based on National Trust Annual Reports, 1980–1990

significant contribution to the running of property (Figure 11.3). There has been a major increase in Trust membership which stood at 2 152 072 in 1991. This membership provides 25 per cent of Trust income but significant sums are received in the form of gifts and legacies, income from investment and grants. Appeals are targeted at specific projects. In 1988–89 these included a Lake District appeal to increase local staff as wardens and teams to repair footpaths and other countryside facilities. The other appeals included seeking support for the Enterprise Neptune project, renovation of landscaped gardens, and a repair to a sea wall at a Trust property (National Trust, 1990, p. 14).

Despite issues relating to the hybrid nature of the National Trust as a quasi-public voluntary body, it is able to count on a great deal of voluntary support. In many ways its practices can be seen as a model for others. Even though established landowners can retain an influence over property when it is acquired by the Trust, this does not 'prevent the National Trust from creating a very different model of land ownership from the norm in rural Britain: it gives a hint of what the countryside might be like if priority were to be accorded to conservation and public access rather than the very different concerns of most other landowners' (Shoard, 1987, pp. 156–157).

COMMENT

There has been a long tradition of the voluntary sector playing a part in countryside recreation, both in terms of providing facilities and in campaigning. The scale and variety of organizations is considerable and in recent years there has been a renewed interest in their value as a challenge and alternative to local government. The review in this chapter has highlighted several issues.

Firstly, it should be recorded that the voluntary sector has been responsible for providing and managing rural recreation on a large scale in a responsible way. Normally groups have no statutory powers; often they are under-resourced and are highly dependent on their powers of persuasion to achieve their goals. Much effort goes unrecorded, and organizations are highly dependent on considerable commitment from people working on a voluntary basis. For many, there is nothing at all unusual in this arrangement; helpers themselves gain a great deal of personal satisfaction in their task of helping others. In many cases there

290

has never been a need for central support and members and organizers would normally not acknowledge the need for support.

A major preoccupation of voluntary groups is with the problem of finding funding support and much effort is spent trying to find out where funding for the next year is going to come from. The idea of environmental trusts being independent and self-funding is often promoted, but in practice such trusts are highly dependent on government support in one form or another. Often voluntary-sector organizations are subject to sudden withdrawals of funding support, as, for example, in the ending of government job-training schemes on which they relied for labour supplies.

Raising income by realizing the development potential of property through land sales is a valuable but also unpredictable method on which to base future development of policies. In addition, such practices can create confusion in the minds of supporters when a voluntary group takes on the role of land developer. Voluntary-sector organizations thus face difficulties in taking a long-term view of future policies. In the case of organizations whose activities parallel most closely those of local authorities, then they may be seen as a threat and as an unsatisfactory substitute for permanent agencies which provide long-term and continuing support for recreation facilities.

A further issue concerns the extent to which voluntary groups are able to contribute to recreation policy-making. At the site level, or within limited geographical areas, groups may be able to resolve difficulties with other users. At higher levels, there can be difficulties in public agencies' accommodating groups' ambitions, making use of their expertise and responding to constructive criticism. At the same time, the agencies themselves would probably agree that were it not for the continued and sustained pressure from, say, the access groups, present-day provision for public enjoyment in the countryside would be much more limited than it is.

Recent changes in government policies in Britain have resulted in voluntary-sector activity being seen as a manifestation of particular political ideologies. To an extent voluntary organizations have had no choice but conform to the latest government ideas on the appropriate balance between state and private interests. However, there is a danger that increased politicization of voluntary-sector effort could diminish all-party support, particularly if the state/private interest balance changes again. There is a need to maintain a careful balance in order to avoid domination of voluntary-sector activity by the government of the day.

Chapter 12

Conclusions

This book has examined the varied factors that have influenced the planning of recreation in the British countryside. In the conclusions which follow, the main threads running through the text are considered in relation to questions which were posed in Chapter 1.

STYLES OF PLANNING

Within the planning system which emerged in Britain after 1947, it was shown to be exceptional for rural recreation to feature as a major topic in the planning and development process. However, the strongly regulatory styles of planning which aimed to contain urban growth have indirectly benefited rural recreation by safeguarding rural land for use by future generations. Where more strongly prescriptive and 'positive' styles of rural recreation planning have been adopted then this has often been because they have been linked closely to other policy-making sectors. In some cases, for example, rural recreation provision has been under-pinned by central government derelict land and environmental improvement programmes. Provision has thus tended to be grant-led with a major influence being central support which emerged with the 1967 and 1968 Countryside Acts. With a relatively weak constituency, rural recreation policy-makers have adopted a variety of ways of achieving their goals. These have involved use of informal planning measures and a widespread use of techniques of countryside management. In some instances 'hybrid' plans and policies have been produced with a blend of statutory and non-statutory measures.

In relation to the models of planning outlined in Chapter 1, rural recreation planning would seem to share characteristics of both the regulatory model at one extreme and the private management planning model at the other. Particularly noticeable are the examples of private and voluntary-sector agencies undertaking tasks which might hitherto have been associated with the public sector. This can be seen as part of a general trend supported by government for placing more responsibility onto individuals or groups and withdrawing state involvement, at least at the local level.

PLANNING TECHNIQUES

Rural recreational planning and provision has been shown to be opportunistic, without a strong theoretical basis and often lacking evidence of systematic analysis as a basis for policy-making. Plan preparation has often taken place only after the implementation of recreational projects. Nevertheless, Chapter 3 demonstrated ways in which specific analytical techniques have a clear role to play in recreational planning. From those investigations, it emerged that the term 'technique' was used in two senses. Firstly, in analysing and prescribing policies, planners have used a well-established body of techniques based on urban plan-making and rural resource management. Such techniques have focused both on forecasting future demands for rural recreation and in searching for 'optimum' patterns of land use. However, a second type of technique for controlling land uses is to be found within recreational planning policies themselves. Zoning and channelling of recreational pressures are techniques which have been widely adopted in statutory and informal plans, providing frameworks for the operation of development control policies.

In discussing the value of planning techniques for plan-making, it is apparent that practitioners face a dilemma. They work in a culture which is dominated by the need to 'make things happen', but they are increasingly faced with the task of scrutinizing both the general viability of their own and developers' projects and the robustness of analytical and prescriptive techniques that might be used to justify them. In addition, an enhanced role for more systematic use of planning techniques has been a consequence of environmental assessment legislation introduced in 1988. These measures now mean that many types of projects, including recreational proposals, are now required to stand up to more detailed evaluation than in the past.

293

CENTRE–LOCAL RELATIONS

In discussing centre–local relations, the tension which exists between national and local levels of government surfaced at several points in this study. While central support for rural recreation policies has been available through the Countryside Commission, direction from government on statutory planning aspects of rural recreation itself has often been seen to be weak and confusing. A major constraint faced by planning authorities is that government has stressed that statutory plans should focus on physical land-use issues only and should not be concerned with rural land management. Despite this, it was shown in practice that statutory plans have sometimes included non-statutory matters, including aspects relating to language, culture, resource management and social impacts of developments.

The investigations revealed the extent to which frequent changes in legislation are affecting local authorities both as recreation plan-makers and as providers. Championship of consumerism, greater accountability and better value for money have been stressed by government. The results have included a heightened concern about the quality of delivery from local government services. The general effect of these moves has been seen as weakening the power of local authorities as providers. However, the legislative changes requiring the increasing separation of client from contractor have also been regarded as ways of freeing providers from inherited internal constraints caused by the policy-maker also being the provider. In this situation, the position of policy-makers, including the planning authority, could well be enhanced in enabling them to concentrate on key strategic issues and to control effectively the provision of recreational services.

A theme which re-occurs at several places in the text concerns attempts to plan for rural recreation at a regional level. Many rural recreation issues may be appropriately considered at district or county level of government. However, provision of long-distance routes, major recreation facilities, including community forests, need to be considered at regional level. Regional and strategic guidance for development plans and regional strategies for sport and recreation currently perform these tasks unsatisfactorily. The former provide only the barest of guidance and the latter deal largely with urban recreation themes and do not form part of any wider strategy for social, physical and economic development within a region. Governments' intentions on local government reform

294

and the ensuing balance in centre–local relations will be the main determinant on whether there will be a strong regional tier perspective on rural recreational planning.

SUSTAINABILITY

A further angle from which it was suggested that rural recreation planning might be viewed was that of 'sustainability'. In Chapter 1 it was noted that at both the local and strategic levels of planning little attention was given to questions of energy efficiency, with ambivalent or negative advice coming from government. Concern for sustainability issues noted in this study has been limited mainly to the impact of tourism on the environment with increasing calls for the adoption of 'green' approaches to tourism development. Isolated instances exist of providers who encourage use of modes of transport such as walking and cycling for travelling to and within the countryside and public expectation of local authorities is that they should be increasingly concerned with green issues. Yet the evidence from the studies reviewed in this present investigation reveal often only token references to achieving greater sustainability.

Thus, a planning authority might rightly argue with others over acceptable levels of recreational use for ecologically valuable habitats, but scanter attention is likely to be paid to the wider environmental damage which may arise because of visitors with interests in wildlife travelling to sites along narrow, unsuitable roads and lanes. Policy-making can, of course, influence the use of sustainable resources including, for example, site policies for country parks, community forests and other major recreational facilities. Sites developed near to urban areas and facilities capable of being reached by foot, bicycle or public transport, may make a modest contribution to the development of sustainable recreation policies. However, for other forms of provision – car-dependent rural tourism enterprises, for example – the opportunities for achieving sustainable policies are much more problematic. More evidence of the operation of 'good practice' may help diffuse ideas on how sustainability might have a more effective presence in recreational planning policies.

A THREAT, THREATENED OR AN OPPORTUNITY?

There is often likely to be strong opposition to proposals to develop a recreation or tourism project, even if modest in size and unlikely to cause more than minimal disturbance. The strength of 'NIMBYism' can be a powerful force in shaping recreation policies. The relegation of rural recreation to a marginal location in plan-making may reflect the desire of decision-makers to avoid contentious policies: for example, provision for motor-based sports.

On several occasions in this study it was shown that implementation of rural recreation policies was likely to be constrained by the 'acceptability' of initiatives to modify visitor behaviour. It was shown that the ability of planning authorities to plan for rural recreation can be strongly influenced by lobbying by local communities. The more 'commercial' a proposal, the greater pressure there is likely to be on the local authority to refuse planning permission for development, although this was shown to be not always the case. A difficulty faced by a planning authority is that it will also need to pay regard to the economic costs that may result from not allowing a development scheme as well as amenity considerations, and resolution of a conflict may only be resolved via a planning appeal inquiry. Ultimately, policies will reflect people's willingness to pay for maintaining or modifying existing environmental standards.

Chapter 5 drew attention to the way in which rural recreation, rather than being a threat or an opportunity, was itself under threat for a variety of reasons. This is an aspect of rural recreation which in the past has been too readily overlooked. Yet it is an important consideration, whether it involves the loss of permissive access on water company or forestry land, or the severance of access routes for walkers and cyclists from town to countryside because of the construction of new roads. Environmental assessment may help to identify potential losses in the case of specified classes of development outlined in the regulations. However, there is a danger that smaller-scale developments outside the provisions of the environmental assessment regulations may gain planning approval without sufficient regard being paid to their impact on recreation. For rural recreation resources to be satisfactorily safeguarded, planning authorities need to be aware of their existence and ensure that their potential value is clearly indicated on the policy agenda. A continuing role for access and recreation campaign groups will doubtless be that of reminding planning authorities of the importance of these issues.

CLASHES OF CULTURE AND RURAL RECREATION

Rural recreation planning has generally sought to champion conservation, to accommodate rural recreation cautiously in specified locations in the countryside, to minimize possible conflict and to bear the stamp of consensus. To an extent this has been a reflection of what has been expected of the planning system by concerned sections of the public. In the 1980s this orthodox approach was challenged on several grounds as a result of external pressures. Planning has been expected to present a much more 'positive' and promotional stance by government itself and by a variety of bodies ranging, in England, from the Sports Council to the Rural Development Commission and the English Tourist Board, and by equivalent bodies in Scotland and Wales. Rural recreational planning has often reluctantly had to respond to changes taking place in these other policy areas. The result seems to be that there is no longer an orthodox view of what might be a proper focus for rural recreational planning. If rural tourism is included within the remit of this study, then there seems little doubt that those involved in recreational planning and management now share a variety of different 'cultures', resulting in different types of response to people's recreational needs. The Gateway project in Nottingham highlighted the conflict between the visitor's and provider's perception of what might be an appropriate form of recreation in a rural setting. The subsequent approaches there and in later policy development by the Countryside Commission suggest the need for a diversity of approaches. The conventional countryside management service needs to be matched by approaches typified by the presence of 'host' staff to welcome visitors to a site. However, a vital issue here concerns the precise image of 'countryside' that planning seeks to provide or safeguard as a backcloth for rural recreation. Is it the countryside which has all the characteristics of a rustic theme park, a setting for recreational pursuits, a place where the worst fears of some are confirmed as the countryside becomes a place for entertainment? The conflict is illustrated, although to a different degree, in the debate about access to wilderness areas in Britain. Attempts to widen opportunities for long-distance walking remind now that even amongst bodies committed to 'orthodox' protectionist stances of recreational planning, major divisions can occur.

This book has recorded increasingly important roles being played by voluntary and private sectors in providing for rural recreation. What role

Plate 12.1   Identifying acceptable sites for commercial leisure activities in the countryside will be a continuing preoccupation of planning authorities: Trago Mills, near Newton Abbot, Devon, 1992

does this leave for the traditional provider of rural recreation services, the local authority? Should its activities simply be confined to those initiatives that the private or voluntary sector is unable to provide? Is its role now to generate opportunities for the private sector to set about its task of providing for the diverse and constantly changing nature of recreational demand? In the past local authorities have traditionally played a major part in mass provision, devising policies which are free of charge to the user and which often incorporate such social objectives as widening access to the countryside for disadvantaged groups. A test of the role played by local authorities as facilitators rather than as providers will be their ability to ensure that the needs of special groups such as the disabled are met satisfactorily. A further test of this more distanced stance of local authorities will be their ability to influence the ways in which payment is made for enjoyment of rural recreation. Increasingly, reliance is placed on the 'user pays' principle, exploiting opportunities to raise revenue on-site, rather than covering costs through general taxation. Such policies raise important questions about the incidence of payment for access, the ability of the less well-off to continue to enjoy access to the countryside and the future of low cost recreation generally.

Uncertainties persist about the role that the voluntary sector can play as a provider. Quite high hopes have been expressed that it will be a significant alternative competitor to local government as a supplier of facilities. Yet, as was discussed in Chapter 11, there are limitations in the tasks that might be undertaken by voluntary organizations. Such bodies can be highly vulnerable to changes in government policy towards the voluntary sector. Fundraising to support their activities is increasingly competitive as new voluntary groups are created with broadly similar aims. Relying as they do on private sponsorship and support, they tend to suffer markedly during periods of economic recession and their activities can be hindered quite considerably. Yet, despite these constraints, there has been a major increase in direct community involvement in recreation provision. The active part played by parish and community councils in maintenance and improvement of public rights of way and adoption of local open spaces suggests that those particular bodies could play an increasingly important role in recreation provision in the future.

In writing this book, the author set out to explore how far there was evidence of planning *for* rural recreation in Britain. Has the statutory planning system paid more than passing regard for rural recreation provision? The evidence indicates that most of a great deal of what might be regarded as rural recreational planning has been undertaken through informal rather than statutory plans and policies. Yet, the investigations show that the statutory planning system also has a role to play in indicating where, when and by whom, public, private and voluntary-sector recreational projects actually take place. In this regulatory role, the statutory planning system, and particularly the development control arm, is of some significance in shaping rural recreation provision.

It must be concluded, therefore, that although 'positive' statutory planning *for* rural recreation is a limited phenomenon in Britain, there is a close and well established relationship between planning *and* rural recreation.

References

Abercrombie, P. (1945) *Greater London Plan 1944*, London: HMSO, 221 pp.

Aldridge, D. (1975) *Guide to Countryside Interpretation, Part 1: Principles of countryside interpretation and interpretive planning*. For Countryside Commission for Scotland and Countryside Commission, London: HMSO, 40 pp.

Anderson, R. (1990) 'The process of plan preparation', in Countryside Commission, *Advice Manual for the Preparation of a Community Forest Plan*, Cheltenham: Countryside Commission, pp. 8–15.

Andrew, D. (1988) 'Creating railway paths', in C. Banister and D. Groome (eds), *Railway Paths – Missed Connections?*, Conference proceedings, Department of Town and Country Planning, University of Manchester, pp. 3–13.

Andrews, J. (1991) 'Planning for visitors on unwardened nature reserves', *British Wildlife*, **2**, (2), 206–213.

Anfield, J. (1971) 'The underprivileged and the countryside', *Countryside Recreation News Supplement*, **4**, 21–22.

Anon (1989) 'Rainstorm that is brewing over a valley in Wales', *The Independent*, 21 November 1989.

Anon (1991) 'Government has gone soft on enforcement', *The Planner*, **77**, (37), 4.

Anon (1991) 'The path to righteousness', *Byway and Bridleway*, journal of the Byway and Bridleway Trust, **9**, 33.

Archer, D. (1988) 'Working with voluntary organisations and volunteers'; in *Report of the third national parks workshop, Llandudno. Harnessing resources for national park purposes*, Cheltenham: Countryside Commission, pp. 37–40.

Arthur Young, McClelland, Moores & Co (1984) *Review of the Eco-*

nomic Efficiency of National Park Authorities, Cheltenham: Countryside Commission, CCP 160, 56 pp.

ASH Partnership and Cousins Stephens in association with Institute of Terrestial Ecology and Centre for Environmental Interpretation (1991) *Development opportunities in the Natural Environment: A report to Highland Regional Council and others. Executive summary*, Glasgow: ASH Partnership, 29 pp.

Audit Commission (1988) *Competitive Management of Parks and Green Spaces*, London: HMSO, 42 pp.

Audit Commission (1989) *Sport for Whom? Clarifying the local authority role in sport and recreation*, London: HMSO, 25 pp.

Audit Commission (1990) *Performance Review in Local Government: Action Guide. A handbook*, London: HMSO, 42 pp.

Audit Commission (1991) *The Citizen's Charter: Local authority performance indicators*, London: HMSO, 5 pp.

Banister, C., Groome, D.M. and Pawson, G. (1992) 'The shared use debate: a discussion on the shared use of canal towing paths by walkers, anglers and cyclists', *Journal of Environmental Management*, **34**, 149–158.

Barker, F. (1991) 'Protect and assert ... a guide to section 130 of the Highways Act, 1980', *Journal of Planning and Environment Law*, January, pp. 3–8.

Beazley, E. (1969) *Designed for Recreation*, London: Faber and Faber, 217 pp.

Bedfordshire County Council (1987) *Development and Management Plan: Harrold-Odell Country Park, Bedfordshire, Leisure Services*, Bedford: The Council, 16 pp.

Bell, P. and Cloke, P. (1989) 'The changing relationship between the private and public sectors: privatisation and rural Britain', *Journal of Rural Studies*, **5**, (1), 1–15.

Bell, S. (1991) 'New National Forest' quoted in *Planning*, **920** (21 May 1991), p. 22.

Benington, J. and White, J. (eds) (1988) *The Future of Leisure Services*, Harlow: Longman 272 pp.

Biggs, W.D. (1990) *Settle–Carlisle Railway: Opportunities for development*, For Standing Conference for the Settle–Carlisle Railway, Kendal: Cumbria County Council, 23 pp.

Binks, G. (1973) *Goodwood Nature Trail for the Blind and Sighted Persons*, Cheltenham: Countryside Commission, CCP 68, 11 pp.

Binks, G. (1987) 'Planning for provision for the disabled at your site: a checklist', *Environmental Interpretation*, **3**, (2), 14–15.

Bishop, K. (1991) 'Community forests: implementing the concept', *The Planner*, **77**, (18), 6–10.

Blatchford, B. (1990) *The Long Distance Walker's Handbook* , London: A & C Black, 160 pp.

Bolton, D. (1991) *Race Against Time: How Britain's waterways were saved*, London: Mandarin, 270 pp.

Boothby, J., Tungatt, M., Townsend, A.R. and Collins, M.F. (1981) *A Sporting Chance: Family and environmental influences on taking part in sport*, Sports Council Study 22, London: The Sports Council, 64 pp.

Bouquet, M. and Winter, M. (eds) (1987) *Who From Their Labours Rest? Conflict and practice in rural tourism*, Aldershot: Avebury, 158 pp.

Bovaird, A.G., Tricker, M.J. and Stoakes, R. (1984) *Recreation Management and Pricing*, Aldershot: Gower, 182 pp.

Bowers, J., O'Donnell, K. and Whatmore, S. (1988) *Liquid Assets: the likely effects of privatisation of the water authorities on wildlife habitats and landscape*, London: Council for the Protection of Rural England, Royal Society for the Protection of Birds, 45 pp.

Breheny, M.J. (1991) 'Sustainable development and urban form: the contradictions of the compact city', *Joint International Conference, Association of Collegiate Schools of Planning and Association of European Schools of Planning, Oxford Polytechnic 1991*, 17 pp.

Brindley, T., Rydin, Y. and Stoker, G. (1989) *Remaking Planning: The politics of urban change in the Thatcher years*, London: Unwin Hyman, 197 pp.

Briscoe, B. (1983) 'Regeneration in West Yorkshire', in D.T. Cross and M.R. Bristow (eds), *Structure Planning in Britain: A commentary on procedure and practice*, London: Pion, pp. 96–124.

British Tourist Authority (1988) *The British Tourism Market*, London: British Tourist Authority, 24 pp.

British Tourist Authority (1990) *Digest of Tourist Statistics No 14*, London: British Tourist Authority, 89 pp.

British Waterways Board (1969) *Annual Report and Accounts for the Year Ended 31st December, 1968*, London: HMSO, 102 pp.

British Waterways Board (1986) *The British Waterways System: Leisure and tourism on inland waterways*, Planning and Research Report No 23, Watford: British Waterways Board, 30 pp.

303

British Waterways Board (1989) *Leeds and Liverpool Canal: Towing path user survey*, Planning and Research Report No 33, Watford: British Waterways Board, 83 pp.

British Waterways Board (1989) *Report and Accounts 1987/88*, London: British Waterways Board, 56 pp.

British Waterways Board (1990) *Research Matters: Planning and Research Unit Annual Review No 1*, Watford: British Waterways Business Planning and Research Unit, 8 pp.

British Waterways Board (1991) *Policy Statement: Towing paths*, Watford: British Waterways Board.

Bromley, P. (1990) *Countryside Management*, London: E. and F. N. Spon, 365 pp.

Broom, G. (1991) 'Environmental management of countryside visitors', *Ecos*, **12**, (1), 14–21.

Brotherton, I. (1973) 'Recreational capacity', *Recreation News Supplement 9*, Countryside Commission, pp. 6–11.

Brotherton, I., Maurice, O., Barrow, G. and Fishwick, A. (1978) *Tarn Hows: An approach to the management of a popular beauty spot*, Cheltenham: Countryside Commission, CCP 106, 53 pp.

Building Design Partnership (1990) *Audenshaw Estate development for a business park, hotel, housing and golf course for NWW Properties Ltd*, Manchester: Building Design Partnership, 66 pp plus appendices.

Bunce, R.G.H. and Barr, J.C. (1988) *Rural Information for Forward Planning*, Grange over Sands: Institute of Terrestial Ecology, 115 pp.

Burton, R.J.C. (1974) *The recreational carrying capacity of the countryside*, Keele University Library, Occasional Paper No 11, 221 pp.

Burton, T.L. (ed) (1970) *Recreation Research and Planning*, London: George Allen and Unwin, 276 pp.

Burton, T.L. (1971) *Experiments in Recreation Research*, London: George Allen and Unwin, 365 pp.

Burton, T.L. (1983) 'Surveys and forecasts', in S.R. Lieber and D.R. Fesenmaier (eds), *Recreation Planning and Management*, London: E. and F.N. Spon Ltd, pp 229–240.

Cabinet Office (Enterprise Unit) (1985) *Pleasure, Leisure and Jobs – The business of tourism*, London: HMSO, 19 pp.

Cairns, C.B. (1982) *An Experiment Continued: Countryside management in the urban fringe of Barnet and South Hertfordshire*, Cheltenham: Countryside Commission, CCP 148, 91 pp.

Cairns, C.B. (1985) *Bridleway Management*, Cheltenham: Countryside Commission, CCP 189, 44 pp.

Central Statistical Office (1990) *Social Trends 20, 1990 Edition*, London: HMSO, 208 pp.

Centre for Leisure Research (1986a) *A digest of Sports Statistics for the UK*, Sports Council Information Series No 7, London: The Sports Council, 166 pp.

Centre for Leisure Research (1986b) *Access Study Summary Report*, Cheltenham: Countryside Commission/Sports Council, CCP 216, 26 pp.

Centre for Leisure Research (1986c) *Access to the Countryside for Recreation and Sport*, Countryside Commission/Sports Council, Cheltenham: Countryside Commission, CCP 217, 174 pp.

Chartered Institute of Public Finance and Accountancy (1990) *Leisure and Recreation 1990–91 Estimates*, London: CIPFA Statistical and Information Services, 120 pp.

Chatters, C. (1991) 'Golf: growth in a vacuum', *Ecos*, **12**, (1), 21–25.

Cherry, G.E. (1975) *Environmental Planning 1939–69 Vol II National Parks and Recreation in the Countryside*, London: HMSO, 173 pp.

Cherry, G.E. (1988) *Cities and Plans: The shaping of urban Britain in the nineteenth and twentieth centuries*, London: Edward Arnold, 210 pp.

Cheshire County Council (1989) *West Heath Country Park Congleton: Proceedings of Libraries and Countryside Committee*, 3 April 1989.

Cheshire County Council (1990) *Cheshire 2001 Structure Plan: Explanatory memorandum*, Chester: Cheshire County Council, 169 pp.

Claridge, C.J. (1988) 'The approach adopted by Highland Council', in R.G.H. Bunce and J.C. Barr (eds), *Rural Information for Forward Planning*, Grange over Sands: Institute of Terrestial Ecology, pp. 21–28.

Clawson, M. (1981) *Methods for Measuring the Demand for the Value of Outdoor Recreation*, RFF reprint 10, fifth printing, Washington DC: Resources for the Future, 36 pp.

Claxton, E. and Dartington Amenity Research Trust (1978) *Cycling to the Countryside*, Cheltenham: Countryside Commission, WP 10, 91 pp.

Cleveland County Council (1991) *Opening the Gateway: A countryside recreation strategy for Cleveland*, Middlesbrough: Cleveland County Council, 34 pp.

Cloke, P. (ed) (1987) *Rural Planning: Policy into Action*, London: Harper and Row, 229 pp.

Coalter, F. with Long, J. and Duffield, B. (1988) *Recreational Welfare: The rationale for public leisure policy*, Aldershot: Avebury, 211 pp.

Cobham Resource Consultants (1988) *A Holiday Village in the Cotswold Water Park: Environmental statement for Granada Group plc*, Oxford: Cobham Resource Consultants, 54 pp.

Colenutt, R. and Sidaway, R. (1973) *Forest of Dean: Day visitor survey*, Forestry Commission Bulletin 46, London: HMSO, 52 pp.

Collis, I. (1990) 'Groundwork – fact and fiction', *Ecos*, **11**, (4), 34–42.

Commission of the European Communities (1985) 'Council Directive of 27 June 1985 on the assessment of the effects of certain public and private projects on the environment', *Official Journal of the European Communities*, **L 175**, 40–48.

Cooper, G. and Hull, A.P. (1978) 'Managing a linear country park', *Town and Country Planning*, **46**, 168–172.

Coopers and Lybrand Associates Ltd (1979) *Rufford Country Park Marketing Study: a report to the Countryside Commission and Nottinghamshire County Council*, Cheltenham: Countryside Commission, CCP 129, 164 pp.

Coppock, J.T. and Duffield, B. (1975) *Recreation in the Countryside: A spatial analysis*, London: Macmillan, 262 pp.

Cornwall County Council (1985) *Cornwall Countryside Local Plan*, Truro: Cornwall County Council, 52 pp.

Cornwall County Council (1988) *Cornwall Structure Plan, 1st Alteration, Explanatory Memorandum 1988*, Truro: Cornwall County Council, 165 pp.

Cotswold District Council (1989) *Local planning inquiry. Application CT6641. Holiday Village: Statement of case by Cotswold District Council*, Cirencester: Cotswold District Council.

Cotswold Water Park Joint Committee (1969) *Cotswold Water Park Review*, Gloucester, Cotswold Water Park Joint Committee, 67 pp.

Cotswold Water Park Joint Committee (1983) *Cotswold Water Park Review*, Gloucester, Cotswold Water Park Joint Committee, 69 pp.

Council for National Parks (1988) *Tourist Complexes in National Parks – A discussion paper*, London: Council for National Parks, 12 pp.

Council for the Protection of Rural England (1989) *Permitted Development: Response to Department of the Environment consultation document*, London: The Council for the Protection of Rural England, 15 pp.

306

Country Landowners Association (1984) *A Guide to the Countryside for Disabled People*, Country Landowners Association, 193 pp.

Countryside Commission (1972) *The Goyt Valley Traffic Experiment*, Cheltenham: Countryside Commission, CCP 55, 114 pp.

Countryside Commission (1974a) *Advisory Notes on Country Park Plans*, Cheltenham: Countryside Commission, CCP 80, 9 pp.

Countryside Commission (1974b) *Advisory Notes on National Park Plans*, Cheltenham: Countryside Commission, CCP 81, 7 pp.

Countryside Commission (1975) *Seventh Report of the Countryside Commission for the year ended 30 September 1974*, London: HMSO, 79 pp.

Countryside Commission (1976a) *The Bollin Valley: A study of land management in the urban fringe*, Cheltenham: Countryside Commission, CCP 97, 47 pp.

Countryside Commission (1976b) *The Lake District Upland Management Experiment*, Cheltenham: Countryside Commission, CCP 93, 41 pp.

Countryside Commission (1977) *SIRSEE: The study of informal recreation in South East England. The Demand report*, Cheltenham: Countryside Commission, 100 pp.

Countryside Commission (1979a) *Interpretive Planning: Advisory series No 2*, Cheltenham: Countryside Commission, 16 pp.

Countryside Commission (1979b) *The Snowdonia Upland Management Experiment*, Cheltenham: Countryside Commission, CCP 122, 39 pp.

Countryside Commission (1981a) *Informal Countryside Recreation for Disabled People*, Advisory series No 15, Cheltenham: Countryside Commission, 79 pp.

Countryside Commission (1981b) *Countryside Management in the Urban Fringe*, Cheltenham: Countryside Commission, CCP 136, 135 pp.

Countryside Commission (1983) *Groundwork North West: The programme*, Manchester: Countryside Commission, 3 pp (pamphlet).

Countryside Commission (1985a) *National Countryside Recreation Survey: 1984*, Cheltenham: Countryside Commission, CCP 201, 20 pp.

Countryside Commission (1985b) *The Wayfarer Project*, Cheltenham: Countryside Commission, CCP 193, 68 pp.

Countryside Commission (1987a) *A Compendium of Recreation Statistics*, CCD 16, Cheltenham: Countryside Commission, CCD 16, 32 pp.

Countryside Commission (1987b) *Forestry in the Countryside*, Cheltenham: Countryside Commission, CCP 245, 24 pp.

Countryside Commission (1987c) *Planning for Countryside in Metropolitan Areas*, Cheltenham: Countryside Commission, CCP 244, 20 pp.

Countryside Commission (1987d) *Public Transport to the Countryside*, Cheltenham: Countryside Commission, CCP 227, 36 pp.

Countryside Commission (1987e) *The Neath Local Access Project: An interim report*, Cheltenham: Countryside Commission, CCP 236, 28 pp.

Countryside Commission (1988a) *Changing the Rights of Way Network*, Cheltenham: Countryside Commission, CCP 254, 20 pp.

Countryside Commission (1988b) *National Park Plans: Second review. Advisory notes*, Cheltenham: Countryside Commission, CCD 30, 9 pp.

Countryside Commission (1988c) *Paths, Routes and Trails: A consultation paper*, Cheltenham: Countryside Commission, CCP 253, 20 pp.

Countryside Commission (1989a) *A Countryside for Everyone*, Cheltenham: Countryside Commission, CCP 265, 31 pp.

Countryside Commission (1989b) *A New National Forest in the Midlands: A consultation document*, Cheltenham: Countryside Commission, CCP 278, 8 pp.

Countryside Commission (1989c) *Enjoying the Countryside: Priorities for action*, Cheltenham: Countryside Commission, CCP 235, 16 pp.

Countryside Commission (1989d) *Managing Rights of Way: An agenda for action*, Cheltenham: Countryside Commission, CCP 273, 24 pp.

Countryside Commission (1989e) *Paths Routes and Trails: Policies and priorities*, Cheltenham: Countryside Commission, CCP 266, 16 pp.

Countryside Commission (1989f) *Principles for Tourism in National Parks*, Countryside Commission with English Tourist Board (leaflet).

Countryside Commission (1989g) *Recreational Cycling in the Countryside*, Cheltenham: Countryside Commission, CCP 259, 40 pp.

Countryside Commission (1989h) *Rights of Way: A challenge for the 1990s*, Cheltenham: Countryside Commission, CCD 48, 14 pp.

Countryside Commission (1989i) *Sites of Conservation and Recreation Value Currently in the Ownership of Water Authorities*, Cheltenham: Countryside Commission, CCD 34, 58 pp.

Countryside Commission (1990a) *Advice Manual for the Preparation of a Community Forest Plan*, Cheltenham: Countryside Commission , CCP 271, 48 pp.

Countryside Commission (1990b) *National Rights of Way Condition Survey 1988*, Cheltenham: Countryside Commission, CCP 284, 28 pp.

308

Countryside Commission (1990c) *The New National Forest: A countryside for the 21st century*, Cheltenham: Countryside Commission, CCP 328, 4 pp.

Countryside Commission (1990d) *The Rights of Way Act 1990: Guidance notes for highway authorities*, Cheltenham: Countryside Commission, CCP 301, 32 pp.

Countryside Commission (1990e) *Training for Tomorrow's Countryside. The Report of the Countryside Staff Training Advisory Group*, Cheltenham: Countryside Commission, CCP 269, 108 pp.

Countryside Commission (1991a) *Environmental Assessment: The treatment of landscape and countryside recreation issues, Technical Report*, Cheltenham: Countryside Commission, CCP 326, 52 pp.

Countryside Commission (1991b) *Visitors to the Countryside*, Cheltenham: Countryside Commission, CCP 341, 23 pp.

Countryside Commission (1992a) *Countrygoer News*, Cheltenham: Countryside Commission, 12 pp.

Countryside Commission (1992b) *Parish Paths Partnership: An outline*, Cheltenham: Countryside Commission, CCP 380, 4 pp.

Countryside Commission for Scotland (1974) *A Park System for Scotland*, Redgorton: Countryside Commission for Scotland, 36 pp.

Countryside Commission for Scotland (1986) *Development of Long Distance Routes in Scotland: Report of working party (CCS and CSLA)*, Redgorton: Countryside Commission for Scotland, 29 pp.

Countryside Commission for Scotland (1988) *Management Plans for Country Parks: A guide to their preparation*, Redgorton: Countryside Commission for Scotland, 10 pp.

Countryside Commission for Scotland (1990) *Day Trips to Scotland's Countryside*, Redgorton: Countryside Commission for Scotland, 44 pp.

Countryside Review Committee (1977) *Leisure and the countryside: A discussion paper*, Topic Paper No 2, London: HMSO, 23 pp.

Cross, D.T. (1983) 'Theory', in D.T. Cross and M.R. Bristow (eds), *English Structure Planning: A commentary on procedure and practice*, London: Pion pp. 285–308.

Cross, D.T. and Bristow, M.R. (eds) (1983) *English Structure Planning: A commentary on procedure and practice*, London: Pion, 342 pp.

Croucher, N. (1981) *Outdoor Pursuits for Disabled People*, London: Woodhead Faulkner for the Disabled Living Foundation, 189 pp.

309

Crowther, A. (1990) 'Countryside planning: the response of the planning system to increased pressures for change with special reference to two districts in Cheshire', Unpublished MTPI dissertation, University of Manchester, 139 pp.

Cumbria Tourist Board (1990) *Regional Tourism Strategy for Cumbria*, Windermere: Cumbria Tourist Board, 34 pp.

Curry, N. (1985) 'Countryside recreation sites policy: a review', *Town Planning Review*, **56**, (1), 70–89.

Curry, N. and Comley, A. (1986a) *Countryside Recreation Policies in Structure Plans: A report to the Countryside Commission*, Gloucester: GLOSCAT School of Environmental Studies, 188 pp.

Curry, N. and Comley, A. (1986b) *Who enjoys the countryside?* Strathclyde papers on planning, Dept of Urban and Regional Planning, University of Strathclyde, 29 pp.

Cyclists' Touring Club (1990) *Mountain bikes: policy statement*, Godalming: The Cyclist's Touring Club.

Cyclists' Touring Club (1991) *British Waterways Bill: Humble Petition of the Cyclists' Touring Club*, Godalming: Cyclists' Touring Club, 4 pp.

Darling, F. and Buchanan, S. (1985) *Doing More than Volunteering: Volunteers in the national park*, Berkhamstead: The Volunteer Centre, 54 pp.

Dartington Amenity Research Trust (1976) *Public Transport for Countryside Recreation*, Cheltenham: Countryside Commission, CCP 94, 52 pp.

Dartington Amenity Research Trust (1977) *A Guide to the Preparation of Initial Regional Recreation Strategies*, Redgorton: Countryside Commission for Scotland, Scottish Sports Council, Scottish Tourist Board and Forestry Commission and others, 84 pp.

Dartington Amenity Research Trust (1979) *Dales Rail*, Cheltenham: Countryside Commission, CCP 120, 33 pp.

Dartington Amenity Research Trust (1982) *Financing of Water-based Recreation.* Wallingford: Hydraulics Research Station, Report IT 236, 175 pp.

Dartington Amenity Research Trust in association with the Department of Psychology, University of Surrey (1978) *Interpretation in visitor centres.* For British Tourist Authority and others, Cheltenham: Countryside Commission, CCP 115, 126 pp.

Davies, H.W. (1989) 'A people's playground', *Countryside Commission News*, 38 (July/August), 88 pp.

Davies, H.W.E., Edwards, D. and Rowley, A.R. (1986) *The Relationship between Development Plans, Development Control, and Appeals*, working papers in land management and development: Environmental policy No. 10, Department of Land Management and Development, University of Reading, 89 pp. plus appendices.

Department of Education and Science (1966) *Report of the Land Use Study Group for Forestry, Agriculture and the Multiple Use of Rural Land (Ellison Report)*, London: HMSO, 110 pp.

Department of the Environment (1974) *Strategic Plan for the North West*, London: HMSO, 283 pp.

Department of the Environment (1975) *Sport and Recreation*, Cmnd 6200, London: HMSO, 20 pp.

Department of the Environment (1977a) *Guidelines for Regional Recreational Strategies*, Circular 73/77, London: HMSO, 11 pp.

Department of the Environment (1977b) *Leisure and the Quality of Life: A report on four experiments*, London: HMSO (two volumes) pp. 142 and 530.

Department of the Environment (1984) *Memorandum on Structure and Local Plans*, Circular 22/84, London: HMSO, 85 pp.

Department of the Environment (1987) *Development Involving Agricultural Land*, Circular 16/87, London: HMSO, 5 pp.

Department of the Environment (1988a) *Environmental Assessment*, Circular 15/88, London: HMSO, 25 pp.

Department of the Environment (1988b) *Planning Policy Guidance 1: Policy and principles*, London: HMSO, PPG 1, 5 pp.

Department of the Environment (1988c) *Planning Policy Guidance 11: Strategic guidance for Merseyside*, London: HMSO, PPG 11, 7 pp.

Department of the Environment (1988d) *Town and Country Planning (Assessment of Environmental Effects) Regulations 1988 (Statutory Instrument No 1199) as amended by Statutory Instrument SI 1990 No 367*, London: HMSO 22 pp.

Department of the Environment (1988e) *Town and Country Planning General Development Order*, Circular 22/88, London: HMSO, 21 pp.

Department of the Environment (1988f) *Unitary Development Plans: Local Government Act 1985: S.4 and Sch 1*, Circular 3/88, London: HMSO, 14 pp.

Department of the Environment (1989a) *Environmental Assessment: A guide to the procedures,* London: HMSO, 64 pp.

Department of the Environment (1989b) *Permitted Use Rights in the Countryside,* Consultation paper, London: Department of the Environment, 14 pp.

Department of the Environment (1989c) *The Future of Development Plans,* Cm 569, London: HMSO, 17 pp.

Department of the Environment (1991a) Application by Park Hall Leisure, The Granada Group plc, and ARC Properties: *Report of planning inquiry and decision letter,* Bristol: Department of the Environment, Ref SW/P/5224/220/2, 188 pp.

Department of the Environment (1991b) *Local Government Financial Statistics, England, No 2 1990,* London: HMSO, 85 pp.

Department of the Environment (1991c) *Permitted Development Rights for Agriculture and Forestry: A report by Land Use Consultants in association with Countryside Planning and Management and Prior and Rickerts Silviculture,* London: HMSO, 52 pp.

Department of the Environment (1991d) *Planning and Compensation Act 1991: Planning obligations,* Circular 16/91, London: HMSO, 8 pp.

Department of the Environment (1991e) *Planning Policy Guidance 17: Sport and recreation,* London: HMSO, 13 pp.

Department of the Environment (1992a) *Planning Policy Guidance 1: General Policy and Principles,* London: HMSO, PPG 1, 9 pp.

Department of the Environment (1992b) *Planning Policy Guidance 12: development plans and regional planning guidance,* London: HMSO, PPG 12, 68 pp.

Department of Transport (1989) *National Road Traffic Forecasts (Great Britain) 1989,* London: HMSO, 39 pp.

Departments of the Environment/Department of Transport (1977) *Roads and Traffic: National parks,* Circular 118/77, London: The Departments, 5 pp.

Derwent Valley Advisory Committee (1972) *Derwent View,* Durham: Durham County Council, 15 pp.

Dickinson, G. (1988) 'Countryside recreation', in P.H. Selman (ed), *Countryside Planning in Practice: The Scottish experience,* Stirling University Press, pp. 89–104.

Dobbs, B. (1984) 'No tourists – no transport?' in C. Banister and D. Groome (eds), *Out and About: Promoting access to countryside recreation by bus, train, bicycle and foot,* Occasional Paper 12, Department of Town and Country Planning, Manchester University, pp. 25–42.

Dodd, T. (1991) *Leisure Day Visits in Great Britain, 1988/89,* A survey carried out by the Social Survey Division of the Office of Population Censuses and Surveys for the Employment Department and the British Tourist Authority/English Tourist Board, London: HMSO, 119 pp.

Dower, M. (1965) 'The Fourth Wave – the challenge of leisure', *Architect's Journal,* 20 January, 123–190.

Drabble, M. (1979) *A Writer's Landscape,* London: Thames and Hudson, 288 pp.

Duffield, B.S. (1982) 'A review of mobility and countryside recreation', *Countryside Recreation Research Advisory Group Conference Proceedings 1982,* London: The Sports Council, pp. 112–138.

Duffield, B.S. and Long, J. (1984) 'Planning local leisure provision in a changing society', in J. Long and R. Hecock (eds), *Leisure, Tourism and Social Change,* Edinburgh: Centre for Leisure Research, pp. 147–175.

Dyke, J., Dagnall, P., Rees, H. and Vasey, T. (1986) *Self Guided Trails: A national survey,* Manchester: Centre for Environmental Interpretation, 46 pp.

Eachus Huckson Partnership (1988) *The Water Industry in the Countryside,* CCP 239, Cheltenham: Countryside Commission, 36 pp.

Eardley, G. (1989) 'The Water Bill: General proposals, recreation and water use', in *Mersey Basin Campaign Seminar: The Water Bill: A briefing for voluntary organisations,* 14 January 1989, Manchester: Mersey Basin Campaign, pp. 3–9.

East Sussex County Council (1987) *Seven Sisters Country Park – Management Plan 1987,* Lewes: The Council, 18 pp.

Ehrman, R. (1988) *Planning Planning – clearer strategies – and environmental controls,* Policy Study 100, London: Centre for Policy Studies, 29 pp.

Eisenschitz, A. (1988) 'The growth of leisure: panacea or political football?, *Planning and Practice Research,* **2,** 14–18.

Elson, M.J. (1977) *A Review and Evaluation of Countryside Recreation Site Surveys,* Cheltenham: Countryside Commission, WP9, 138 pp.

Elson, M.J. (1986) *Green Belts: Conflict mediation in the urban fringe,* London: Heinemann, 304 pp.

Elson, M.J., Buller, H. and Stanley, P. (1986) *Providing for Motor Sports: From image to reality,* Sports Council Study 28, 281 pp.

Elson, M.J. (1990) 'Planning gain; the implications for conservation', *Ecos*, **11** (2), 2–6.

English Tourist Board (1981) *Planning for Tourism in England*, London: English Tourist Board, 102 pp.

English Tourist Board (1985a) *Holiday Motivations: A special report on the British Tourism Survey*, London: English Tourist Board, 32 pp.

English Tourist Board (1985b) *Kielder Tourism Development Action Programme*, London: English Tourist Board, 9 pp.

English Tourist Board (1988a) *The Business Makers: ETB Development Division and Section Four Funding*, London: English Tourist Board, 8 pp.

English Tourist Board (1988b) *Visitors in the Countryside: Rural tourism: A development strategy*, London: English Tourist Board, 24 pp.

English Tourist Board (1989a) *Tourism For All: A report of the working party chaired by Mary Baker*, London: English Tourist Board, 64 pp.

English Tourist Board (1989b) *Tourism Investment Report*, London: English Tourist Board, 74 pp.

English Tourist Board and Employment Department Group (1991) *Tourism and the Environment: Maintaining the balance*, London: English Tourist Board, 56 pp.

Essex County Council (1991) *Essex Protected Lanes: Preservation of minor rural roads*, Colchester: County Planning Department, 7 pp.

Eversley, Lord (1910) *Commons, Forests and Footpaths*, London: Cassell and Co., 356 pp.

Field, B. and MacGregor, B. (1987) *Forecasting Techniques for Urban and Regional Planning*, London: Hutchinson, 238 pp.

Fieldfare Trust (undated) The Fieldfare Trust: *Countryside access design competition: country gate; adapted picnic table*, Sheffield: The Trust, pamphlets.

Flanagan, B. (1990) 'The competitive environment', *The Ranger Magazine*, **20**, 3.

Forestry Commission (1984) *Cycling in Forestry Commission Forests; Policy statement*, Edinburgh: Forestry Commission, 2 pp.

Forestry Commission (1989) *Great Britain: Great Forest*, Edinburgh: Forestry Commission (pamphlet).

Forestry Commission (1991) *70th Annual Report and Accounts 1989–90*, London: HMSO, 93 pp.

Frater, J. (1982) *Farm Tourism in England and Overseas*, Research Memorandum 93, CURS, Birmingham University, 55 pp.

Friends of the Earth (1984) *Environmental and other implications of the growth in off highway cycling: a paper for consultation*, London: Friends of the Earth, 8 pp.

Friends of the Lake District (1990) *On the Right Road?*, Kendal: Friends of the Lake District, 8 pp.

Getz, D. (1982) *The Impact of Tourism in Badenoch and Strathspey*, Inverness: Highland Regional Council, 102 pp.

Gibbons, R. (1991) 'Reserve focus: Cuckmere Haven, Seven Sisters Country Park, East Sussex', *British Wildlife*, **2**, (2), 230–232.

Gloucestershire County Council (1985) *Upper Thames Plan: Minerals, agriculture, recreation and tourism and conservation local plan*, Gloucester: Gloucestershire County Council, 78 pp.

Glyptis, S. (1991) *Countryside Recreation*, Harlow: Longman Group UK, 180 pp.

Glyptis, S.A. (1981) 'Leisure life-styles', *Regional Studies*, **15**, (5), 311–326.

Goodwin, P., Hallett, S., Kenny, F. and Stokes, G. (1991) *Transport: The New Realism: Summary and Conclusions*, Oxford: Transport Studies Unit, University of Oxford, 6 pp.

Graham, D. (1988) *Extending public bridleways in Essex*, Horndon on the Hill: Essex Bridleways Association, 11 pp.

Gratton, C. and Taylor, P. (1985) *Sport and Recreation: An economic analysis*, London: E. and F.N. Spon, 261 pp.

Greater Manchester Council (1985a) *Mersey Valley Local Plan: Report of the Inspector on objections and representations to the plan*, Manchester: Greater Manchester Council, 56 pp.

Greater Manchester Council (1985b) *Mersey Valley Local Plan: Deposited plan*, Manchester: Greater Manchester Council, 79 pp.

Greater Manchester Countryside Unit (1991) Greater Manchester Countryside Information Unit, Ashton under Lyne: personal communication.

Green, B.H. (1985) *Countryside Conservation: The protection and management of amenity ecosystems*, London: George Allen and Unwin, 253 pp.

Green, B.H. and Marshall, I.C. (1987) 'An assessment of the role of golf courses in Kent, England, in protecting wildlife and landscapes', *Landscape and Urban Planning*, **14**, 143–154.

Green, R. and Holliday, J. (1991) *Country Planning: A time for action*, London: Town and Country Planning Association, 21 pp.

Greening, P.A.K. and Slater, P. (1981) *Rural Recreational Transport:*

The Sunday bus experiment, TRRL Report 1026, Crowthorne: Transport and Road Research Laboratory, 47 pp.

Greer, J.V. and Murray, M.R. (1988) *A Recreation Strategy for Mourne Area of Outstanding Natural Beauty*, Sports Council for Northern Ireland, 52 pp.

Gregory, R. (1971) *The Price of Amenity: Five studies in conservation and government*, London: Macmillan, 319 pp.

Gregory, D.G. (1970) *Green Belts and Development Control: A case study in the West Midlands*, Occasional Paper No 12, Centre for Urban and Regional Studies, University of Birmingham, 69 pp.

Grimshaw, J. (1988) 'Railway paths: construction matters', in C. Banister and D. Groome, (eds) *Railway Paths – Missed connections?*, Conference proceedings, Department of Town and Country Planning, Manchester University, pp. 40–46.

Groome, D. and Tarrant, C. (1985) 'Countryside Recreation: Achieving access for all?', in A. Gilg (ed.), *Countryside Planning Yearbook*, Norwich: Geo Books, pp. 72–100.

Groome, D.M. (1986) *Recreation 2000 – the Prospects for Recreational Cycling*, Consultant's report, Cheltenham: The Countryside Commission, 112 pp.

Groome, D.M. (1990) 'Green corridors: A discussion of a planning concept', *Landscape and Urban Planning*, **19**, 383–387.

Groome, D.M. (1991) 'Land trusts: the conservation potential', *Ecos*, **12**, (1), 56–59.

Gunn, C. (1988) *Tourism Planning*, 2nd edn, New York: Taylor & Francis, 357 pp.

Gwynedd County Council (1989) *Gwynedd Structure Plan: Draft explanatory memorandum*, Caernarfon: Gwynedd County Council, 58 pp.

Hall, J. (1974) 'Forests as recreation resources', in P. Lavery (ed.), *Recreational Geography*, Newton Abbot: David and Charles, pp. 145–166.

Hammitt, W.E. and Cole, D.N. (1987) *Wildland Recreation Ecology and Management*, New York: John Wiley and Sons, 341 pp.

Hampshire County Council (1968) *East Hampshire AONB: A study in countryside conservation*, Winchester: Hampshire County Council, 62 pp.

Hampshire County Council (1988) *Noisy Sports Hampshire: Rural De-*

velopment Strategy Conference working party on noisy sports, Winchester: Hampshire County Council, 51 pp.

Hampshire County Council (1989) *Highway Strategy for the New Forest*, County Surveyor, Winchester: Hampshire County Council, 33 pp.

Hampshire County Council (1991) *New Forest Highway Strategy: Report of the County Surveyor 11 January 1991*, Winchester: Hampshire County Council.

Hansard (1989) Response by Secretary of State for Scotland to question from Sir Hector Munro, Parliamentary Debates, House of Commons, 16 June 1989, Volume 154, Session 1988–89, London: HMSO, columns 542–543.

Hansard (1990) Written answer by Secretary of State for Scotland to question from Sir Hector Munro, Parliamentary Debates, House of Commons, 21 November 1990, Volume 181, Session 1990–91, London: HMSO, columns 164–166.

Hardy, D. and Ward, C. (1985) *Arcadia for All: The legacy of a makeshift landscape*, London: Mansell, 307 pp.

Harrison, A.J.M. (1978) 'Waterways provide good value as a leisure resource', *The Surveyor*, 12 January, 18–22.

Harrison, C. (1983) 'Countryside recreation and London's urban fringe', *Transactions of the Institute of British Geographers*, NS 8, (3), 295–313.

Harrison, C., Limb, M. and Burgess, J. (1986) 'Recreation 2000: Views of the country from the city', *Landscape Research*, 11 (2), 19–24.

Hartwright, T.U. (1985) 'A private enterprise case – Thorpe Park', in *Planning for Leisure in the Countryside, Journal of Planning and Environmental Law Occasional Papers*, London: Sweet and Maxwell, pp. 58–69.

Hatton, C. (1991) 'Wargames and wildlife: jeux sans frontières', *Ecos*, 12, (1), 26–30.

Healey, P., Doak, A., McNamara, P. and Elson, M. (1985) *The Implementation of Planning Policies and the Role of Development Plans, Volume 1: Final report to the Department of the Environment on the implementation of development plans*, Department of Town Planning, Oxford Polytechnic, 117 pp.

Hencke, D. (1991) 'Speculator warning over canal sales', *The Guardian*, 24 June 1991.

Hewison, R. (1987) *The Heritage Industry – Britain in a climate of decline*, London: Methuen, 160 pp.

317

Heytze, J.C. (1976) 'Recreation research – results and techniques', *XVI World Congress of the International Union of Forest Research Organisations Oslo 1976*, State Forest Service in the Netherlands, p. 23.

Highlands Regional Council (1989) *Summary and Land Use Strategy: Caithness and Sutherland HRC Working Party*, Inverness: Highlands Regional Council, 27 pp.

Highlands Regional Council (1990) *Structure Plan: Written statement*, Inverness: Highlands Regional Council, 115 pp.

Hill, E.A. and Healey, P. (1985) 'Local plans for the countryside: the first decade', in A. Gilg (ed), *Countryside Planning Year Book 1985*, Norwich: Geo Books, pp. 46–71.

Hillary, W. (1984) 'Leisure and the developer', *Journal of Planning and Environmental Law, Occasional Papers: Planning for leisure in the countryside*, London: Sweet and Maxwell, 91–105.

Hillman, M. (1984) 'Personal mobility and access to leisure,' in C. Banister and D. Groome (eds), *Out and About: Promoting access to countryside recreation by bus, train, bicycle and foot*, Occasional Paper 12, Department of Town and Country Planning, Manchester University, pp. 13–18.

Hillman, M. (1992) *Cycling: Towards health and safety*, London: British Medical Association, 159 pp.

Hockin, R., Goodall, B. and Whittow, J. (1979) *The site requirements and planning of outdoor recreational activities*, Geographical papers 54, Department of Geography, University of Reading, 52 pp.

Hodge, I.D. (1988) 'Property institutions and environmental improvement', *Journal of Agricultural Economics*, **39**, (3), 369–375.

Hoggett, P. and Bishop, J. (1983) 'Purposes, style and orientations of the voluntary sector in the countryside', in *Countryside Recreation Research Advisory Group Conference Proceedings 1983*, London: Sports Council, pp. 23–40.

Holt, A. (1989) 'Introduction', in T. Stephenson (ed.), *Forbidden Land: The struggle for access to mountain and moorland*, Manchester University Press, pp. 40–55.

Hookway, R. (1967) 'The management of Britain's rural land', *Town and Country Planning Summer School: Report of proceedings*, London: Royal Town Planning Institute, pp. 63–75.

Hookway, R. (1977) 'Countryside management: the development of techniques', *Town and Country Planning Summer School*, London: Royal Town Planning Institute, pp. 7–10.

House of Commons Agriculture Committee (1990) *Second Report of the Agriculture Committee on Land Use and Forestry: Vol 2. Minutes of evidence and appendices*, London: HMSO, 440 pp.

House of Lords (1973) *Second Report from the Select Committee on Sport and Leisure*, London: HMSO, 135 pp.

Irving, J.A. (1985) *The Public in Your Woods: An owner's guide to managing urban fringe woodland for recreation*, Chichester: Packard Publishing, 147 pp.

Jackson, M.J. (1986) *Economic Impact Studies: The methodology applied to tourism*, Occasional Research Paper in Economics, Bristol Polytechnic, 97 pp.

Jenkinson, A. (1990) 'The countryside experience: Part 2. Some further thoughts on environmental interpretation', *Heritage Interpretation,* **45**, 10–11.

Johnstone, M. and Tivy, J. (1981) 'Assessment of the physical capability of land for rural recreation', in M.F. Thomas and J. Coppock (eds), *Land Assessment in Scotland*, Aberdeen: Aberdeen University Press, pp. 89–104.

Joint Centre for Land Development Studies (1985) *Ploughing Footpaths and Bridleways: A study of the law and practice*, Cheltenham: Countryside Commission, CCP 190, 104 pp.

Jones, C.F., Lee, N. and Wood, C. (1991) *UK Environmental Statements 1988–1990: An analysis*, Occasional Paper 29, EIA Centre/Department of Planning and Landscape, University of Manchester, 79 pp.

Jones, P. (1990) 'Groundwork projects', *Planning Outlook*, **33**, (1), 62–64.

Jowell, J. and Millichap, D. (1987) 'Enforcement: the weakest link in the planning chain', in M.L. Harrison and K. Mordey (eds), *Planning Control: Philosophies, prospects and practice*, London: Croom Helm, pp. 175–194.

Jubenville, A., Twight, B.W. and Becker, R.H. (1987) *Outdoor Recreation Management: Theory and application*, State College: Venture Publishing, 290 pp.

Kent County Council (1990) *Kent Public Rights of Way Strategy*, Maidstone: Highways and Transportation Department, Kent County Council, 28 pp.

Kenyon, V. (1970) Background paper in *The Demand for Outdoor Recreation in the Countryside*, report of a seminar, 15 January 1970, London: Countryside Commission, pp. 1–8.

Kirby, A. (1985) 'Leisure as commodity: the role of the state in leisure provision', *Progress in Human Geography*, **9**, (1), 64–75.

Knightsbridge, R. (1986) 'Amenity and nature conservation in the urban fringe; competing or complementary land uses', in J.G. Sykes (ed) *Recreation and ecology in the urban fringes*, Recreation Ecology Research Group Report No. 11, pp. 17–35.

L & R plc with Transport for Leisure and Groundwork Associates (1990) *Trans-Pennine Trail – A strategy for Action, Final Report*, Selby: Selby District Council, 29 pp. plus appendices.

Lake District Special Planning Board (1976) *Lake District National Park Plan: Response to ideas for discussion*, Kendal: Lake District Special Planning Board, 52 pp.

Lake District Special Planning Board (1986) *Promoting the Public Enjoyment of the Lake District: Tourism*, Kendal: Lake District Special Planning Board, 14 pp.

Lake District Special Planning Board (1990) *New Policies and Initiatives for the Lake District National Park: Your contribution counts*, Kendal: Lake District Special Planning Board, 34 pp.

Lake District Special Planning Board (1991) *Board meeting report on Borrowdale Traffic Management Experiment 22 February 1991*, Kendal: Lake District Special Planning Board.

Lancashire County Council (1980) *West Pennine Moors: Draft recreation and conservation subjects plan*, Preston: Lancashire County Council, 293 pp.

Lancashire County Council (1988) *A Strategy for Tourism in Lancashire*. Four volumes: 1,2,3 *Strategy and Opportunities*; 4 *Review and Assessment*, Preston: Lancashire County Council, pp. 59 and 106.

Lancashire County Council (1989) *A Countryside Recreation Strategy for Lancashire*, Preston: The County Planning Officer, 40 pp.

Land Use Consultants with Berger, R. (1985) *Management Schemes for Commons*, Cheltenham: The Countryside Commission, CCP 197, 84 pp.

Lane, B. (1988) 'What is rural tourism?' in *Countryside Recreation Research Advisory Group Conference Proceedings 1988*, School of Advanced Urban Studies, University of Bristol, pp. 60–63.

Lane, B. (1991) 'Sustainable tourism: a new concept for the interpreter', *Interpretation Journal*, **49**, 2–4.

Lapping, M. and Hoagland, G. (1985) 'The private option for open space retention: the case for land trusts', *Loisir et Société*, **8**, (1), 171–195.

Laurie, I. (1983) 'Bolam Lake Country Park Northumberland: Recreation design 3', *Landscape Design*, **146**, 42–45.

Lavery, P. (ed) (1974) *Recreational Geography*, Newton Abbot: David and Charles, 335 pp.

Lavery, P. (1982) 'Countryside management schemes in the urban fringe', *Planning Outlook*, **25**, (2), 52–59.

Le Grand, J. (1982) *The Strategy of Equality: Redistribution and the social services*, London: George Allen and Unwin, 192 pp.

Leay, M.J., Rowe, J. and Young, J.D. (1986) *Management Plans: A guide to their preparation and use*, Cheltenham: The Countryside Commission, CCP 206, 52 pp.

Lee, D. (1976) *The Flixton Footpath Battle*, Manchester: Peak and Northern Footpaths Society, 23 pp.

Lee, N. and Colley, R. (1990) *Reviewing the Quality of Environmental Statements*, Occasional Paper 24, EIA Centre/Department of Planning and Landscape, University of Manchester, 46 pp.

Lee, T. (1991) 'Some thoughts on interpreting, revealing and presenting', *Interpretation Journal*, **47**, 15–17.

Lee Valley Regional Park Authority (1986) *Lee Valley Park Plan*, Enfield: Lee Valley Regional Park Authority, 126 pp.

Lee Valley Regional Park Authority (1989) *Annual Report 1988–89*, Enfield: Lee Valley Regional Park Authority, 29 pp.

Leicestershire County Council (1987) *Planning for Change in the Leicestershire Countryside, 2. Household questionnaire survey, Report of findings August 1986*, Leicester: Leicestershire County Council, 24 pp.

Leicestershire County Council (1991) *Leicestershire County Recreation Strategy: Golf in Leicestershire*, Leicester: Leicestershire County Council, 16 pp.

LeMottee, S. (1984) *Operation Gateway, Report no. 2, Pilot implementation stage*, Nottinghamshire County Council Leisure Services/ Countryside Commission, 10 pp.

Limna, T. (1985) 'The experience of a regional park authority in the southeast of England', in A.S. Travis and J. Towner (eds), *Regional Parks for the West Midlands*, Conference and Seminar Papers No 8, Centre for Urban and Regional Studies, University of Birmingham, pp. 23–29.

Lincolnshire County Council (1982) *Approved Structure Plan and Explanatory Memorandum*, Lincoln: Lincolnshire County Council, 74 pp.

Lock, D. (1991) 'Future definitive', *The Planner*, **77**, (26), 5–8.

London Planning Advisory Committee (1988) *Strategic Planning Advice for Greater London: Policies for the 1990s*, Romford: London Planning Advisory Committee, 76 pp.

Long Distance Paths Advisory Service (undated) Constitution clauses 2a and 2b, Kendal.

Lovett-Jones, G. (1988) *English Country Lanes: A celebration of travelling slowly*, Aldershot: Wildwood House, 303 pp.

Lowe, P. and Goyder, J. (1983) *Environmental Groups in Politics*, London: George Allen and Unwin, 208 pp.

Lowenthal, D. (1985) *The Past is a Foreign Country*, Cambridge University Press, 489 pp.

Lumsdon, L. (1984) 'Traffic not for travelling alone', *Town and Country Planning*, **53**, (4), 112–113.

Macclesfield and Vale Royal Groundwork Trust (1984–89) *Annual Report and Accounts*, Bollington: Macclesfield and Vale Royal Groundwork Trust, 19 pp.

MacEwen, A. and MacEwen M. (1987) *Greenprints for the Countryside: The story of Britain's national parks*, London: Allen and Unwin, 248 pp.

McHarg, I. (1969) *Design with Nature*, New York: Doubleday, 198 pp.

Mather, A.S. (1991) 'Pressures on British forestry policy: prologue to the post-industrial forest?' *Area*, **23**, (3), 245–253.

Matheson, J. (1991) *Participation in Sport*, Office of Population Censuses and Surveys Social Survey Division Series GHS, no 17, Supplement B, London: HMSO, 33 pp.

Maund, R. (1982) 'The Greater Manchester adventure: an exercise in strategic environmental improvement', *Environmental Education and Information*, **2**, (2), 79–96.

McKay, D.H. and Cox, A.W. (1979) *The Politics of Urban Change*, London: Croom Helm, 297 pp.

Mersey Basin Campaign (1989) *Mersey Basin Campaign Seminar: the Water Bill: a briefing for voluntary organisations 14 January 1989*, Manchester: Mersey Basin Campaign, 33 pp. plus appendices.

Mersey Valley Partnership (1989) *Countryside Recreation Strategy*, Runcorn: Mersey Valley Partnership, 8 pp.

Miles, C.N.W. and Seabrooke, W. (1977) *Recreational Land Management*, London: E. and F.N. Spon, 147 pp.

Ministry of Agriculture (1987) *Farming UK*, London: HMSO, 40 pp.

Ministry of Housing and Local Government (1955) *Green Belts*, Circular no 42/55, London: HMSO, 2 pp.

Ministry of Housing and Local Government (1965) *The Future of Development Plans: Report of the Planning Advisory Group*, London: HMSO, 62 pp.

Ministry of Housing and Local Government (1970) *Development Plans: A manual on form and content*, London: HMSO, 105 pp.

Ministry of Town and Country Planning (1945) *National Parks in England and Wales (The Dower Report)*, Cmnd 6626, London: HMSO, 57 pp.

Ministry of Town and Country Planning (1947a) *Footpaths and Access to the Countryside: Report of the Special Committee (England and Wales)*, Cmnd 7207, London: HMSO, 64 pp.

Ministry of Town and Country Planning (1947b) *Report of the National Parks Committee (England and Wales) (The Hobhouse Report)*, Cmnd 7121, London: HMSO, 134 pp.

Morgan, G. (1991) *A Strategic Approach to the Planning and Management of Parks and Open Spaces*, Basildon: Institute of Leisure and Amenity Management, 21 pp.

Morris, H. (1989) 'Ironing out the traffic', *The Surveyor*, 10 August, 16–18.

Muller, H.-R. (1990) 'The case for developing tourism in harmony with man and nature', in W. Bramwell (ed), *Shades of Green: Conference proceedings*, Countryside Commission, English Tourist Board, Rural Development Commission, pp. 11–22.

Murphy, F. (1983) 'The range and scope of voluntary activity in the countryside', in *Countryside Recreation Research Advisory Group Conference Proceedings 1983*, London: Sports Council, pp. 4–22.

Mutch, W.E.S. (1967) *Public Recreation in National Forests: A factual study*. Forestry Commission Booklet No 21, London: HMSO, 100 pp.

Mynors, C. (1991) 'The Planning and Compensation Act, 1991: (2) enforcement', *The Planner*, **77**, (30), 10–11.

National Economic Development Council (1991) 'The planning system and large-scale tourism and leisure developments'. Press release. London: National Economic Development Council.

National Parks Policy Review Committee (1974) *Report of the National Park Policies Review Committee*, London: HMSO, 130 pp.

National Parks Review Panel (1991) *Fit for the Future: Report of the*

National Parks Review Panel, CCP 334, Cheltenham: Countryside Commission, 151 pp.

National Rivers Authority (1990) *Corporate Plan 1990/91*, London: National Rivers Authority, 108 pp.

National Trust (1990) *Annual Report 1989*, London: National Trust, 33 pp.

Nature Conservancy Council (1989) *On Course Conservation: Managing golf's natural heritage*, Peterborough: The Nature Conservancy Council, 46 pp.

Neate, S. (1987) 'The role of tourism in sustaining farm structures and communities on the Isles of Scilly', in M. Bouquet and M. Winter, (eds), *Who From Their Labours Rest?* Aldershot: Avebury, pp. 9–21.

New Forest District Council (1990) *New Forest 2000: A strategy for the New Forest*, Lyndhurst: New Forest District Council, 64 pp.

New Forest Joint Steering Committee (1971) *Conservation of the New Forest: Final recommendations*, Lyndhurst: New Forest Joint Steering Committee, 62 pp.

New Forest Review Group (1988) *Report of the New Forest Review Group 1988: Recommendations made in the light of comments received on the New Forest Review Consultation Draft Report 1987*, Lyndhurst: The Group, 64 pp.

New York State Office of Parks, Recreation and Historic Preservation (1989) *People Resources Recreation: New York statewide comprehensive outdoor recreation plan and generic environmental impact statement*, Albany, NY: The State Office, 160 pp plus appendices.

Newman, P. (1981) 'Access to the "urban fringe" for informal countryside recreation', in D. Halsall (ed), *Transport for Recreation*, Transport Geography Study Group, Institute of British Geographers, c/o Department of Geography, Edge Hill College of Higher Education, Lancashire, pp. 36–62.

North Hertfordshire District Council (1991) *North Hertfordshire District Local Plan No. 2, Draft, Supplementary Planning Guidance, Golfcourses and Facilities, Policy and Advice Note, November 1991*, Letchworth: North Hertfordshire District Council, 3 pp.

North Regional Planning Committee (1969) *Outdoor Leisure Activities in the Northern Region: A survey carried out by NOP Ltd*, Newcastle upon Tyne: North Regional Planning Committee, 154 pp.

North West Council for Sport and Recreation (1989) *Regional Strategy for Sport and Recreation*, Manchester: North West Council for Sport and Recreation, 94 pp.

North West Water Authority (1986) *12th Annual Report 1985–86*, Great Sankey: North West Water Authority, 23 pp.

North West Water Group plc (1990) *Annual Report 1990*, Great Sankey: North West Water Group, 52 pp.

North West Water Ltd (1990) *Green Portfolio Conservation, Access and Recreation*, Great Sankey: North West Water Ltd (pamphlet).

North Yorkshire Moors National Park Authority (1982) *Roads and Traffic. Review, national park plan consultation paper*, Helmsley: North Yorkshire Moors National Park Authority, 43 pp.

North Yorkshire Moors National Park Committee (1990) *North Yorkshire Moors National Park Plan: Second review draft for consultation*, Helmsley: The National Park Officer, 151 pp.

Northern Motorsports Project (1989) *Issues report*, Newcastle: Northern Motorsports Project, 45 pp.

Office of Population and Censuses Surveys (1989a) *The General Household Survey 1986*, London: HMSO 324 pp.

Office of Population and Censuses Surveys (1989b) *The General Household Survey 1987*, London: HMSO, 291 pp.

Ortolano, L. (1984) *Environmental Planning and Decision-making*, New York: John Wiley, 431 pp.

Owens, P.L. (1978) 'Conflict between Norfolk Broads coarse anglers and boat users: a managerial issue', in M.J. Moseley (ed), *Social Issues in Rural Norfolk*, Norwich: Centre of East Anglian Studies, University of East Anglia, pp. 123–143.

Owens, P.L. (1984) 'Rural leisure and recreation research: A retrospective evaluation', *Progress in Human Geography*, **8**, (2), 157–188.

Owens, S. (1991) *Energy Conscious Planning: The case for action. A report commissioned by the Council for the Protection of Rural England*, London: The Council for the Protection of Rural England, 60 pp.

PA Cambridge Economic Consultants Ltd (1987) *A Study of Rural Tourism*, London: English Tourist Board and Rural Development Commission, 64 pp.

Palmer, J. and Bradley, J. (1974) 'Planning for outdoor recreation', in P. Lavery (ed), *Recreational Geography*, Newton Abbot: David and Charles, pp. 270–296.

Parker, D.J. and Penning-Rowsell, E.C. (1980) *Water Planning in Britain*, London: George Allen and Unwin, 277 pp.

325

Parker, D.J. and Sewell, D.W.R. (1988) 'Evolving water institutions in England and Wales: an assessment of 2 decades of experience', *Natural Resources Journal*, **28**, (4), 751–786.

Parker, S. (1976) *The Sociology of Leisure*, London: George Allen and Unwin, 157 pp.

Parkinson, M. (ed) (1987) *Reshaping Local Government*, Hermitage: Policy Journals, 170 pp.

Patmore, J.A. (1970) *Land and Leisure in England and Wales*, Newton Abbot: David and Charles, 235 pp.

Patmore, J.A. (1983) *Recreation and Resources: Leisure patterns and leisure places*, Oxford: Blackwell, 280 pp.

Patmore, J.A. and Rodgers, H.B. (1972) *Leisure in the North West*, Manchester: North West Sports Council, 257 pp.

Pawson, G. and Groome, D. (1987) *Access to countryside recreation in Greater Manchester*, Report 1, Department of Town and Country Planning, Manchester University/Greater Manchester Countryside Unit, 105 pp.

Payne, A. (1991) 'The green side of the water business', *The Planner*, **77**, (21), 7–8.

Peak District National Park (1955) *Peak District National Park Development Plan Report and Analysis of Survey*, Bakewell: Peak Park Planning Board, 119 pp.

Peak Park Joint Planning Board (1988) *Peak National Park Visitor Survey 1986/87*, Bakewell: Peak Park Joint Planning Board, 64 pp.

Peak Park Joint Planning Board (1989) *National Park Plan: First review*, Bakewell: Peak Park Joint Planning Board, 224 pp.

Peak Park Joint Planning Board (1991a) *Annual Report 1990–91*, Bakewell: Peak Park Joint Planning Board, 32 pp.

Peak Park Joint Planning Board (1991b) *Peak District National Park Structure Plan Review and Replacement: Consultation draft*, Bakewell: Peak Park Joint Planning Board, 109 pp.

Peak Park Planning Board/Derbyshire County Council (1972) *Routes for People: An environmental approach to rural highway planning*, Bakewell: Peak Park Planning Board, 8 pp.

Peter Scott Planning Services (1989) *Review of Countryside Recreation Strategies for Wales: for Countryside Commission, Wales Office*, Edinburgh: Peter Scott Planning Services, 128 pp.

Pigram, J. (1983) *Outdoor Recreation and Resource Management*, Beckenham: Croom Helm, 262 pp.

Planning Appeal Decisions (1985) *Planning Appeal Decisions Involving Recreational and Leisure Developments*, PAD 1, pp. 59–68.

Plowden, S. and Hillman, M. (1985) *Danger on the Road: The needless scourge*, Report no 627, London: PSI Publications, 239 pp.

Porter, M. (1991) *The Pennine Way Management Project: A study of the condition and management requirements of the southern part of the Pennine Way 1991*, Cheltenham: Countryside Commission, CCP 297, 77 pp.

Quinion, M.B. and Glen, M.H. (1989) 'The invaders as allies: information and interpretation in the New Forest', *Heritage Interpretation*, **42**, 18–19.

Raikes, G. (1990) 'Clocking up the miles', *The National Trust Magazine*, No. 59, Spring, p. 19.

Ramblers' Association (1978) *Roads Fit to Walk On*, London: Ramblers' Association, 16 pp.

Ramblers' Association (1988) *Paths, Routes and Trails: Response to the Countryside Commission's consultation paper by the Ramblers' Association*, London: The Ramblers' Association, 7 pp.

Reade, E. (1987) *British Town and Country Planning*, Milton Keynes: Open University Press, 270 pp.

Reiling, S.D., Anderson, M.W. and Gibbs, K.C. (1983) 'Measuring the costs of publicly supplied outdoor recreational facilities: a methodological note', *Journal of Leisure Research*, **15**, (3), 203–218.

Research Surveys (1990) *Ironbridge Park and Ride Survey 1990*, Telford: Research Surveys, 20 pp. plus appendices.

Roberts, M. (1974) *Town Planning Techniques*, London: Hutchinson, 414 pp.

Rodgers, H.B. (1967) *Pilot National Recreation Survey Report No. 1*, London: British Travel Association, 104 pp.

Rodgers, H.B. (1969) *Pilot National Recreation Survey Report No. 2, Regional Analysis*, London: British Travel Association, 59 pp.

Roehl, W. and Fesenmaier, D. (1987) 'Tourism and land use conflict in the United States', *Annals of Tourism Research*, **14**, (4), 471–485.

Rothman, B. (1982) *The 1932 Kinder Trespass: A personal view of the Kinder Scout Mass Trespass*, Timperley: Willow Publishing, 56 pp.

Rowson, N.J. and Thoday, P.R. (1985) *Landscape Design for Disabled People in Public Open Space*, University of Bath, 129 pp.

Royal and Ancient Golf Club of St Andrews (1989) *The Demand for Golf*, St Andrews, 69 pp.

Royal Institution of Chartered Surveyors (1989) *Managing the Countryside: Access, recreation and tourism. The policy framework. Proposals by the RICS*, London: The Royal Institute of Chartered Surveyors, 10 pp.

Royal National Institute for the Blind (1986) *Nature Trails for Blind People*, London: The Institute, 25 pp.

Royal Society of Arts (1970) *The Countryside in 1970: Proceedings of the Third Conference, October 1970*, London: Royal Society of Arts, 193 pp.

Rural Development Commission (1989) *Practical Assistance for Tourism and Leisure Businesses*, Salisbury: Rural Development Commission, pamphlet.

Salford City Council (1989) *A Countryside Recreation Strategy for Salford*, Swinton: Salford City Council, 31 pp.

Scott, A. (1989) 'The changing forestry scene in Britain', in *Proceedings of Countryside Recreation Research Advisory Group Conference 1989*, School of Advanced Urban Studies, University of Bristol, pp. 15–18.

Scottish Office Inquiry Reporters (1988) *Reporter's decision letter. Appeal by Scottish Rights of Way Society: erection of footbridge at Fords of Avon*, Edinburgh: Scottish Office Ref: P/PPA/GE/97, 5 pp.

Selman, P.H. (1987) 'Countryside management plans in Britain: a preliminary appraisal', *Landscape and Urban Planning*, **14**, (2), 155–162.

Shaw, G., Williams, A. and Greenwood, J. (1988) 'Tourism and economic development: policy implications from a case study of Cornwall', *Planning Practice and Research*, 6/88, 4–11.

Sheail, J. (1981) *Rural Conservation in Inter-war Britain*, Oxford: Clarendon Press, 263 pp.

Shercliff, W.H. (1987) *Nature's Joys are Free for All: A history of countryside recreation in north east Cheshire*, Poynton, Cheshire: W.H. Shercliff, 131 pp.

Sherwood Forest Study Group (1974) *Sherwood Forest Study*, Nottingham: Sherwood Forest Study Group, 115 pp.

Shoard, M. (1979) 'Metropolitan escape routes', *London Journal*, **5**, (1), 87–112.

Shoard, M. (1987) *This Land is our Land: The struggle for Britain's countryside*, London: Paladin, 592 pp.

Sidaway, R. (1982) 'Trends and issues in countryside recreation in the 1970s and 1980s', *Countryside Recreation Research Advisory Group Conference Proceedings 1982*, London: Sports Council, pp. 2–32.

Sidaway, R. (1988) *Sport Recreation and Nature Conservation*, Study No. 32, London: The Sports Council, 98 pp.

Sidaway, R. (1991) *A Review of Marina Developments in Southern England*, Godalming: World Wide Fund for Nature UK and Royal Society for the Protection of Birds, 75 pp.

Sillitoe, J. (1969) *Planning for Recreation*, London: HMSO, 261 pp. plus appendices.

Simpson, R. (1983) 'How local authorities national parks and water authorities work with volunteers', in *Countryside Recreation Research Group Conference Proceedings 1983*, London: Sports Council, pp. 92–101.

Skelly, D. (1985) 'Clyde–Muirshiel Regional Park', in A.S. Travis and J. Towner (eds), *Regional Parks for the West Midlands*, Conference and Seminar Papers No. 8, Centre for Urban and Regional Studies, University of Birmingham, pp. 17–22.

Slee, B. (1989) *Alternative Farm Enterprises*, Ipswich: Farming Press Books, 208 pp.

Smart, A.D.G. (1990) 'Areas of outstanding natural beauty and the wider countryside', in J. Blunden and N. Curry (eds), *A People's Charter*, London: HMSO Books, pp. 158–190.

Smith, D. (1990) 'Restructuring Cheshire's countryside management service', *The Ranger Magazine*, **20**, 5.

Smith, R. (1990) 'Access' in J. Blunden and N. Curry (eds), *A People's Charter*, London: HMSO Books, pp. 129–157.

Smith, S.L.J. (1983) *Recreation Geography*, Harlow: Longman, 220 pp.

Smiths Gore (1989) *Review 1989–90,* London, 33 pp.

Snowdonia National Park Authority (1989) *Bala and Penllyn Local Plan*, Penrhyndeudraeth: Snowdonia National Park Authority (pamphlet).

Solesbury, W. (1974) *Policy in Urban Planning: Structure plans, programmes and local plans*, Urban and Regional Planning Series No. 8, Oxford: Pergamon Press, 186 pp.

South Hams District Council (1985) *Kingsbridge District Plan Draft Written Statement*, Totnes: South Hams District Council, 167 pp.

South West Water Authority (1989) *Annual Report and Accounts 1988–89*, Exeter: South West Water Authority, 59 pp.

Sports Council (1990) *A Countryside for Sport: Towards a policy for sport and recreation in the countryside. A consultation*, London: Sports Council, 15 pp.

Sports Council for Wales (1986) *Changing Times; Changing Needs: 10 year strategy for sport in Wales*, Cardiff: Sports Council for Wales, 85 pp.

Stephenson, T. (1989) *Forbidden Land: The struggle for access to mountain and moorland*, Manchester University Press, 243 pp.

Stokes, G., Goodwin, P. and Kenny, F. (1992) *Trends in Transport and the Countryside*, Cheltenham: Countryside Commission, CCP 382, 24 pp.

Surrey County Council (1992) *Traffic Regulation Orders on Byways Open to all Traffic: Report of the Director of Highways and Transportation*, 17 January 1992, Kingston: Surrey County Council, 2 pp.

Survey Research Associates (1989) *Ridgeway Users Study: Summary report*, Cheltenham: The Countryside Commission, CCD 52, 61 pp. plus appendices.

Sustrans Ltd (1990) *Annual Report 1989/90*, Bristol: Sustrans Ltd, 24 pp.

Sustrans Ltd (1991a) *Financial Statements Year Ended 31 March 1989*, Bristol: Sustrans Ltd.

Sustrans Ltd (1991b) *Newsletter*, Bristol: Sustrans Ltd.

Tanner, M.F. (1987) 'Recreation in the rural–urban fringe', in D. Lockhart and B. Ilbery (eds), *The Future of the British Rural Landscape*, Norwich: Geo Abstracts Ltd, pp. 184–207.

Thames Chase Team (1992) *Thames Chase Plan: Draft for consultation*, Brentwood: Thames Chase Team, 120 pp. plus appendices.

Thomas, M.F. and Coppock, J. (eds) (1981) *Land Assessment in Scotland*, Aberdeen University Press, 143 pp.

Thomson, K.J. and Whitby, M.C. (1976) 'The economics of public access in the countryside', *Journal of Agricultural Economics*, **27**, 307–320.

Tilden, F. (1977) *Interpreting Our Heritage*, Chapel Hill: University of North Carolina Press, 119 pp.

Tompkins, S. (1990) 'Forestry lobby lashes out', *Ecos*, **11**, (4), 70.

Torkildsen, G. (1983) *Leisure and Recreation Management*, London: E. and F.N. Spon, 492 pp.

Tourism and Recreation Research Unit (1980) *A study of four parks in and around Glasgow*. Report of surveys carried out in 1977 and 1978, sponsored by Countryside Commission for Scotland, City of Glasgow Parks Department and Strathclyde Regional Council, Research Report 44, Edinburgh: Tourism and Recreation Research Unit, University of Edinburgh, 184 pp.

Tourism and Recreation Research Unit (1981) *The Economy of Rural*

Communities in the National Parks of England and Wales. For Countryside Commission, Department of the Environment, English Tourist Board, Ministry of Agriculture Fisheries and Food Research. The Unit Edinburgh: Edinburgh University, Tourism and Recreation Research Unit, Report No. 47, 400 pp.

Tourism and Recreation Research Unit (1983a) *A Digest of Sports Statistics for the UK. Information series No. 7*, London: Sports Council, 101 pp.

Tourism and Recreation Research Unit (1983b) *Recreation Site Survey Manual: Methods and techniques for conducting visitor surveys*, London: E. and F.N. Spon, 146 pp.

Trade and Industry, Secretary of State for (1988) *Releasing Enterprise*, Cm 512, London: HMSO, 44 pp.

Transport for Leisure and Department of Planning and Landscape University of Manchester (1990) *Cycle Transport Network Study: A study undertaken for the Countryside Commission North West England office*, Manchester: Countryside Commission, 44 pp.

Travis, A.S. (1985) 'Introduction to the needs, problems and possibilities of regional parks', in A.S. Travis and J. Towner, (eds), *Regional Parks for the West Midlands*, Conference and Seminar Papers No. 8, Centre for Urban Regional Studies, University of Birmingham, pp. 3–4.

Travis, A.S. (1989) 'Recreation in the woods today: a United Kingdom review', in *Proceedings of Countryside Recreation Research Advisory Group Conference 1989*, School of Advanced Urban Studies, University of Bristol, pp. 19–36.

Trépanier, M.-O. and Ouellet, B. et al. (1986) 'La contribution des organisations locales à la gestion d'un parc national: trois études de cas', *Loisir et Société*, **9**, (1), 125–164.

Tubbs, C. (1987) *New Forest Review: Survey of horse riding damage*, Lyndhurst: Nature Conservancy Council, 3 pp.

Tunbridge, J.E. (1981) 'Conservation trusts as geographic agents: their impact upon landscape, townscape and land use', *Transactions of the Institution of British Geographers N S*, **6**, (1), 103–135.

Turner, T. (1988) 'Lee Valley: assessment', *Landscape Design*, **171**, 33.

Vaughan, D.R. (1977) *The Economic Impact of Tourism in Edinburgh and the Lothian Region*, Edinburgh: Scottish Tourist Board, 49 pp.

Veal, A.J. (1979) *Sport and Recreation in England and Wales: An analysis of adult participation patterns in 1977*, Centre for Urban and Re-

331

gional Studies Research Memorandum 74, Birmingham: The University, 101 pp.

Veal, A.J. (1982) *Planning for Leisure: Alternative approaches*, Polytechnic of North London, Papers in leisure studies No. 5, 55 pp.

Veal, A.J. (1986) 'Planning for leisure: alternative approaches', *The Planner*, **72**, (6), 9–12.

Wager, J.F. (1976) *Management Agreements in Principle and Practice: A case study in Monsal Dale*, Bakewell: Peak Park Joint Planning Board, 36 pp.

Wales Tourist Board (1990) *Tourist Accommodation Resources*, Research Information Factsheet 7, Cardiff: Wales Tourist Board, 3 pp.

Walshe, P. (1990) 'The philosophy of zoning', in Countryside Commission, *Advice Manual for the Preparation of a Community Forest Plan*, Cheltenham: Countryside Commission, pp. 5–7.

Warburton, D. and Wilcox, D. of Partnership Ltd with Bailey, N., Davidson, J., Robinson, L., Thomson, K. and Tyler, D. (1987) *Creating Development Trusts: Case studies of good practice in urban regeneration*. For Department of the Environment, London: HMSO, 54 pp.

Water Authorities Association (1988) *Water Facts 1988*, London: The Water Authorities Association, 63 pp.

Wathern, P. (ed) (1988) *Environmental Impact Assessment*, London: Unwin Hyman, 332 pp.

Watkins, S. (1984) *Cycling Accidents*, Godalming: Cyclists' Touring Club, 106 pp.

Webster, P. (1985) 'Regional park development in the Greater Manchester region, north west England', in A.S. Travis and J. Towner (eds), *Regional Parks for the West Midlands*, Conference and Seminar Papers No. 8, Centre for Urban and Regional Studies, University of Birmingham, pp. 31–38.

Weisbrod, B.A. (1988) *The Nonprofit Economy*, Cambridge, Mass: Harvard University Press, 251 pp.

Wells, S. (1987) 'Pugney's country park', *Landscape Design*, 165, 43–46.

Welsh Office (1988) *The Welsh Language and Planning Control*, Circular 53/88, Cardiff: Welsh Office, 1 p.

Welsh Office (1989) *Application by Snowdonia Leisure plc: Public Inquiry Inspector's Report*, Cardiff: Ref p44/452, 30 pp.

Welsh Water plc (1989) *Welsh Water Elan Trust: Press statement*, Brecon: Welsh Water plc, 2 pp.

Williams, A.F. and Tanner, M.F. (1982) 'From conurbation to countryside: a day out by bus or rail in the West Midlands', in D. Halsall (ed), *Transport for Recreation*, Transport Geography Study Group, Institute of British Geographers, c/o Department of Geography, Edge Hill College of Higher Education, Lancashire, pp 84–123.

Wilson, H. and Womersley, L. (1972) *Traffic Management in the Lake District National Park: A report to the Friends of the Lake District*, Kendal: Friends of the Lake District, 115 pp.

Woodman, D. (1985) 'Holiday parks', in *Countryside Recreation Research Advisory Group Conference Proceedings 1988*, School of Advanced Urban Studies, University of Bristol, pp. 64–65.

Woolerton Truscott (1992) *AONB Management Plans: Advice on their format and content*, Cheltenham: Countryside Commission, CCP 352, 38 pp.

Worth, J. (1984) 'A resource all can share', *Town and Country Planning*, **53**, (4), 98–99.

Yorkshire Dales National Park Committee (1989) *The Condition of Green Lanes: Report of survey 1988*, Skipton: The Committee, 3 pp. plus appendices.

Index

DATE DUE

DEMCO 38-297